OUTLAWS AND PEACE OFFICERS

OUTLAWS AND PEACE OFFICERS

Memoirs of Crime and Punishment in the Old West

Edited by

STEPHEN BRENNAN

Skyhorse Publishing

Skyhorse Publishing books may be purchased in bulk at special discounts for sales promotion, corporate gifts, fund-raising, or educational purposes. Special editions can also be created to specifications. For details, contact the Special Sales Department, Skyhorse Publishing, 307 West 36th Street, 11th Floor, New York, NY 10018 or info@skyhorsepublishing.com.

Skyhorse® and Skyhorse Publishing® are registered trademarks of Skyhorse Publishing, Inc.®, a Delaware corporation.

Visit our website at www.skyhorsepublishing.com.

10 9 8 7 6 5 4 3 2 1

Library of Congress Cataloging-in-Publication Data is available on file.

Cover design by Anthony Morais

Print ISBN: 978-1-63450-436-2
Ebook ISBN: 978-1-5107-0038-3

Printed in the United States of America

CONTENTS

Chapter I.

DODGE

By William MacLeod Raine

It was in the days when the new railroad was pushing through the country of the plains Indians that a drunken cowboy got on the train at the way station in Kansas. John Bender, the conductor, asked him for his ticket. He had none, but he pulled out a handful of gold pieces.

"I wantta—go-go to—h-hell," he hiccuped.

Bender did not hesitate an instant. "Get off at Dodge. One dollar, please."

Dodge did not get its name because so many of its citizens were or had been, in the Texas phrase, on the dodge. It came quite respectably by way of its cognomen. The town was laid out by A. A. Robinson, chief engineer of the Atchison, Topeka & Santa Fe, and it was called for Colonel Richard I. Dodge, commander of the post at Fort Dodge and one of the founders of the place. It is worth noting because it is one of the few respectable facts in the early history of the cowboy capital. Dodge was a wild and uncurried prairie wolf, and it howled every night and all night long. It was gay and young and lawless. Its sense of humor was exaggerated and worked overtime. The crack of the six-shooter punctuated its hilarity ominously. Those who dwelt there were the valiant vanguard of civilization. For good or bad they were strong and forceful, many of them generous and big-hearted in spite of their lurid lives. The town was a hive of energy. One might justly use many adjectives about it, but the word respectable was not among them.

1

There were three reasons why Dodge won the reputation of being the wildest town the country had ever seen. In 1872 it was the end of the track, the last jumping-off spot into the wilderness, and in the day when the transcontinental railroads were building across the desert the temporary terminus was always a gathering place of roughs and scalawags. The payroll was large, and gamblers, gunmen, and thugs gathered for the pickings. This was true of Hays, Abilene, Ogalala, and Kit Carson. It was true of Las Vegas and Albuquerque.

A second reason was that Dodge was the end of the long trail drive from Texas. Every year hundreds of thousands of longhorns were driven up from Texas by cowboys scarcely less wild than the hill steers they herded. The great plains was being opened, and cattle were needed to stock a thousand ranches as well as to supply the government at Indian reservations. Scores of these trail herds were brought to Dodge for shipment, and after the long, dangerous drive the punchers were keen to spend their money on such diversions as the town could offer. Out of sheer high spirits they liked to shoot up the town, to buck the tiger, to swagger from saloon to gambling hall, their persons garnished with revolvers, the spurs on their high-heeled boots jingling. In no spirit of malice they wanted it distinctly understood that they owned the town. As one of them once put it, he was born high up in the Guadaloupe, raised on prickly pear, had palled with alligators and quarreled with grizzlies.

Also, Dodge was the heart of the buffalo country. From here great quantities of hides were shipped back on the new railroad. R. M. Wright, one of the founders of the town and always one of its leading citizens, says that his firm alone shipped two hundred thousand hides in one season. He estimates the number of buffaloes in the country at more than twenty-five million, admitting that many as well informed as he put the figure at four times as many.

Many times he and others traveled through the vast herd for days at a time without ever losing sight of them. The killing of buffaloes was easy, because the animals were so stupid. When one was shot, they would mill round and round. Tom Nicolson killed 120 in forty minutes; in a little more than a month he slaughtered 2,713 of them. With good luck a man could earn one hundred dollars a day. If he had bad luck he lost his scalp.

The buffalo was to the plains Indian food, fuel, and shelter. As long as there were plenty of buffaloes he was in Paradise. But he saw at once that this slaughter would soon exterminate the supply. He hated the hunter and battled against his encroachments. The buffalo hunter was an intrepid plainsman. He fought the Kiowas, Comanches, and the staked plain Apaches, as well as the Sioux and the Arapahoe. Famous among these hunters were Kirk Jordan, Charles Rath, Emanuel Dubbs, Jack Bridges, and Curly Walker. Others even better known were the two Buffalo Bills (William Cody and William Mathewson) and Wild Bill.

These three factors then made Dodge: it was the end of the railroad, the terminus of the cattle trail from Texas, and the center of the buffalo trade. Together they made "the beautiful bibulous Babylon of the frontier," in the words of the editor of the *Kingsley Graphic*. There was to come a time later when the bibulous Babylon fell on evil days and its main source of income was old bones. They were buffalo-bones, gathered in wagons, and piled beside the track for shipment, hundreds and hundreds of carloads of them, to be used for fertilizer. It used to be said by way of derision that buffalo bones were legal tender in Dodge.

But that was in the far future. In the early years Dodge rode the wave of prosperity. Hays and Abilene on Ogalala had their day, but Dodge had its day and its night too. For years it did a tremendous business. The streets were so blocked that one could hardly get through. Hundreds of wagons were parked in them, outfits belonging to freighters, hunters, cattlemen, and the government. Scores of camps surrounded the town in every direction. The yell of the cowboy and the weird oath of the bull-whacker and muleskinner were heard in the land. And for a time there was no law nearer than Hays City, itself a burg not given to undue quiet and peace.

Dodge was no sleepy village that could drowse along without peace officers. Bob Wright has set it down that in the first year of its history twenty-five men were killed and as many wounded. The elements that made up the town were

too diverse for perfect harmony. The freighters did not like the railroad graders. The soldiers at the fort fancied themselves as scrappers. The cowboys and the buffalo hunters did not fraternize a little bit. The result was that Boot Hill began to fill up. Its inhabitants were buried with their boots on and without coffins.

There was another cemetery for those who died in their beds. The climate was so healthy that it would have been very sparsely occupied those first years if it had not been for the skunks. During the early months Dodge was a city of camps. Every night the fires flamed up from the vicinity of hundreds of wagons. Skunks were numerous. They crawled at night into the warm blankets of the sleepers and bit the rightful owners when they protested. A dozen men died from these bites. It was thought at first that the animals were a special variety, known as the hydrophobia skunk. In later years I have sat around Arizona campfires and heard the subject discussed heatedly. The Smithsonian Institute, appealed to as referee, decided that there was no such species and that deaths from the bites were probably due to blood poisoning caused by the foul teeth of the animal.

In any case, the skunks were only half as venomous as the gunmen, judging by comparative staff statistics. Dodge decided it had to have law in the community. Jack Bridges was appointed first marshal.

Jack was a noted scout and buffalo hunter, the sort of man who would have peace if he had to fight for it. He did his sleeping in the afternoon, since this was the quiet time of the day. Someone shook him out of slumber one day to tell him that cowboys were riding up and down Front Street shooting the windows out of buildings. Jack sallied out, old buffalo gun in hand. The cowboys went whooping down the street across the bridge toward their camp. The old hunter took a long shot at one of them and dropped him. The cowboys buried the young fellow next day.

There was a good deal of excitement in the cow camps. If the boys could not have a little fun without some old donker, an old vinegarroon who couldn't take a joke, filling them full of lead it was a pretty howdy-do. But Dodge stood pat. The coroner's jury voted it justifiable homicide. In future the young Texans were more discreet. In the early days whatever law there was did not interfere with casualties due to personal differences of opinion provided the figure had no unusually sinister aspect.

The first wholesale killing was at Tom Sherman's dance hall. The affair was between soldiers and gamblers. It was started by a trooper named Hennessey, who had a reputation as a bad guy and a bully. He was killed, as were several others. The officers of the fort glossed over the matter, perhaps because they felt the soldiers had been to blame.

One of the lawless characters who drifted into Dodge the first year was Billy Brooks. He quickly established a reputation as a killer. My old friend Emanuel Dubbs, a buffalo hunter who "took the hides off'n" many a bison, is authority for the statement that Brooks killed or wounded fifteen men in less than a month after his arrival. Now, Emanuel is a preacher (if he is still in the land of the living; I saw him last at Clarendon, Texas, ten years or so ago), but I cannot quite swallow that "fifteen." Still, he had a man for breakfast now and then and on one occasion four.

Brooks, by the way, was assistant marshal. It was the policy of the officials of these wild frontier towns to elect as marshal some conspicuous killer, on the theory that desperadoes would respect his prowess or if they did not would get the worst of the encounter.

Abilene, for instance, chose "Wild Bill" Hickok. Austin had its Ben Thompson. According to Bat Masterson, Thompson was the most dangerous man with a gun among all the bad men he knew—and Bat knew them all. Ben was an Englishman who struck Texas while still young. He fought as a Confederate under Kirby Smith during the Civil War and under Shelby for Maximilian. Later he was city marshal at Austin. Thompson was a man of the most cool effrontery. On one occasion, during a cattlemen's convention, a banquet was held at a leading hotel. The local congressman, a friend of Thompson, was not invited. Ben took exception to this and attended in person. By way of pleasantry he shot the plates in front of the diners. Later one of those present made a humorous comment: "I always thought Ben was a game man. But what did he do? Did he hold up a whole convention of a thousand cattlemen? No, sir. He waited until he got forty of fifty of us poor fellows alone before he turned loose his wolf."

Of all the bad men and desperadoes produced by Texas, not one of them, not even John Wesley Hardin himself, was more feared than Ben Thompson. Sheriffs avoided serving warrants of arrest on him. It is recorded that once, when the county court was in session with a charge against him on the docket, Thompson rode into the room on a mustang. He bowed pleasantly to the judge and court officials.

"Here I am, gents, and I'll lay all I'm worth that there's no charge against me. Am I right? Speak up, gents, I'm a little deaf."

5

There was a dead silence until at last the clerk of the court murmured, "No charge."

A story is told that on one occasion Ben Thompson met his match in the person of a young English remittance man playing cards with him. The remittance man thought he caught Thompson cheating and discreetly said so. Instantly Thompson's .44 covered him. For some unknown reason the gambler gave the lad a chance to retract.

"Take it back—and quick," he said grimly.

Every game in the house was suspended while all eyes turned on the daredevil boy and the hard-faced desperado. The remittance man went white, half rose from his seat, and shoved his head across the table towards the revolver.

"Shoot and be damned. I say you cheat," he cried hoarsely.

Thompson hesitated, laughed, shoved the revolver back into its holster, and ordered the youngster out of the house.

Perhaps the most amazing escape on record is that when Thompson, fired at by Mark Wilson at a distance of ten feet from a double-barreled shotgun loaded with buckshot, whirled instantly, killed him, and an instant later shot through the forehead Wilson's friend Mathews, though the latter had ducked behind the bar to get away. The second shot was guesswork plus quick thinking and accurate aim. Ben was killed a little later in company with his friend King Fisher, another bad man, at the Palace Theatre. A score of shots were poured into them by a dozen men waiting in ambush. Both men had become so dangerous that their enemies could not afford to let them live.

King Fisher was the humorous gentleman who put up a signboard at the fork of a public road bearing the legend:

THIS IS KING FISHER'S ROAD. TAKE THE OTHER.

It is said that those traveling that way followed his advice. The other road might be a mile or two farther, but they were in no hurry. Another amusing little episode in King Fisher's career is told. He had some slight difficulty with a certain bald-headed man. Fisher shot him and carelessly gave the reason that he wanted to see whether a bullet would glance from a shiny pate.

El Paso in its wild days chose Dallas Stoudenmire for marshal, and after he had been killed, John Selman. Both of them were noted killers. During Selman's regime, John Wesley Hardin came to town. Hardin had twenty-seven notches on his gun and was the worst man killer Texas had ever produced. He was at the bar of a saloon shaking dice when Selman shot him from behind. One year later Deputy United States Marshal George Scarborough killed Selman in a duel. Shortly after this, Scarborough was slain in a gunfight by "Kid" Curry, an Arizona bandit.

What was true of these towns was true, too, of Albuquerque and Las Vegas and Tombstone. Each of them chose for peace officers men who were "sudden death" with a gun. Dodge did exactly the same thing. Even a partial list of its successive marshals reads like a fighting roster. In addition to Bridges and Brooks may be named Ed and Bat Masterson, Wyatt Earp, Bill Tilghman, Ben Daniels, Mysterious Dave Mathers, T. C. Nixon, Luke Short, Charlie Bassett, W. H. Harris, and the Sughrue brothers, all of them famous as fighters in a day when courage and proficiency with weapons were a matter of course. On one occasion the superintendent of the Santa Fe suggested to the city dads of Dodge that it might be a good thing to employ marshals less notorious. Dodge begged leave to differ. It felt that the best way to "settle the hash" of desperadoes was to pit against them fighting machines more efficient, bad men more deadly than themselves.

The word "bad" does not necessarily imply evil. One who held the epithet was known as dangerous to oppose. He was unafraid, deadly with a gun, and hard as nails. He might be evil, callous, treacherous, revengeful as an Apache. Dave Mathers fit this description. He might be a good man, kindly, gentle, never taking more than his fighting chance. This was Billy Tillman to a T.

We are keeping Billy Brooks waiting. But let that go. Let us look first at "Mysterious Dave." Bob Wright has set it down that Mathers had more dead men to his credit than any other man in the West. He slew seven by actual count in one night, in one house, according to Wright. Mathers had a very bad reputation. But his courage could blaze up magnificently. While he was deputy marshal word came that the Henry gang of desperadoes were terrorizing a dance hall. Into that hall walked Dave beside his chief Tom Carson. Five minutes later out reeled Carson, both arms broken, his body shot through and through, a man with only five minutes to live. When the smoke in the hall cleared away Mathers might have been seen beside two handcuffed prisoners, one of them wounded. In a circle around him were four dead cowpunchers of the Henry outfit.

"Uncle" Billy Tilghman died the other day at Cornwall, Oklahoma, a victim of his own fearlessness. He was shot to death while taking a revolver from a drunken prohibition agent. If he had been like many other bad men he would have shot the fellow down at the first sight of danger. But that was never Tilghman's way. It was his habit to make arrests without drawing a gun. He cleaned up Dodge during the three years while he was marshal. He broke up the Dooley gang, killing Bill Raidler and "Little" Dick in personal duels and capturing Bill Doolin, the leader. Bat Masterson said that during Tilghman's term as sheriff of Lincoln County, Oklahoma, he captured, or drove from the county more criminals than any other official that section ever had. Yet "Uncle" Billy never used a gun except reluctantly. Time and again he gave the criminal the first shot, hoping the man would surrender rather than fight. Of all the old frontier sheriffs none holds a higher place than Billy Tilghman.

After which diversion we turn to Billy Brooks, a "gent" of an impatient temperament, not used to waiting, and notably quick on the trigger. Mr. Dubbs reports that late one evening in the winter of '72–'73 he returned to Dodge with two loads of buffalo meat. He finished his business, ate supper, and started to smoke a postprandial pipe. The sound of a fusillade in an adjoining dance hall interested him since he had been deprived of the pleasures of metropolitan life for some time and had come to depend upon Indians for excitement. (Incidentally, it may mentioned that they furnished him with a reasonable amount. Not long after this three of his men were caught, spread-eagled, and tortured by Indians. Dubbs escaped after a hair-raising ride and arrived at Adobe Walls in time to take part in the historic defense of that post by a handful of buffalo hunters against many hundred tribesmen.) From the building burst four men. They started across the railroad track to another dance hall, one frequented by Brooks. Dubbs heard the men mention the name of Brooks, coupling it with an oath. Another buffalo hunter named Fred Singer joined Dubbs. They followed the strangers, and just before the four reached the dance hall Singer shouted a warning to the marshal. This annoyed the unknown four, and they promptly exchanged shots with the buffalo hunters. Then what took place was startling in the sudden drama of it.

Billy Brooks stood in bold relief in the doorway, a revolver in each hand. He fired so fast that Dubbs says the sounds were like a company discharging weapons. When the smoke cleared Brooks still stood in the same place. Two of the strangers were dead and two mortally wounded. They were brothers. They had come from Hays City to avenge the death of a fifth brother shot down by Brooks some time before.

Mr. Brooks has a fondness for the fair sex. He and Browney, the yardmaster, took a fancy to the same girl. Captain Drew, she was called, and she preferred Browney. Whereupon Brooks naturally shot him in the head. Perversely, to the surprise of everybody, Browney recovered and was soon back at his old job.

Brooks seems to have held no grudge at him for making light of his marksmanship in this manner. At any rate, his next affair was with Kirk Jordan, the buffalo hunter. This was a very different business. Jordan had been in a hundred tight holes. He had fought Indians time and time again. Professional killers had no terror for him. He drew down his big buffalo gun on Brooks, and the latter took cover. Barrels of water had been placed along the principal streets for fire protection. These had saved several lives during shooting scrapes. Brooks ducked behind one, and the ball from Jordan's gun plunged into it. The marshal dodged into a store, out of the rear door, and into a livery stable.

He was hidden under a bed. Alas! For a reputation gone glimmering. Mr. Brooks fled to the fort, took the train from the siding, and shook forever the dust of Dodge from his feet. Whither he departed a deponent sayeth not.

How do I explain this? I don't. I record a fact. Many gunmen were at one time or another subject to these panics during which the yellow streak showed. Not all of them by any means, but a very considerable percentage. They swaggered boldly, killed recklessly. Then one day some quiet little man with a cold grey eye called the turn on them, after which they oozed out of the surrounding scenery.

Owen P. White gives it on the authority of Charlie Siringo that Bat Masterson sang small when Clay Allison of the Panhandle, he of the well-notched gun, drifted into Dodge and inquired for the city marshal. But the old timers at Dodge do not bear this out. Bat was at the Adobe Walls fight, one of fourteen men who stood of the hundred bucks of the Cheyenne, Comanche, and Kiowa tribes. He scouted for miles. He was elected sheriff of Ford County, with headquarters at Dodge when only twenty-seven years of age. It was a tough assignment, and Bat executed it to the satisfaction of all concerned except the element he cowed.

Personally, I never met Bat until his killing days were past. He was dealing faro at a gambling house in Denver, when I, a young reporter, first had the pleasure of looking into his cold blue eyes. It was a notable fact that all the frontier bad men had eyes either grey or blue, often a faded blue, expressionless, hard as jade.

It is only fair to Bat that the old-timers of Dodge do not accept the Siringo point of view about him. Wright said about him that he was absolutely fearless and no trouble hunter. "Bat is a gentleman by instinct, of pleasant manners, good address, and mild until aroused, and then for God's sake, look out. He is a leader of men, has much natural ability, and good hard common sense. There is nothing low about him. He is high-toned and broad-minded, cool and brave." I give this opinion for what it is worth.

In any case, he was a most efficient sheriff. Dave Rudabaugh, later associated with Billy the Kid in New Mexico, staged a train robbery at Kingsley, Kansas, a territory not in Bat's jurisdiction. However, Bat set out in pursuit with a posse. A near-blizzard was sweeping the country. Bat made for Lovell's cattle camp, on the chance that the bandits would be forced to take shelter there. It was a good guess. Rudabaugh's outfit rode in, stiff and half frozen, and

Bat captured the robbers without firing a shot. This was one of many captures that Bat made.

He had a deep sense of loyalty to his friends. On two separate occasions he returned to Dodge, after having left the town, to straighten out difficulties for his friends or to avenge them. The first time was when Luke Short, who ran a gambling house in Dodge, had difficulty with Mayor Webster and his official family. Luke appears to have held the opinion that the cards were stacked against him and that this was a trouble out of which he could not shoot himself. He wired Bat Masterson and Wyatt Earp to come to Dodge. They did, accompanied by another friend or two. The Mayor made peace on terms dictated by Short.

Bat's second return to Dodge was caused by a wire from his brother James, who ran a dance hall in partnership with a man named Peacock. Masterson wanted to discharge the bartender, Al Updegraph, a brother-in-law of the other partner. A serious difficulty loomed in the offing. Wherefore James called for help. Bat arrived at eleven one sunny morning, another gunman at heel. At three o'clock he entrained for Tombstone, Arizona. James beside him. The interval had been a busy one. On the way up from the station (always known then as the depot), the two men met Peacock and Updegraph. No amenities were exchanged, it was strictly business. Bullets began to sing at once. The men stood across the street from each other and emptied their weapons. Oddly enough, Updegraph was the only one wounded. This little matter attended to, Bat surrendered himself, was fined three dollars for carrying concealed weapons, and released. He ate dinner, disposed of his brother's interest in the saloon, and returned to the station.

Bat Masterson was a friend of Theodore Roosevelt, who was given to admiring men with "guts," such men as Pat Garrett, Ben Daniels, and Billy Tilghman. Mr. Roosevelt offered Masterson a place as United States Marshal of Arizona. The ex-sheriff declined it. "If I took it," he explained, "I'd have to kill some fool boy who wanted to get a reputation for killing me." The President then offered Bat a place as Deputy United States Marshal of New York, and this was accepted. From that time Masterson became a citizen of the Empire State. For seventeen years he worked on a newspaper there and died a few years since with a pen in his hand. He was respected by the entire newspaper fraternity.

Owing to the pleasant habit of cowboys of shooting up the town, they were required, when entering the city limits, to hand over their weapons to the marshal. The guns were deposited at Wright & Beverly's Store, in a rack built for the purpose, and receipts given for them. Sometimes a hundred six-shooters would be there at once. These were never returned to their owners unless the cowboys were sober.

To be a marshal of one of these fighting frontier towns was no post to be sought for by a supple politician. The place called for a chilled iron nerve and an uncanny skill with the Colt. Tom Smith, one of the gamest men and best officers who ever wore a star on the frontier, was killed in performance of his duty. Colonel Breackenridge says that Smith, marshal of Abilene before "Wild Bill," was the gamest man he ever knew. He was a powerful, athletic man who would arrest, himself unarmed, the most desperate characters. He once told Breackenridge that anyone could bring a dead man back but it took a good officer to take lawbreakers while they were alive. In this he differed from Hickok, who did not take chances. He brought his men in dead. Nixon, assistant marshal at Dodge, was murdered by "Mysterious Dave" Mathers, who himself once held the same post. Ed Masterson, after displaying conspicuous courage many times, was mortally wounded April 9, 1878, by two desperate men, Jack Wagner and Alf Walker, who were terrorizing Front Street. Bat reached the scene a few minutes later and heard the story. As soon as his brother died Bat went after the desperadoes, met them, and killed them both.

The death of Ed Masterson shocked the town. Civil organizations passed resolutions of respect. During the funeral, which was the largest ever held in Dodge, all business houses were closed. It is not on record that anybody regretted the demise of the marshal's assassins.

Among those who came to Dodge each season to meet the Texas cattle drive were Ben and Bill Thompson, gamblers who ran a faro bank. Previously they had been accustomed to go to Ellsworth, while that point was the terminus of the drive. Here they had ruled with a high hand, killed the sheriff, and made their getaway safely. Bill got into a shooting affray at Ogalala. He was badly wounded and was carried to the hotel. It was announced openly that he would never leave town alive. Ben did not dare go to Ogalala, for his record there outlawed him. He came to Bat Masterson.

Bat knew Bill's nurse and arranged a plan for campaign. A sham battle was staged at the big dance hall, during the excitement of which Bat and the nurse carried the wounded man to the train, got him to a sleeper, and into a bed. Buffalo Bill met the next day at North Platte. He had relays of teams stationed on the road, and he and Bat guarded the sick man during the long ride, bringing him safely to Dodge.

Emanuel Dubbs ran a roadhouse not far from Dodge about this time. He was practicing with his six-shooter one day when a splendidly built young six-footer rode up to his place. The stranger watched him as he fired at the tin cans he had put on fence posts. Presently the young fellow suggested he throw a couple of cans up in the air. Dubbs did so. Out flashed the stranger's revolver. There was a roar of exploding shots. Dubbs picked up the cans. Four shots had been fired. Two bullets had drilled through each can.

"Better not carry a six-shooter till you learn to shoot," Bill Cody suggested, as he put his guns back into their holsters. "You'll be a living temptation to some bad man." Buffalo Bill was on his way to the North Platte.

Life at Dodge was not all tragic. The six-shooter roared in the land a good deal, but there were many citizens who went quietly about their business and took no part in the nightlife of the town. It was entirely optional with the individual. The little city had its legitimate theatres as well as its hurdy-gurdy houses and gambling dens. There was the Lady Gay, for instance, a popular vaudeville resort. There were well attended churches. But Dodge boiled so with exuberant young life, often inflamed by bad liquor, that both theatre and church were likely to be scenes of unexpected explosions.

A drunken cowboy became annoyed at Eddie Foy. While the comedian was reciting "Kalamazoo in Michigan" the puncher began bombarding the frail walls from the outside with a .45 Colt's revolver. Eddie made a swift strategic retreat. A deputy marshal was standing near the cow-puncher, who was astride a plunging horse. The deputy fired twice. The first shot missed. The second brought the rider down. He was dead before he hit the ground. The deputy apologized later for his marksmanship, but he added by way of explanation, "the bronc sure was sunfishin' plenty."

The killing of Miss Dora Head, a handsome young actress of much promise, was regretted by everybody in Dodge. A young fellow named Kennedy, son of a rich cattleman, shot her unintentionally while he was trying to murder James Kelly. He fled. A posse composed of sheriff Masterson, William Tilghman, Wyatt Earp, and Charles Bassett took the trail. They captured the man after wounding him desperately. He was brought back to Dodge, recovered, and escaped. His pistol arm was useless, but he used the other well enough to slay several other victims before someone made an end of him.

The gay good spirits of Dodge found continual expression in practical jokes. The wilder these were the better pleased was the town. "Mysterious Dave" was the central figure in one. An evangelist was conducting a series of meetings. He made a powerful magnetic appeal, and many were the hard characters who walked the sawdust trail. The preacher set his heart on converting Dave Mathers, the worst of bad men and a notorious scoffer. The meetings prospered. The church proved too small for the crowds and adjourned to a dance hall. Dave became interested. He went to hear brother Johnson preach. He went a second time, and a third. "He certainly preaches

like the Watsons and goes for sin all spraddled out," Dave conceded. Brother Johnson grew hopeful. It seemed possible that this brand could be snatched from the burning. He preached directly at Dave, and Dave buried his head in his hands and sobbed. The preacher said he was willing to die if he could convert this one vile sinner. Others of the deacons agreed that they too would not object to going straight to heaven with the knowledge that Dave had been saved.

"They were right excited an' didn't know straight up," an old-timer explained. "Dave, he looked so whipped his ears flopped. Finally, he rose an' said 'I've got your company, friends. Now, while we're all saved I reckon we'd better start straight for heaven. First off the preacher, then the deacons; me last.' Then Dave whips out a whoppin' big gun and starts to shootin'. The preacher went right through a window an' took it with him. He was sure in some hurry. The deacons hunted cover. Seemed like they was willin' to postpone taking that through ticket to heaven. After that they never did worry anymore about Dave's soul."

Many rustlers gathered around Dodge in those days. The most notorious of these was a gang of more than thirty under the leadership of Dutch Henry and Tom Owens, two of the most desperate outlaws ever known in Kansas. A posse was organized to run down this gang under the leadership of Dubbs, who had lost some of his stock. Before starting, the posse telephoned Hays City to organize a company to head off the rustlers. Twenty miles west of Hays the posse overtook the rustlers. A bloody battle ensued, during which Owens and several outlaws were killed and Dutch Henry wounded six times. Several of the posse were also shot. The story has a curious sequel. Many years later, when Emanuel Dubbs was county judge of Wheeler County, Texas, Dutch Henry came to his house and stayed several days. He was a thoroughly reformed man. Not many years ago Dutch Henry died in Colorado. He was a man with many good qualities. Even in his outlaw days he had many friends among the law-abiding citizens.

After the battle with the Owens gang rustlers operated much more quietly, but they did not cease stealing. One night three men were hanged on a cottonwood on Saw Creek, ten or twelve miles from Dodge. One of these was a young man of a good family who had drifted into rustling and had been carried away by the excitement of it. Another of the three was the son of Tom Owens. To this day the pace is known as Horse Thief Canyon. During its years of prosperity many eminent men visited Dodge, including Generals Sherman and Sheridan, President Hayes, and General Miles. Its reputation had extended far and wide. It was the wild and woolly cowboy capital of the Southwest, a place to quicken the blood of any man. Nearly all that gay, hard-riding company of cow-punchers, buffalo hunters, bad men, and pioneers have vanished into yesterday's seven thousand years. But Certainly Dodge once had its day and night of glory. No more rip-roaring town ever bucked the tiger.

Chapter II.

COWBOY DETECTIVE

By Charles Siringo

A rest of a few days in Denver, and Supt. A instructed me to get ready for a trip among the Ute Indians who were then reported to be on the warpath.

It was the fall of 1887. The work was to be done for a wealthy widow by the name of Mrs. Tice. She and a Mr. C owned a small cattle ranch in western Colorado. She suspicioned that she was being robbed by their foreman and her partner. So, for there I started out in my cowboy rigging.

In Rifle, on Grande River, I left the Denver & Rio Grande train and on the upper deck of a civilized pony I started north over the mountains for Meeker, on White River. A moderate ride of a day and a half brought me to the town made famous by the "Meeker Massacre." On my arrival in Meeker the excitement of a late Indian war had subsided. A week or ten days previous, a battle had been fought on the head of White River, a day's ride from Meeker, and on leaving Denver I was instructed to investigate this battle for an official of the US government, after finishing the cattle operation.

From Meeker, a day's ride down the river brought me to the cattle ranch owned by Mrs. Tice and C. With the foreman and cowboys I played myself off as an outlaw Texan, and by being an expert with a lasso I soon won their friendship.

In the course of two weeks I had secured sufficient evidence to show that our friend, Mrs. Tice, was being robbed.

I then returned to Meeker and from there went to the head of White River to investigate the killing of some Ute Indians by the sheriff and a crowd of ranchmen.

Before leaving Meeker I wrote a letter to Mr. Geo. L. Golding, of Denver, asking that my name be put on the list of wild-horse riders and steer ropers, in the grand Cowboy Tournament soon to take place. I signed myself "Dull Knife," with Meeker as my home, so that no one would know me.

The name "Dull Knife" was selected on account of it once having been my nickname on the cattle ranges of Texas. It was given to me by cowboy companions who were in the habit of borrowing my pearl-handled bowie knife, and always finding it dull, from having killed so many rattlesnakes. Through years of practice I had become an expert in throwing the knife from my horse's back. By holding the point between my thumb and forefinger I would throw it at the snake's neck and seldom failed to pin his snakeship to the earth by burying the blade through his neck or head into the ground. Often the blade would sever the snake's head from his body. Of course the knife was kept dull from being stuck into the earth so often.

On the head of White River I visited the few ranchmen and hunters and was shown the battle ground where the Ute Indians were murdered by the blood-thirsty Whites. From what I could learn from eyewitnesses, it was cold-blooded murder. The fight was started by the long-legged, wild and woolly sheriff of Garfield County, who soon after absconded with the county's funds. The excitement of the "Great Indian Uprising" caused the militia to be called out, and made fat pocket-books for the ranchers who had horses, hay, and grain for sale. Besides, the sheriff lined his pockets with free silver at the county's expense.

This was my first peep behind the curtain of a great Indian war, as illustrated by glaring headlines in the daily press. We wondered who are the real savages, the Whites or the Reds.

On leaving the head of White River for Denver, I concluded to take a shortcut across the Flattop mountains, a distance of sixty miles between ranches.

The start was made from the cabin of a hunter at the head of White River. From him I had bought an extraordinary fine pair of elk horns. These I undertook to carry on my pony by holding them up in front of me with the skull resting on the saddle-horn. In traveling that lonely sixty mile stretch over the old Ute Indian trail, I had plenty of leisure to ponder over that wise saying: "What fools these mortals be."

Crossing the "Flattops," I saw more deer than I ever expect to see again. There were hundreds of them in sight at all times and they were very tame. Often they would stand by the side of the trail and allow me to pass within fifty paces of them. I saw one herd of elk, but they ran into the heavy timber near by before I could get out my Winchester rifle and shoot. I would have followed on their trail, as I had never killed an elk, if it hadn't been for the pair of elk horns. I pitched camp about sundown and killed a fat buck for supper. I had brought with me some salt and cold biscuits. The venison was broiled on a stick over the fire.

By daylight next morning the horns and I headed south. We got off on the wrong trail and were lost part of the day, but by hard swearing and a little patience we managed to get down over the rim-rock of the "Flattops" into the Grand Valley about half way between Newcastle and Glenwood Springs. On the road in the valley a boy leading a bronco overtook us. The boy was persuaded to allow me to make a pack-horse out of his bronco, so "Mr. Bronc" was blindfolded and the horns put astride of his back. When securely fastened with a rope the blind was raised and Hades broke loose. The bronco began bucking and running and the rope which was fastened to the horn of my saddle broke. Then the horns had a swift ride for quite a distance, but as the run was made towards Glenwood Springs no time was lost. The boy and I caught the bronco after he had become exhausted. Then the horns were strapped onto my civilized pony and I rode the uncivilized brute. It was long after dark when we landed in Glenwood Springs. Next day the horns were crated and expressed to Denver, and after selling my pony and saddle I took passage on the same train with the antlers.

On my arrival in Denver I secured permission from my superintendent to enter the Cowboy Tournament at River Side Park. It was to take place in a couple of days and I had no time to lose.

After making a search of all the livery stables in the city I finally found a small white cow-pony which I thought would answer my purpose. He was quick and active, but too light in weight for such work. I also secured an old Texas saddle, as I couldn't get used to the high horn kind in use by northern cowboys. This old Texas saddle was the cause of my losing the steer roping prize, as the horn flew off when the weight of the steer and pony went against it. I feel confident that I would have won the prize, as the best time made was many seconds slower than the time made by me at a Caldwell, Kansas, fair several years previous, at which time I won a silver cup; and in the Kansas contest I lost valuable time by having to throw the steer twice.

In the wild-horse riding contest luck was also against me. After throwing the big bay bronco in quick time, I sprang off the white pony onto the bronco's head. Then to prevent him from choking to death, I cut the rope, knowing that he was in my power with both my knees on his neck and a good hand hold on his nose. But when I reached for the hackamore (a cowboy halter) and the leather blind which had been carried under my pistol belt, I found they were gone. They had slipped out from under the belt when I leaped out of the saddle. I saw them lying on the ground just out of my reach. According to the rules, no one could hand them to me, therefore I could do nothing but free the bronco and lose my chance at the prize. In reporting the matter the newspaper reporters had failed to comprehend my situation: They were green and didn't know why I held the struggling bronco by the nose for several minutes before turning him loose. Of course my cowboy opponents realized the cause of my predicament and cheered with joy, as it made their chances of winning more secure. I had been told that they feared the "dark horse," "Dull Knife," from Meeker, and had made much inquiry as to my identity.

This is what two of the leading daily papers of the city The Rocky Mountain News and the Republican had to say about "Dull Knife" the next morning. One paper stated:

> None knew who the next man was who rode out on a white pony. They called him Dull Knife, and he was from Meeker. That was all the information obtainable. But Dull Knife was a daisy. With new white sombrero, Mexican saddle, leather-fringed chaparejos, flaming red 'kerchief, belt and pearl handled revolver and knife, he was all that the eastern imagination of the typical cowboy could picture. As a bronco breaker, however, he wasn't a brilliant success. A bay was pointed out to him and away they flew. It didn't take that cunning bay bronco more than a minute to

find out that he was wanted. With all the natural cussedness of his breed it didn't take him more than a second to determine that he would fool somebody. Dashing here and there, with flashing eyes and streaming mane and tail, the animal was a pretty picture. The white pony was too cunning for him though, and soon put his rider in a position where the rope could be thrown and the arched neck caught in the running loop. The captive was thrown by twining the rope around his limbs and then Dull Knife made a skillful move. He cut the rope loose and held the struggling animal by the nose. But while he was subduing the horse, the man had gotten too far away from his saddle and couldn't get back to it. The judges at length called time and the pretty bay was free.

The other paper gave this account:

When Dull Knife rode in armed with pearl-handled pistol and knife, a gold embroidered Mexican sombrero on his head and mounted on a beautiful, quick-reined, white pony, he was such a perfect and graceful type of a Texas cowboy that the audience gave one spontaneous Ah-h-h! of admiration. The little white was a daisy and ran up on Dull Knife's bronco easy. Dull Knife was the only man this day to rope and throw his bronco on horseback. But the rope had fouled in the bronco's mane, and it was choking to death, so Dull Knife cut the rope, mercifully, freed the bronco and lost his time to ride. Dull Knife assayed roping and tying, but luck was against him. The horn of his light Texas saddle broke off close to the fork. Regaining his rope he tied it in the forks of his saddle and tried it again, but his beautiful little cut horse was too light and tried to hold the big burly steer which dragged it all over the corral, so Dull Knife, chafing with chagrin, had to give in to hard luck and call it a draw.

Dull Knife and E. A. Shaeffer next stretched a steer in quick time.

Several days after the tournament George Golding and Mr. B. G. Webster, while riding in a buggy, happened to see me on the street. Hailing me as "Dull Knife" they called me to them. They said they had been trying to find me but no one knew who "Dull Knife" was or where a letter would reach him. I was then informed that the judges had voted me fifteen dollars for skillful cowboy performance and that a check for that amount awaited me at headquarters. Of course I went after the check and still retain it as a relic, as it states that it was presented to "Dull Knife" for skillful cowboy work.

For many years afterwards, and even up to the present time, I meet men who call me "Dull Knife," from having seen me at this Cowboy Tournament.

It was several years after, before Geo. Golding, who is still proprietor of the City Sale Yards and Stables, and has since served as Denver's Chief of Police learned of my identity.

In the course of a week or two Mrs. Tice brought suit in a Denver Court to annul her partnership with Mr. C or for damages, I have forgotten which. I was the star witness, and on the strength of my testimony as to the way cattle were being stolen, Mrs. Tice won. The foreman and one of his cowboys who were present in court, were surprised on finding that I was a detective instead of an outlaw.

A few days after ending Mrs. Tice's case I was off for Wyoming as a cowboy outlaw.

Kalter Skoll, the Cheyenne, Wyoming, attorney, who has lately won fame through the conviction and execution of Tim Corn, the stock detective, had written my superintendent to send him a cowboy detective who could make friends with a gang of tough characters on the Laramie River.

Before starting, my superintendent informed me that I was going up against a hard proposition, as Gen. Dave Cook, head of the Rocky Mountain Detective Agency, had sent three of his men up into Wyoming to get in with this gang, but had failed, they being on the lookout for detectives, hence wouldn't allow strangers to enter their camp.

On my arrival in Cheyenne I called on District Attorney Skoll. He explained the case on which I was to work. He told how Bill McCoy had shot and killed Deputy Sheriff Gun in Lusk, Wyoming, and of McCoy being sentenced to hang for the crime, but that he broke jail in Cheyenne just before he was to be executed, and was trailed up to the Keeline ranch, which was run by Tom Hall, a Texas outlaw and his gang of cowboys, who were supposed to be ex-convicts from Texas. He felt sure that McCoy was in hiding at the Keeline ranch, but he said it would be a difficult matter to get in with them as they were on their guard against officers and detectives.

I boarded the Cheyenne northern train and went north to its then terminus. There I bought a horse and saddle and struck out, ostensibly for Fort Douglas, about one hundred miles north.

The second day out I stopped for dinner at "Round Up No. 5 Saloon." This place was run by Howard, an ex-policeman and saloon keeper from Cheyenne. His wife was an ex-prize fighter and dance hall "girl" during the palmy days of the Black Hill excitement in Cheyenne. She was now getting old, but could still hide large quantities of liquor under her belt. After dinner I proceeded to get drunk so as to kill time. Mr. and Mrs. Howard drank with me. In telling of my past I told just enough to lead them to believe that I was a Texas outlaw headed for the north.

About 4 p.m. I saddled my horse and made a start for Fort Douglas, but on shaking hands with Mr. and Mrs. Howard, they being the only people beside myself present, and bidding them goodbye, they persuaded me to have one more drink at their expense. Then, of course, I had to treat before making another start. This program was kept up for half an hour.

I had never mentioned the Keeline ranch, which I knew lay over a small range of mountains five miles east. As winter had set in, there was very little travel on this Fort Douglas road, and the cowboys had all gone into winter quarters. Howard depended on the summer cattle round-ups for his business. He said he and his wife merely existed during the winter seasons. His saloon was located at No. 5 round-up grounds.

Finally, I mounted and made another start, pretending to be drunker than I really was. As I rode off, Howard wished me well. Checking up my horse I remarked that I would be all right if I could run across some Texas boys up at Douglas. Then I asked if he knew of any Texas boys in that part of the country. He replied: "There are several Texas fellers not far from here, but they are in trouble and won't let strangers into their camp." At this I wheeled my horse around and rode back. I asked where they could be found. He replied: "No use going there, for they would run you off and perhaps kill you. The officers have been trying to get detectives in with them. They swear they will kill the next that looks suspicious."

I answered: "If they are from Texas I'm not afraid of them. Just tell me where they are and I'll take chances on the killing part."

He pointed out a bridle path around a high peak and said I would find their camp on the other side of this on the edge of a clump of cottonwood timber. We then went into the saloon and had two more drinks and I bought a quart of his best whiskey, which was the same as his worst, though labeled differently.

I explained that the boys could drink with me and then run me off if they wanted to; but Howard plead with me not to go.

On mounting I buried the spurs into my horse's flanks and gave a cowboy yell and away we flew through the heavy grove of cottonwood timber. There was no trail, and my horse had to jump fallen logs and trees and I dodged projecting limbs. I wanted to prove to Howard that I was a reckless cowboy who had no fear of danger. Looking back I saw Howard and his wife watching me. The saloon was finally lost to view and then I rode slowly and began to lay plans, though it was quite an effort as the whiskey had gone to my head.

Howard had told me that there were fourteen men at the Keeline ranch, but he wouldn't tell me what kind of trouble they were in.

On reaching the foot of the high peak I struck the bridle trail which had been pointed out. This I followed over the range. When on the opposite side, my horse was made to gallop in the most dangerous places, for I figured that my horse's tracks would be examined. In a rocky place where the trail went around a point and where a horse on a gallop could hardly keep his feet, I stopped. Here I knew the horse's tracks couldn't be seen. At this point I got above the horse and gave him a shove over the rocky bluff. He landed on his side in the soft sand in the dry arroyo, twenty feet below. The fall knocked the wind out of him, but he soon recovered and jumped to his feet. I held one end of the rope so that he couldn't get away. The impression of the horse and saddle showed plainly in the sand. Climbing down on the rocks I fell on my left side, leaving the impression of my body in the sand where it would have been had I fallen with the horse. I then jumped up, and dragging my crippled left leg through the sand, led the horse to a place where we could get back to the trail. Here I pulled off my left boot and ripped the seam of my pants' leg nearly to the knee. Then I rolled the knit woolen drawer's leg up above the knee. This made a tight roll which checked the flow of blood, causing the knee to become red. It also had a tendency to shove the flesh downward and make the knee look swollen. I then rubbed the knee with dry grass and poured some of Howard's "rattle-snake juice" on. After tying the left boot to the saddle I mounted and headed for the large grove of cottonwood timber on the bank of the Laramie River.

Just after the sun had set I came in sight of a group of log houses on the edge of the grove. Not a breath of air was stirring and a column of smoke from a chimney pierced the lead-colored clouds above. I was riding slowly across an open flat. Soon I saw a man come out of the large log house. Then others followed until there were about a dozen lined up against the yard fence. I wondered what kind of a game I was running up against and where it would end. It was a case of forward march, with me, even though it led to death "all same," a fool soldier who marches up to the cannon mouth to have his head shot off so that posterity can weep and plant flowers on his grave.

As I drew near my body reeled as though drunk. My left leg was kept stiff and out of the stirrup. When within sixty paces of the yard gate where all the men stood, a fine looking six-footer, who proved to be the boss, Tom Hall, asked: "What in the h—are you doing here?" I replied that my leg was broken and I needed some help. Hall sprang out of the gate and running up to me asked in a soft, sympathetic voice, how it happened. There was a wonderful change in his looks as well as voice, when he found I was crippled.

Soon the whole gang, all heavily armed, were around me and I was taken off the horse and carried into the house where I was seated before a blazing log fire in the large fire-place. Then Hall got down on his knees before me to examine the wound. I took pains to roll up the pants' leg which was only ripped part way to the knee, so as to hide the roll of knit drawers, this being the secret of my swollen knee. I had previously been shot with a large caliber bullet through this knee, and there was a large scar where the bullet entered, and another on the opposite side where it was cut out by the doctor. This helped to brand me as an outlaw in their minds.

After pressing the swollen flesh with his hand, Hall asked me to move my toes. I did so, as I didn't want the leg to appear broken for fear they might haul me off to a doctor. On moving my toes he said my leg was not broken. I asked how he could tell by the moving of the toes, and he explained. Then he asked me to bend my knee and also to twist it around, but this I couldn't do on account of the pain. He decided that my leg was badly sprained or out of joint. He ordered hot water and a towel brought and my knee was bathed and the hot towel bound around it. Then he demanded an explanation as to how I came to leave the Douglas road to visit them. I explained matters fully, and told the place where my horse fell over the bluff. He asked why I left Texas to come up to such a cold country so late in the season. With a smile I told him that the people of Texas tried to get me to stay, and even followed me to Red River on the Indian Territory border in hopes of overtaking me so as to compel me to stay. This caused a laugh, as it meant that officers of the law had chased me to the State line.

Here I looked over towards a sullen, dark complexioned young man whom I had recognized as Jim McChesney, a boy raised in Southern Texas, and I asked him what he had done with his old sweetheart Matilda Labaugh.

He was surprised and asked who in the h—I was, that I should know he courted Matilda Labaugh over twenty years previous. I wouldn't tell him, but did say that he could call me Charlie Henderson. He then asked if I knew his name. I told him, yes, that it ought to be Jim McChesney. This was another surprise, and he wanted to know when I left the part of Texas where Matilda had lived. I told him that I pulled out one night in 1872 when a boy, but that I had slipped back to see my friends many times since then. His face brightened, and walking up to me he shook my hand, saying: "I know you." Then he whispered in my ear and asked if I wasn't one of the Pumphry boys. I told him that my name was Henderson now. I had chosen the year 1872, for at that time two of the Pumphry boys, mere children, had committed murder and left the country. McChesney felt sure that I was one of these boys, and that suited me.

Finally, all left the room to hold a consultation. Two men were dispatched with a lantern to examine the place where I said my horse had fallen over the bluff, and to ride to Howard's saloon to find out if I had told the truth. Another man was sent in haste to a small ranch three miles down the river, after some linament. Supper was then brought in and set before me. In the course of an hour and a half the man returned with the linament and Hall applied it to the supposed wound, and he bound up the knee so tight with bandages that it pained, but the tight bandages did good in preventing me from thoughtlessly bending my leg and thereby giving myself away.

About ten o'clock the two "boys" returned from Howard's. Then all went outside and held a long consultation. Next day Jim McChesney told me confidentially that Howard had confirmed the truthfulness of my story and had told of the reckless manner in which I had run through the woods. He said he was not surprised at hearing of my being hurt, that he expected to see me killed before I got out of his sight.

Several days later McChesney told me of their long council of war, after the two "boys" had returned from Howard's. He said most of the "boys," especially the three escaped convicts from the penitentiary in Huntsville, Texas, were afraid that I might be a detective and insisted that I be taken out to a tree and hung up by the neck, just to frighten me into a confession in case I was a detective; but said he and Tom Hall argued against it as they felt confident that I was all right. Hall argued that it would be a shame to take advantage of a poor crippled man. He said if I was a detective that I couldn't help from showing it before many days and then I could be hung for "keeps."

All the men slept on camp beds spread on the floor, except Hall. He had a private room cut off from a corner of the kitchen, and in it he had a single bedstead. This he kindly turned over to me and he slept with one of the "boys" on the floor.

It was after 1:00 a.m. when I went to bed, as I pretended that my leg was paining so that I could not sleep, anyway. After being put to bed by Hall I took off the bandages from my leg so that I could rest my knee by bending it. I retired with my Colt's 45 pistol in the shoulder scabbard under my overshirt, and my bowie knife was swung to my waist by a small belt under my drawers. Therefore no one had seen my gun and knife. The cartridge belt containing my supply of ammunition was in my "war-bag," and this I put under my head. I slept very little during the night. Before daylight next morning, I fastened the bandages back on my leg so as to keep it stiff while hobbling about the house. After breakfast, Hall and McChesney made me a pair of crutches.

A few of the "boys" seemed suspicious of me, especially Johnny Franklin, a bowlegged Texan, who had escaped from the penitentiary in that State, so McChesney told me.

During the day Hall played "foxy" and tried to find out more about me. In speaking of Texas cowboys he asked if I ever knew Bill Gatlin. I told him yes, that I had worked with him in the Panhandle country until he got into trouble and had to skip and change his name again. I told him that Bill Gatlin was a name he had adopted after coming to northern Texas. These were facts, as I had known Gatlin well, but I never dreamed that he was the Bill McCoy I was now trying to locate.

A few days later, after I had convinced Hall that I was all right and was really acquainted with Gatlin and many of his Texas friends, he confided in me and told me how Bill Gatlin, under the name of Bill McCoy, had killed Deputy Sheriff Gunn, and was sentenced to hang, and that he (Hall) and others paid a slick jail breaker from the East $500 to commit a petty crime in Cheyenne so as to be put in jail. The result was that he sawed the bars and liberated McCoy and the other prisoners. A horse was kept in hiding for McCoy and he came direct to the Keeline ranch where they had kept him hid out in the hills until a few days before my arrival, when he was mounted on Hall's pet roan race-horse and skipped for New Orleans, there to take a sailing vessel for Buenos Aires, South America. For a pack animal McCoy used a large-hoofed bay horse that he had stolen from the sheriff's posse who were searching for him. Later,

Hall and McChesney told many incidents of how they had fooled the sheriff's posse of one hundred men who were scouring the hills for McCoy.

A week later we all rode forty miles to attend a dance at John Owens's ranch, a mile above the "Hog ranch" (a tough saloon and sporting house) at Fort Laramie. I was still walking on crutches, therefore couldn't dance. The crutches were tied to my saddle en route. Late at night when the "boys" were pretty well loaded with liquor, I rode to Fort Laramie and secured a room at the hotel where my first reports were written. About daylight my reports were mailed to Denver, and then I rode back to the dance. The crowd had simmered down to just a few ladies and many drunken cowboys who kept the air outside full of smoke from their revolvers. My friends, McChesney and Franklin, were the worst. I finally succeeded in getting my drunken friends into a room to lay down, but McChesney raised such a racket breaking the windows and furniture with his pistol, that we had to abandon sleep and start back to the Keeline ranch. As I was sober, it fell to my lot to get them all on their horses and headed for home. Hall and the cook had not come with us.

A supply of whiskey was taken along, and my life was made miserable keeping the men from fighting. To prevent McChesney from killing someone, I slipped the cartridges out of his pistol without letting him know it. Soon after this, McChesney and one of the "boys" got into a fuss while riding along, and McChesney pulled his pistol and began snapping it at the fellow, who pulled his loaded pistol and would have killed McChesney if I hadn't shoved my cocked revolver into his face just in time. I made him ride on ahead while I kept McChesney behind with me. We arrived at the Keeline ranch before night, and were a hungry, sleepy crowd.

Our next excitement came a few days later, when Howard came running over on horseback one evening to tell us that his wife was dying. He had left her alone while he came after help. All of us, Hall and the cook included, rode over to Howard's and spent the night. What happened would have made angels weep. Howard turned the saloon over to us and the liquor was free. Whiskey was poured down the poor woman's throat up to the last breath. She died before midnight and then the "Irish wake" began in dead earnest. Poor Howard, a large fine-looking, middle-age man, cried as though his heart would break. Between drinks he "harked back" to the time when he first met the corpse. Then he was on the police force of Cheyenne, and she was a beautiful young woman who made a living by boxing and singing on the saloon stages.

Until morning, whiskey and wine flowed like water, and my friend McChesney was in clover. Cowboy songs, both nice and vulgar, were sung over the corpse. Tom Hall was the champion singer of the crowd.

Next day the body was put in a rough box and lowered to its last resting place amid the drinking of toasts and the singing of "There's a land that beats this all to h—, etc." One of the songs which was sung at the burial amused me. It ran thus:

Oh, see the train go 'round the bend,
Goodby, my lover, goodby;
She's loaded down with Dickenson men,
Goodby, my lover, goodby

When we took our departure the Howard saloon looked like a cyclone had struck it. The walls were shot full of holes and the liquors were gone. Howard left for Cheyenne when he sobered up. Of course, I didn't have as much fun as the rest, owing to the fact that I had to use one crutch.

With Mrs. Howard under the sod, "Calamity Jane" had the field to herself. These two women were noted characters in that part of Wyoming.

Finally my crutch was discarded and we made another forty-mile ride to a dance at Fort Laramie. This time I danced, and pretended to fall in love with a young lady who lived at the terminus of the Cheyenne Northern Railway. I wanted to make the excuse of riding over to the railroad station to see this girl when my work was finished at the Keeline ranch.

Reports were written, and much liquor destroyed, the same as on our previous trip.

Soon after, Hall received a letter from Bill McCoy in New Orleans. He was ready to sail for South America. Hall had given him a letter of introduction to a dentist in Buenos Ayres, South America. This answered the purpose of a passport into a tough gang of outlaws in the cattle country 1200 miles from this seaport, Buenos Ayres. Hall showed me letters from one of the gang there. His name was Moore and he was a Texas murderer. He wrote that they were over one hundred strong, and that double their number of officers couldn't come in there and arrest them.

Hall had been reared at Austin, Texas, and had to skip out and change his name on account of a killing. He also told me of his ups and downs in New Mexico when he was a chum to the noted outlaw, Joe Fowler, who was

hung by a mob at Socorro, New Mexico. He told how Fowler, after killing one of his own cowboys in Socorro, had placed the $50,000 received for his cattle and ranch to the credit of his sweetheart, Belle, and that on the day when the mob was collecting to hang Fowler that night, Belle drew $10,000 out of the bank and turned it over to him (Hall) so that he could bribe the jailer and liberate Fowler. Hall said he had the jailor "fixed" but when the time for liberating Fowler came, the mob was collecting and the jailer backed out for fear they would hang him, if Fowler was gone. Then Hall said he hit the "high places" and came North. I didn't ask if he brought the $10,000 with him, but took it for granted that he did.

It happened that I was already familiar with Joe Fowler's crimes. He murdered Jim Greathouse, who was a friend of mine, and at White Oaks, New Mexico, in 1880, I knew of his murdering a cowboy whom he had never seen before. Two cowboys had a pistol duel in Bill Hudgen's Pioneer Saloon. One of them was mortally wounded when Fowler, who had heard the shooting, came running in. He asked the cause of the shooting. Someone pointed to the wounded cowboy on the floor. Then Fowler pulled out his pistol and shot him through the head. The other cowboy was caught and hung to a tree by Fowler and his gang, and by the rope route Fowler's life was ended.

Finally, I struck out from the Keeline ranch to see my girl at the railroad station. There my horse and saddle were sold and I boarded the train for Cheyenne.

The Grand Jury were in session and I appeared before them as a witness. Hall and his gang were indicted. The sheriff and a large posse surrounded the Keeline ranch at daylight one morning, and the Hall gang were arrested. I was told that Hall remarked when arrested:

"That Henderson is at the bottom of this." The fact that I did not come back had created a suspicion.

They were all landed in jail at Cheyenne and I felt sorry for them, especially for Hall and McChesney. My sympathy was overflowing for Hall because he is a prince, and has a heart in him like an ox. The sympathy for McChesney was on account of having known him when a boy, and having known his father in Caldwell, Kansas, years later.

I lay in Denver waiting to be called as a witness against Hall and his gang. But before the case was tried, District Attorney Skoll, who at that time was trying to get away with all the liquor in Cheyenne, had a row with the judge on the bench, McGinnis, and the cases were nolle prossed by Skoll. At least, this is the story told by my superintendent, who was in Cheyenne at the time. Thus my friends were liberated to my great joy, as I didn't want to see them sent to the pen. I heard afterwards that three of the escaped convicts from Texas were returned there, but as to its truthfulness I do not know.

CHAPTER III.

SLADE

from *Roughing It*

By Mark Twain

We passed Fort Laramie in the night, and on the seventh morning out we found ourselves in the Black Hills, with Laramie Peak at our elbow (apparently) looming vast and solitary—a deep, dark, rich indigo blue in hue, so portentously did the old colossus frown under his beetling brows of storm-cloud. He was thirty or forty miles away, in reality, but he only seemed removed a little beyond the low ridge at our right. We breakfasted at Horse-Shoe Station, six hundred and seventy-six miles out from St. Joseph. We had now reached a hostile Indian country, and during the afternoon we passed Laparelle Station, and enjoyed great discomfort all the time we were in the neighborhood, being aware that many of the trees we dashed by at arm's length concealed a lurking Indian or two. During the preceding night an ambushed savage had sent a bullet through the pony-rider's jacket, but he had ridden on, just the same, because pony-riders were not allowed to stop and inquire into such things except when killed. As long as they had life enough left in them they had to stick to the horse and ride, even if the Indians had been waiting for them a week, and were entirely out of patience. About two hours and a half before we arrived at Laparelle Station, the keeper in charge of it had fired four times at an Indian, but he said with an injured air that the Indian had "skipped around so's to spile everything—and ammunition's blamed skurse, too." The most natural inference conveyed by his manner of speaking was, that in "skipping around," the Indian had taken an unfair advantage.

The coach we were in had a neat hole through its front—a reminiscence of its last trip through this region. The bullet that made it wounded the driver slightly, but he did not mind it much. He said the place to keep a man "huffy" was down on the Southern Overland, among the Apaches, before the company moved the stage line up on the northern route. He said the Apaches used to annoy him all the time down there, and that he came as near as anything to starving to death in the midst of abundance, because they kept him so leaky with bullet holes that he "couldn't hold his vittles." This person's statements were not generally believed.

We shut the blinds down very tightly that first night in the hostile Indian country, and lay on our arms. We slept on them some, but most of the time we only lay on them. We did not talk much, but kept quiet and listened. It was an inky-black night, and occasionally rainy. We were among woods and rocks, hills and gorges—so shut in, in fact, that when we peeped through a chink in a curtain, we could discern nothing. The driver and conductor on top were still, too, or only spoke at long intervals, in low tones, as is the way of men in the midst of invisible dangers. We listened to raindrops pattering on the roof; and the grinding of the wheels through the muddy gravel; and the low wailing of the wind; and all the time we had that absurd sense upon us, inseparable from travel at night in a close-curtained vehicle, the sense of remaining perfectly still in one place, notwithstanding the jolting and swaying of the vehicle, the trampling of the horses, and the grinding of the wheels. We listened a long time, with intent faculties and bated breath; every time one of us would relax, and draw a long sigh of relief and start to say something, a comrade would be sure to utter a sudden "Hark!" and instantly the experimenter was rigid and listening again. So the tiresome minutes and decades of minutes dragged away, until at last our tense forms filmed over with a dulled consciousness, and we slept, if one might call such a condition by so strong a name—for it was a sleep set with a hair-trigger. It was a sleep seething and teeming with a weird and distressful confusion of shreds and fag-ends of dreams—a sleep that was a chaos. Presently, dreams and sleep and the sullen hush of the night were startled by a ringing report, and cloven by such a long, wild, agonizing shriek! Then we heard—ten steps from the stage—

"Help! Help! Help!" (It was our driver's voice.)

"Kill him! Kill him like a dog!"

"I'm being murdered! Will no man lend me a pistol?"

"Look out! Head him off! Head him off!"

(Two pistol shots; a confusion of voices and the trampling of many feet, as if a crowd were closing and surging together around some object; several heavy, dull blows, as with a club; a voice that said appealingly, "Don't, gentlemen, please don't—I'm a dead man!" Then a fainter groan, and another blow, and away sped the stage into the darkness, and left the grisly mystery behind us.)

What a startle it was! Eight seconds would amply cover the time it occupied—maybe even five would do it. We only had time to plunge at a curtain and unbuckle and unbutton part of it in an awkward and hindering flurry, when our whip cracked sharply overhead, and we went rumbling and thundering away, down a mountain "grade."

We fed on that mystery the rest of the night—what was left of it, for it was waning fast. It had to remain a present mystery, for all we could get from the conductor in answer to our hails was something that sounded, through the clatter of the wheels, like "Tell you in the morning!"

So we lit our pipes and opened the corner of a curtain for a chimney, and lay there in the dark, listening to each other's story of how he first felt and how many thousand Indians he first thought had hurled themselves upon us, and what his remembrance of the subsequent sounds was, and the order of their occurrence. And we theorized, too, but there was never a theory that would account for our driver's voice being out there, nor yet account for his Indian murderers talking such good English, if they were Indians.

So we chatted and smoked the rest of the night comfortably away, our boding anxiety being somehow marvelously dissipated by the real presence of something to be anxious about.

We never did get much satisfaction about that dark occurrence. All that we could make out of the odds and ends of the information we gathered in the morning, was that the disturbance occurred at a station; that we changed drivers there, and that the driver that got off there had been talking roughly about some of the outlaws that infested the region ("for there wasn't a man around there but had a price on his head and didn't dare show himself in the settlements," the conductor said); he had talked roughly about these characters, and ought to have "drove up there with his pistol cocked and ready on the seat alongside of him, and begun business himself, because any softy would know they would be laying for him."

That was all we could gather, and we could see that neither the conductor nor the new driver were much concerned about the matter. They plainly had little respect for a man who would deliver offensive opinions of people and then be so simple as to come into their presence unprepared to "back his judgment," as they pleasantly phrased the killing of any fellow-being who did not like said opinions. And likewise they plainly had a contempt for the man's poor discretion in venturing to rouse the wrath of such utterly reckless wild beasts as those outlaws—and the conductor added:

"I tell you it's as much as Slade himself want to do!"

This remark created an entire revolution in my curiosity. I cared nothing now about the Indians, and even lost interest in the murdered driver. There was such magic in that name, SLADE! Day or night, now, I stood always ready to drop any subject in hand, to listen to something new about Slade and his ghastly exploits. Even before we got to Overland City, we had begun to hear about Slade and his "division" (for he was a "division-agent") on the Overland; and from the hour we had left Overland City we had heard drivers and conductors talk about only three things—"Californy," the Nevada silver mines, and this desperado Slade. And a great deal of most of the talk was about Slade. We had gradually come to have a realizing sense of the fact that Slade was a man whose heart and hands and soul were steeped in the blood of offenders against his dignity; a man who awfully avenged all injuries, affront, insults or slights, of whatever kind—on the spot if he could, years afterward if lack of earlier opportunity compelled it; a man whose hate tortured him day and night till vengeance appeased it—and not an ordinary vengeance either, but his enemy's absolute death—nothing less; a man whose face would light up with a terrible joy when he surprised a foe and had him at a disadvantage. A high and efficient servant of the Overland, an outlaw among outlaws and yet their relentless scourge, Slade was at once the most bloody, the most dangerous, and the most valuable citizen that inhabited the savage fastnesses of the mountains.

Really and truly, two thirds of the talk of drivers and conductors had been about this man Slade, ever since the day before we reached Julesburg. In order that the eastern reader may have a clear conception of what a Rocky Mountain desperado is, in his highest state of development, I will reduce all this mass of overland gossip to one straightforward narrative, and present it in the following shape:

Slade was born in Illinois, of good parentage. At about twenty-six years of age he killed a man in a quarrel and fled the country. At St. Joseph, Missouri, he joined one of the early California-bound emigrant trains, and was given the post of train-master. One day on the plains he had an angry dispute with one of his wagon-drivers, and both drew their revolvers. But the driver was the quicker artist, and had his weapon cocked first. So Slade said it was a pity to waste life on so small a matter, and proposed that the pistols be thrown on the ground and the quarrel settled by a fist-fight. The unsuspecting driver agreed, and threw down his pistol—whereupon Slade laughed at his simplicity, and shot him dead!

He made his escape, and lived a wild life for awhile, dividing his time between fighting Indians and avoiding an Illinois sheriff, who had been sent to arrest him for his first murder. It is said that in one Indian battle he killed three savages with his own hand, and afterward cut their ears off and sent them, with his compliments, to the chief of the tribe.

Slade soon gained a name for fearless resolution, and this was sufficient merit to procure for him the important post of overland division-agent at Julesburg, in place of Mr. Jules, removed. For some time previously, the company's horses had been frequently stolen, and the coaches delayed, by gangs of outlaws, who were wont to laugh at the idea of any man's having the temerity to resent such outrages. Slade resented them promptly.

The outlaws soon found that the new agent was a man who did not fear anything that breathed the breath of life. He made short work of all offenders. The result was that delays ceased, the company's property was let alone, and no matter what happened or who suffered, Slade's coaches went through, every time! True, in order to bring about this wholesome change, Slade had to kill several men—some say three, others say four, and others six—but the world was the richer for their loss. The first prominent difficulty he had was with the ex-agent Jules, who bore the reputation of being a reckless and desperate man himself. Jules hated Slade for supplanting him, and a good fair occasion for a fight was all he was waiting for. By and by Slade dared to employ a man whom Jules had once discharged. Next, Slade seized a team of stage-horses which he accused Jules of having driven off and hidden somewhere for his own use. War was declared, and for a day or two the two men walked warily about the streets, seeking each other, Jules armed with a double-barreled shot gun, and Slade with his history-creating revolver. Finally, as Slade stepped into a store, Jules poured the contents of his gun into him from behind the door. Slade was plucky, and Jules got several bad pistol wounds in return.

Then both men fell, and were carried to their respective lodgings, both swearing that better aim should do deadlier work next time. Both were bedridden a long time, but Jules got to his feet first, and gathering his possessions together, packed them on a couple of mules, and fled to the Rocky Mountains to gather strength in safety against the day of reckoning. For many months he was not seen or heard of, and was gradually dropped out of the remembrance of all save Slade himself. But Slade was not the man to forget him. On the contrary, common report said that Slade kept a reward standing for his capture, dead or alive!

After awhile, seeing that Slade's energetic administration had restored peace and order to one of the worst divisions of the road, the overland stage company transferred him to the Rocky Ridge division in the Rocky Mountains, to see if he could perform a like miracle there. It was the very paradise of outlaws and desperadoes. There was absolutely no semblance of law there. Violence was the rule. Force was the only recognized authority. The commonest misunderstandings were settled on the spot with the revolver or the knife. Murders were done in open day, and with sparkling frequency, and nobody thought of inquiring into them. It was considered that the parties who did the killing had their private reasons for it; for other people to meddle would have been looked upon as indelicate. After a murder, all that Rocky Mountain etiquette required of a spectator was, that he should help the gentleman bury his game— otherwise his churlishness would surely be remembered against him the first time he killed a man himself and needed a neighborly turn in interring him.

Slade took up his residence sweetly and peacefully in the midst of this hive of horse-thieves and assassins, and the very first time one of them aired his insolent swaggerings in his presence he shot him dead! He began a raid on the outlaws, and in a singularly short space of time he had completely stopped their depredations on the stage stock, recovered a large number of stolen horses, killed several of the worst desperadoes of the district, and gained such a dread ascendancy over the rest that they respected him, admired him, feared him, obeyed him! He wrought the same marvelous change in the ways of the community that had marked his administration at Overland City. He captured two men who had stolen overland stock, and with his own hands he hanged them. He was supreme judge in his district, and he was jury and executioner likewise—and not only in the case of offences against his employers, but against passing emigrants as well. On one occasion some emigrants had their stock lost or stolen, and told Slade, who chanced to visit their camp. With a single companion he rode to a ranch, the owners of which he suspected, and opening the door, commenced firing, killing three, and wounding the fourth.

From a bloodthirstily interesting little Montana book—*The Vigilantes of Montana* by Prof. Thomas J. Dimsdale—I take this paragraph:

> While on the road, Slade held absolute sway. He would ride down to a station, get into a quarrel, turn the house out of windows, and maltreat the occupants most cruelly. The unfortunates had no means of redress, and were compelled to recuperate as best they could.
>
> On one of these occasions, it is said he killed the father of the fine little half-breed boy Jemmy, whom he adopted, and who lived with his widow after his execution. Stories of Slade's hanging men, and of innumerable assaults, shootings, stabbings and beatings, in which he was a principal actor, form part of the legends of the stage line. As for minor quarrels and

shootings, it is absolutely certain that a minute history of Slade's life would be one long record of such practices.

—*The Vigilantes of Montana* by Prof. Thomas J. Dimsdale

Slade was a matchless marksman with a navy revolver. The legends say that one morning at Rocky Ridge, when he was feeling comfortable, he saw a man approaching who had offended him some days before—observe the fine memory he had for matters like that—and, "Gentlemen," said Slade, drawing, "it is a good twenty-yard shot—I'll clip the third button on his coat!" Which he did. The bystanders all admired it. And they all attended the funeral, too.

On one occasion a man who kept a little whisky-shelf at the station did something which angered Slade—and went and made his will. A day or two afterward Slade came in and called for some brandy. The man reached under the counter (ostensibly to get a bottle—possibly to get something else), but Slade smiled upon him that peculiarly bland and satisfied smile of his which the neighbors had long ago learned to recognize as a death-warrant in disguise, and told him to "none of that!—pass out the high-priced article." So the poor bar-keeper had to turn his back and get the high-priced brandy from the shelf; and when he faced around again he was looking into the muzzle of Slade's pistol. "And the next instant," added my informant, impressively, "he was one of the deadest men that ever lived."

The stage-drivers and conductors told us that sometimes Slade would leave a hated enemy wholly unmolested, unnoticed, and unmentioned, for weeks together—had done it once or twice at any rate. And some said they believed he did it in order to lull the victims into unwatchfulness, so that he could get the advantage of them, and others said they believed

he saved up an enemy that way, just as a schoolboy saves up a cake, and made the pleasure go as far as it would by gloating over the anticipation. One of these cases was that of a Frenchman who had offended Slade. To the surprise of everybody, Slade did not kill him on the spot, but let him alone for a considerable time. Finally, however, he went to the Frenchman's house very late one night, knocked, and when his enemy opened the door, shot him dead—pushed the corpse inside the door with his foot, set the house on fire and burned up the dead man, his widow, and three children! I heard this story from several different people, and they evidently believed what they were saying. It may be true, and it may not. "Give a dog a bad name," etc.

Slade was captured, once, by a party of men who intended to lynch him. They disarmed him, and shut him up in a strong log-house, and placed a guard over him. He prevailed on his captors to send for his wife, so that he might have a last interview with her. She was a brave, loving, spirited woman. She jumped on a horse and rode for life and death. When she arrived they let her in without searching her, and before the door could be closed she whipped out a couple of revolvers, and she and her lord marched forth defying the party. And then, under a brisk fire, they mounted double and galloped away unharmed!

In the fullness of time Slade's myrmidons captured his ancient enemy Jules, whom they found in a well-chosen hidingplace in the remote fastnesses of the mountains, gaining a precarious livelihood with his rifle. They brought him to Rocky Ridge, bound hand and foot, and deposited him in the middle of the cattle-yard with his back against a post. It is said that the pleasure that lit Slade's face when he heard of it was something fearful to contemplate. He examined his enemy to see that he was securely tied, and then went to bed, content to wait till morning before enjoying the luxury of killing him. Jules spent the night in the cattle-yard, and it is a region where warm nights are never known. In the morning Slade practiced on him with his revolver, nipping the flesh here and there, and occasionally clipping off a finger, while Jules begged him to kill him outright and put him out of his misery. Finally Slade reloaded, and walking up close to his victim, made some characteristic remarks and then dispatched him. The body lay there half a day, nobody venturing to touch it without orders, and then Slade detailed a party and assisted at the burial himself. But he first cut off the dead man's ears and put them in his vest pocket, where he carried them for some time with great satisfaction. That is the story as I have frequently heard it told and seen it in print in California newspapers. It is doubtless correct in all essential particulars.

In due time we rattled up to a stage-station, and sat down to breakfast with a half-savage, half-civilized company of armed and bearded mountaineers, ranchmen and station employees. The most gentlemanly-appearing, quiet, and affable officer we had yet found along the road in the Overland Company's service was the person who sat at the head of the table, at my elbow. Never youth stared and shivered as I did when I heard them call him SLADE!

Here was romance, and I sitting face to face with it!—looking upon it—touching it—hobnobbing with it, as it were! Here, right by my side, was the actual ogre who, in fights and brawls and various ways, had taken the lives of twenty-six human beings, or all men lied about him! I suppose I was the proudest stripling that ever traveled to see strange lands and wonderful people.

He was so friendly and so gentle-spoken that I warmed to him in spite of his awful history. It was hardly possible to realize that this pleasant person was the pitiless scourge of the outlaws, the raw-head-and-bloody-bones the nursing mothers of the mountains terrified their children with. And to this day I can remember nothing remarkable about Slade except that his face was rather broad across the cheek bones, and that the cheek bones were low and the lips peculiarly thin and straight. But that was enough to leave something of an effect upon me, for since then I seldom see a face possessing those characteristics without fancying that the owner of it is a dangerous man.

The coffee ran out. At least it was reduced to one tin-cupful, and Slade was about to take it when he saw that my cup was empty.

He politely offered to fill it, but although I wanted it, I politely declined. I was afraid he had not killed anybody that morning, and might be needing diversion. But still with firm politeness he insisted on filling my cup, and said I had traveled all night and better deserved it than he—and while he talked he placidly poured the fluid, to the last drop. I thanked him and drank it, but it gave me no comfort, for I could not feel sure that he would not be sorry, presently, that he had given it away, and proceed to kill me to distract his thoughts from the loss. But nothing of the kind occurred. We left him with only twenty-six dead people to account for, and I felt a tranquil satisfaction in

the thought that in so judiciously taking care of No. 1 at that breakfast table I had pleasantly escaped being No. 27. Slade came out to the coach and saw us off, first ordering certain rearrangements of the mailbags for our comfort, and then we took leave of him, satisfied that we should hear of him again, some day, and wondering in what connection.

And sure enough, two or three years afterward, we did hear him again. News came to the Pacific coast that the Vigilance Committee in Montana (whither Slade had removed from Rocky Ridge) had hanged him. I find an account of the affair in the thrilling little book I quoted a paragraph from in the last chapter—*The Vigilantes of Montana; being a Reliable Account of the Capture, Trial and Execution of Henry Plummer's Notorious Road Agent Band* by Prof. Thomas J. Dimsdale, Virginia City, M.T. Mr. Dimsdale's chapter is well worth reading, as a specimen of how the people of the frontier deal with criminals when the courts of law prove inefficient. Mr. Dimsdale makes two remarks about Slade, both of which are accurately descriptive, and one of which is exceedingly picturesque: "Those who saw him in his natural state only, would pronounce him to be a kind husband, a most hospitable host and a courteous gentleman; on the contrary, those who met him when maddened with liquor and surrounded by a gang of armed roughs, would pronounce him a fiend incarnate." And this: "From Fort Kearney, west, he was feared a great deal more than the almighty." For compactness, simplicity, and vigor of expression, I will "back" that sentence against anything in literature. Mr. Dimsdale's narrative is as follows:

> After the execution of the five men on the 14th of January, the Vigilantes considered that their work was nearly ended. They had freed the country of highwaymen and murderers to a great extent, and they determined that in the absence of the regular civil authority they would establish a People's Court where all offenders should be tried by judge and jury. This was the nearest approach to social order that the circumstances permitted, and, though strict legal authority was wanting, yet the people were firmly determined to maintain its efficiency, and to enforce its decrees. It may here be mentioned that the overt act which was the last round on the fatal ladder leading to the scaffold on which Slade perished, was the tearing in pieces and stamping upon a writ of this court, followed by his arrest of the Judge Alex. Davis, by authority of a presented Derringer, and with his own hands.
>
> J. A. Slade was himself, we have been informed, a Vigilante; he openly boasted of it, and said he knew all that they knew. He was never accused, or even suspected, of either murder or robbery, committed in this Territory (the latter crime was never laid to his charge, in any place); but that he had killed several men in other localities was notorious, and his bad reputation in this respect was a most powerful argument in determining his fate, when he was finally arrested for the offence above mentioned. On returning from Milk River he became more and more addicted to drinking, until at last it was a common feat for him and his friends to "take the town." He and a couple of his dependents might often be seen on one horse, galloping through the streets, shouting and yelling, firing revolvers, etc. On many occasions he would ride his horse into stores, break up bars, toss the scales out of doors and use most insulting language to parties present. Just previous to the day of his arrest, he had given a fearful beating to one of his followers; but such was his

influence over them that the man wept bitterly at the gallows, and beg-ged for his life with all his power. It had become quite common, when Slade was on a spree, for the shop-keepers and citizens to close the stores and put out all the lights; being fearful of some outrage at his hands. For his wanton destruction of goods and furniture, he was always ready to pay, when sober, if he had money; but there were not a few who regarded payment as small satisfaction for the outrage, and these men were his personal enemies.

From time to time Slade received warnings from men that he well knew would not deceive him, of the certain end of his conduct. There was not a moment, for weeks previous to his arrest, in which the public did not expect to hear of some bloody outrage. The dread of his very name, and the presence of the armed band of hangers-on who followed him alone prevented a resistance which must certainly have ended in the instant murder or mutilation of the opposing party.

Slade was frequently arrested by order of the court whose organiza-tion we have described, and had treated it with respect by paying one or two fines and promising to pay the rest when he had money; but in the transaction that occurred at this crisis, he forgot even this caution, and goaded by passion and the hatred of restraint, he sprang into the embrace of death.

Slade had been drunk and "cutting up" all night. He and his com-panions had made the town a perfect hell. In the morning, J. M. Fox, the sheriff, met him, arrested him, took him into court and commenced reading a warrant that he had for his arrest, by way of arraignment. He became uncontrollably furious, and seizing the writ, he tore it up, threw it on the ground and stamped upon it.

The clicking of the locks of his companions' revolvers was instantly heard, and a crisis was expected. The sheriff did not attempt his reten-tion; but being at least as prudent as he was valiant, he succumbed, leaving Slade the master of the situation and the conqueror and ruler of the courts, law and law-makers. This was a declaration of war, and was so accepted. The Vigilance Committee now felt that the question of social order and the preponderance of the law-abiding citizens had then and there to be decided. They knew the character of Slade, and they were well aware that they must submit to his rule without murmur, or else that he must be dealt with in such fashion as would prevent his being able to wreak his vengeance on the committee, who could never have hoped to live in the Territory secure from outrage or death, and who could never leave it without encountering his friend, whom his victory would have emboldened and stimulated to a pitch that would

44

have rendered them reckless of consequences. The day previous he had ridden into Dorris's store, and on being requested to leave, he drew his revolver and threatened to kill the gentleman who spoke to him. Another saloon he had led his horse into, and buying a bottle of wine, he tried to make the animal drink it. This was not considered an uncommon performance, as he had often entered saloons and commenced firing at the lamps, causing a wild stampede.

A leading member of the committee met Slade, and informed him in the quiet, earnest manner of one who feels the importance of what he is saying: "Slade, get your horse at once, and go home, or there will be——to pay." Slade started and took a long look, with his dark and piercing eyes, at the gentleman. "What do you mean?" said he. "You have no right to ask me what I mean," was the quiet reply, "get your horse at once, and remember what I tell you." After a short pause he promised to do so, and actually got into the saddle; but, being still intoxicated, he began calling aloud to one after another of his friends, and at last seemed to have forgotten the warning he had received and became again uproarious, shouting the name of a well-known courtezan in company with those of two men whom he considered heads of the committee, as a sort of challenge; perhaps, however, as a simple act of bravado. It seems probable that the intimation of personal danger he had received had not been forgotten entirely; though fatally for him, he took a foolish way of showing his remembrance of it. He sought out Alexander Davis, the Judge of the Court, and drawing a cocked Derringer, he presented it at his head, and told him that he should hold him as a hostage for his own safety. As the judge stood perfectly quiet, and offered no resistance to his captor, no further outrage followed on this score. Previous to this, on account of the critical state of affairs, the committee had met, and at last resolved to arrest him. His execution had not been agreed upon, and, at that time, would have been negatived, most assuredly. A messenger rode down to Nevada to inform the leading men of what was on hand, as it was desirable to show that there was a feeling of unanimity on the subject, all along the gulch.

The miners turned out almost en masse, leaving their work and forming in solid column about six hundred strong, armed to the teeth, they marched up to Virginia. The leader of the body well knew the temper of his men on the subject. He spurred on ahead of them, and hastily calling a meeting of the executive, he told them plainly that the miners meant "business," and that, if they came up, they would not stand in the street to be shot down by Slade's friends; but that they would take him and hang him. The meeting was small, as the Virginia men were loath to act at all. This momentous announcement of the feeling of the Lower Town was made to a cluster of men, who were deliberation behind a wagon, at the rear of a store on Main Street.

The committee were most unwilling to proceed to extremities. All the duty they had ever performed seemed as nothing to the task before them; but they had to decide, and that quickly. It was finally agreed that if the whole body of the miners were of the opinion that he should be hanged, that the committee left it in their hands to deal with him. Off, at hot speed, rode the leader of the Nevada men to join his command.

Slade had found out what was intended, and the news sobered him instantly. He went into P. S. Pfouts' store, where Davis was, and apologized for his conduct, saying that he would take it all back.

The head of the column now wheeled into Wallace Street and marched up at quick time. Halting in front of the store, the executive officer of the committee stepped forward and arrested Slade, who was at once informed of his doom, and inquiry was made as to whether he had any business to settle. Several parties spoke to him on the subject; but to all such inquiries he turned a deaf ear, being entirely absorbed in the terrifying reflections on his own awful position. He never ceased his entreaties for life, and to see his dear wife. The unfortunate lady referred to, between whom and Slade there existed a warm affection, was at this time living at their ranch on the Madison. She was possessed of considerable personal attractions; tall, well-formed, of graceful carriage, pleasing manners, and was, withal, an accomplished horsewoman.

A messenger from Slade rode at full speed to inform her of her husband's arrest. In an instant she was in the saddle, and with all the energy that love and despair could lend to an ardent temperament and a strong physique, she urged her fleet charger over the twelve miles of rough and rocky ground that intervened between her and the object of her passionate devotion.

Meanwhile a party of volunteers had made the necessary preparations for the execution, in the valley traversed by the branch. Beneath the site of Pfouts and Russell's stone building there was a corral, the gate-posts of which were strong and high. Across the top was laid a beam, to which the rope was fastened, and a dry-goods box served for the platform. To this place Slade was marched, surrounded by a guard, composing the best armed and most numerous force that has ever appeared in Montana Territory.

The doomed man had so exhausted himself by tears, prayers and lamentations, that he had scarcely strength left to stand under the fatal beam. He repeatedly exclaimed, "My God! My God! Must I die? Oh, my dear wife!"

On the return of the fatigue party, they encountered some friends of Slade, staunch and reliable citizens and members of the committee, but who were personally attached to the condemned. On hearing of his sentence, one of them, a stout-hearted man, pulled out his handkerchief and walked away, weeping like a child. Slade still begged to see his wife, most piteously, and it seemed hard to deny his request; but the bloody consequences that were sure to follow the inevitable attempt at a rescue, that her presence and entreaties would have certainly incited, forbade the granting of his request. Several gentlemen were sent for to see him, in his last moments, one of whom (Judge Davis) made a short address to the people; but in such low tones as to be inaudible, save to a few in his immediate vicinity. One of his friends, after exhausting his powers of entreaty, threw off his coat and declared that the prisoner could not be hanged until he himself was killed. A hundred guns were instantly leveled at him; whereupon he turned and fled; but, being brought back, he was compelled to resume his coat, and to give a promise of future peaceable demeanor.

Scarcely a leading man in Virginia could be found, though numbers of the citizens joined the ranks of the guard when the arrest was made. All lamented the stern necessity which dictated the execution.

Everything being ready, the command was given, "Men, do your duty," and the box being instantly slipped from beneath his feet, he died almost instantaneously.

The body was cut down and carried to the Virginia Hotel, where, in a darkened room, it was scarcely laid out, when the unfortunate and bereaved companion of the deceased arrived, at headlong speed, to find that all was over, and that she was a widow. Her grief and heart-piercing cries were terrible evidences of the depth of her attachment for her lost husband, and a considerable period elapsed before she could regain the command of her excited feelings.

There is something about the desperado-nature that is wholly unaccountable—at least it looks unaccountable. It is this: The true desperado is gifted with splendid courage, and yet he will take the most infamous advantage of his enemy; armed and free, he will stand up before a host and fight until he is shot all to pieces, and yet when he is under the gallows and helpless he will cry and plead like a child. Words are cheap, and it is easy to call Slade a coward (all executed men who do not "die game" are promptly called cowards by unreflecting people), and when we read of Slade that he "had so exhausted himself by tears, prayers and lamentations, that he had scarcely strength left to stand under the fatal beam," the disgraceful word suggests itself in a moment—yet in frequently defying and inviting the vengeance of banded Rocky Mountain cut-throats by shooting down their comrades and leaders, and never offering to hide or fly, Slade showed that he was a man of peerless bravery. No coward would dare that. Many a notorious coward, many a chicken-livered poltroon, coarse, brutal, degraded, has made his dying speech without a quaver in his voice and been swung into eternity with what looked liked the calmest fortitude, and so we are justified in believing, from the low intellect of such a creature, that it was not moral courage that enabled him to do it. Then, if moral courage is not the requisite quality, what could it have been that this stout-hearted Slade lacked?—this bloody, desperate, kindly-mannered, urbane gentleman, who never hesitated to warn his most ruffianly enemies that he would kill them whenever or wherever he came across them next! I think it is a conundrum worth investigating.

CHAPTER IV.

WILD BILL HICKOK

By J. W. Buel

In the latter part of 1865, Wild Bill went to Springfield, Missouri, where he remained some time. It was while at this place that he fought a duel with Dave Tutt in the public square, and, as usual, killed his man, and came out of the encounter scatheless. The particulars of this affair are as follows: Springfield became a meeting place, after the war, of Confederates and Union men. Both sides recruited their forces from this section, and though the war had ended, many of the animosities then engendered still remained. Another peculiarity of the place consisted in the excess of border ruffianism, which made the town notorious. Murders had been so frequent in that section that the value of a life could scarcely be computed for its smallness. Among the rowdies was one Dave Tutt, a man of terrible passion, strong revenge, and one withal who had his private graveyard. He and Bill had met before; in fact, had shared the smiles of the same woman, a few years previous; but Bill had won "in a square court," and Dave was anxious to meet Bill with pistols to settle the point finally. Some months passed while the two were in Springfield before any opportunity was presented for Dave to introduce a row, and when it came it was of Dave's own manufacture. It is claimed that Bill killed a particular friend of Dave's some years before, but of the truth of this we have no proof. One of the strong points of difference between the men consisted in the fact that Bill had been a Union scout and spy, and Dave had performed a similar duty for the Confederates.

Springfield was a great place for gamblers, and Bill and Dave belonged to the profession. One night, the two met in a saloon on the north side of the square, and Dave proposed a game with Bill, which, not being agreeable, Dave offered to stake a friend to play Bill. Thus the game was started. When Bill sat down to the game he drew out his heavy gold watch and laid it on the table, remarking that he intended to quit the game promptly at twelve o'clock. After nearly two hours playing he had won two hundred dollars, the greater part of which had come from Dave as a loan to his friend. Having broke the friend and Dave also, the latter remarked, "Bill, you've got money now, so pay me that forty dollars you've been owing me so long."

"All right," replied Bill, "there's your money," and thereupon passed the forty dollars to Dave.

"Now," remarked Dave, further, "I want that thirty-five dollars I won off you Friday night."

Bill's reply was very courteous: "Beg your pardon, Dave, it was only twenty-five dollars; I put the amount down in my memorandum-book at the time."

Receiving this mild reply, Dave reached across the table and took Bill's watch, with the remark, "You'll never get this watch until you pay me that thirty-five dollars."

This threw Bill into a violent passion, although he restrained himself. Rising from his chair and looking piercingly into Dave's eyes, he said: "I am anxious to avoid a row in this gentleman's house. You had better put that watch back on the table."

Dave returned an ugly look, and walked out of the room with the watch.

It was the only time, perhaps, in Bill's life, that he permitted himself to be thus bullied. Everyone who knew him thought he had lost his pluck. It was indeed a seven days' wonder with the people.

Dave kept the watch two days, during which time Bill remained in his room closely, revolving in his mind whether he should add another to his already long list of victims, or stop there and begin a life which flows in a more peaceful current. But he was not permitted to think and resolve without the advice of his friends. Almost every hour one or more of them would come to him with a new story about Dave's boasts and intentions.

On the morning of the third day after the row, Dave sent word to Bill that he intended "to carry the watch across the square at noon, and to call the hour from Wild Bill's watch." Bill sent back the following reply: "Dave Tutt will not carry my watch across the square today unless dead men can walk."

This reply satisfied everybody that there was going to be a death fight. Accordingly, shortly before noon, an immense crowd had assembled on the public square to see the duel.

At five minutes to twelve Wild Bill made his appearance on one side of the square opposite the crowd, where he could command a view of Tutt and his many friends, nearly all of whom were standing with their revolvers in their hands.

Just before twelve Dave stepped out from the crowd and started across the square. When he had proceeded a few steps and placed himself opposite to

Bill, he drew his pistol; there was a report as of a single discharge, and Dave Tutt fell dead with a bullet through his heart. The moment Bill discharged his pistol—both pistols having been fired at the same instant—without taking note of the result of his shot, he turned on the crowd with his pistol leveled, and asked if they were satisfied; twenty or more blanched faces said they were, and pronounced the fight a square one. Bill expected to have to kill more than one man that day, but none of Dave's friends considered it policy to appeal the result.

Bill was arrested, but at the preliminary examination he was discharged on the ground of self-defense. The verdict may not have been in accordance with the well-defined principles of criminal jurisprudence, but it was sufficient, for all who know the circumstances believe that Tutt got his deserts.

* * *

Bill remained in Springfield several months after killing Tutt, and until he was engaged, in 1866, to guide the Peace Commission, which visited the many tribes of Indians that year. Henry M. Stanley, the African explorer, accompanied the commission as correspondent of the New York *Herald*, and wrote some amusing sketches of Bill during the trip, but none of a nature which would make them appropriate in the history of his escapades. They related chiefly to his feats of markmanship, knowledge of Indian cunning, and droll humor.

Upon the return of the Peace Commission, Bill made a trip into the eastern part of Nebraska, and in the spring of 1867, fought a remarkable duel in Jefferson county, with four men as his antagonists. The particulars of this fight were obtained from a gentleman now living in St. Louis, who, at the time, lived within a few miles of where the fight occurred, and heard the details from eyewitnesses.

The origin of the difficulty was in bad whisky and ruffian nature. Bill went into a saloon—which was well filled with cattle drivers, who were half drunk and anxious for a fight—and called for a drink without inviting any one to join him. While raising the glass to his mouth one of the ruffians gave him a push in the back which caused him to drop the glass. Without saying a word, Bill turned and struck the rowdy a desperate blow, felling him outside the door. Four of the rowdy's friends jumped up from their chairs and drew their pistols. Bill appreciated his situation at once, and with wonderful coolness, said: "Gentlemen, let us have some respect for the proprietor. You are anxious for a fight, and I will accommodate you if you will consent to step outside. I will fight all four of you at fifteen paces with pistols." There was a general consent, and the crowd filed out of the saloon. The distance was stepped off, and the four men stood five feet apart, facing Bill. The saloon-keeper was to give the word "fire," and the arrangements were conducted in as fair a manner as four men can fight one. Bill stood as calmly as though he were in church. Not a flush nor tremor. All parties were to allow their pistols to remain in their belts until the word "fire" was given, when each was then to draw and fire at will, and as often as circumstances permitted. The saloon-keeper asked if all were ready, and receiving an affirmative reply, began to count slowly, pausing at least ten seconds between each count: "one, two, three—fire!" Bill had fired almost before the call had died from the saloon-keeper's lips. He killed the man on the left, but a shot also struck Bill in the right shoulder, and his right arm fell helpless.

In another instant he had transferred his pistol to his left hand, and three more successive shots dropped his antagonists. Three of the men were shot in the head and instantly killed. The other was shot in the right cheek, the ball carrying away a large portion of the cheek bone. He afterwards recovered, and may be living yet. The names of the four were: Jack Harkness, the one who recovered; Jim Slater, Frank Dowder, and Seth Beeber.

Bill was lionized by the others in the crowd in a moment after the fight; his wound was carefully bandaged and his wants administered to; but he considered it safer to quit the county at once, and returned to Kansas, going direct to Hays City, where he remained until he recovered the use of his arm, none of the bones having been broken, and in the latter part of the same year he was made city marshal, as he was the only one capable of dealing with the lawless class which had often overrun the town and set law and decency at defiance.

* * *

In 1868, Wild Bill was engaged to guide a party of thirty pleasure-seekers, headed by Hon. Henry Wilson, deceased ex-Vice-President, through some of the Western territories. Mrs. Wilson, wife of the Vice-President, was among the party, and being of a most vivacious and entertaining disposition, added greatly to the enjoyment of the trip. Wild Bill's introduction to her resulted in a pleasing episode at the conclusion of the trip. She requested Bill to carefully scrutinize the party, and then give her his impartial opinion of Yankees. Bill replied that it was not customary for him to form rash conclusions, but if it were her wish he would deliver his opinion upon their return.

The thirty days roaming through the canyons and over the mountains furnished a most enjoyable diversion to the entire party. There was scarcely a day passed but that Bill gave them samples of his unerring aim, killing enough game with his pistol to provision the company. The ladies, who composed nearly one-half the party, never tired of praising him, listening to his stories of border life, and wondering at his marvelous escapes. Bill naturally felt elated, and could not refrain from evincing his very deep interest in the pretty girls from the states. The gentlemen exhibited equal interest in the exploits of Bill, and gave him full credit for his performances. There was one thing about the party which Bill could not comprehend, viz.: the tight-legged pants which they wore—which at that time were the prevailing fashion in the East—and gave to the wearer the appearance of skeleton legs, wrapped with checked bandages, or a grasshopper dressed in an overcoat.

Upon the return of the party, Mrs. Wilson, in bidding Bill good-bye, asked for a fulfillment of his promise. He rather reluctantly responded, "Well, madam, I always like to keep my promise, but in this instance I should like to be excused." But no excuse would answer; his disinclination only excited a more anxious interest in Mrs. Wilson to obtain his opinion.

Being pressingly importuned, Bill at length gave his opinion as follows: "If you Yankee women have as small legs as the sample of Yankee men we have here, then I have a d—d poor opinion of the tribe."

The frankness with which Bill spoke, no less than his remarks, threw the entire party into disorder.

The young ladies hid their faces, and the men generally exhibited their umbrage, but Mr. and Mrs. Wilson were fairly convulsed with laughter. The sting was taken out of Bill's opinion by Mrs. Wilson exclaiming, "Well, Mr. Hickok, that is just my sentiment."

After Bill's return from the trip with the Wilson company of wealthy "Yankees," he resumed his duties as city marshal of Hays City. It would be difficult for anyone not familiar with the terrorism of border life to form an approximate estimate of the condition of society in Hays City when Bill became the

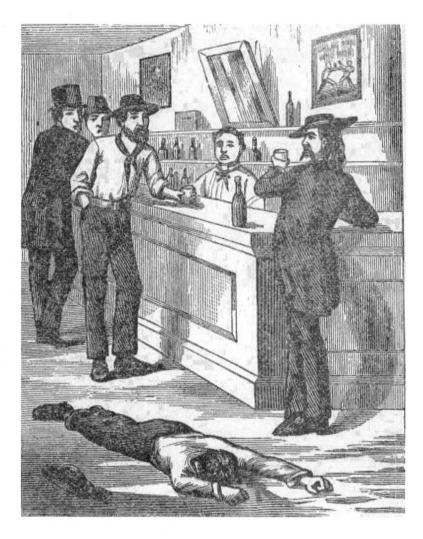

custodian of its peace. Saloons and gambling hells were the most flourishing branches of business, and never closed their doors. The Sabbath was ignored, and the revelry of ruffians continued day and night. The population, it is true, was not a large one, but it was an exceedingly vicious and lively one. There were, of course, many good citizens, but, to use a border expression, "they never aired themselves," yet it was through their instrumentality that Bill became marshal. Among the most violent and dangerous of the rowdy element in Hays City was Jack Strawhan, a large, double-fisted bully who boasted that he could clean out the town, and who had his record well made by killing several men.

Some months previous to the occurrence about to be related, Strawhan had visited Ellsworth, and after getting fighting drunk, he and his gang undertook to "clean out the place," as they expressed it. Capt. Kingsbury, the gentleman before referred to, was sheriff of Ellsworth county at the time, and being a man of equally desperate pluck, he called his deputy, Whitney, and Wild Bill, who was also in Ellsworth on that day, to his assistance, and after a slight skirmish arrested the gang. Strawhan was so violent and abusive that it became necessary, owing to there being no secure jail in the place, to tie him to a post, his arms being thrown around it and fastened in front. This position was a punishment as well as a secure one, and he was kept there until thoroughly sober and subjugated.

This severe treatment caused Jack to take a public oath to kill Kingsbury, Whitney, and Wild Bill at the first opportunity, and every one who knew the man felt that he would keep his word.

The day of fate arrived in 1869, and under the following circumstances: Wild Bill was in Tommy Drum's saloon, in company with a crowd of drinking characters, indulging, as was his wont, when Strawhan entered by a side door. Bill's eyes were always on the lookout for danger, and they caught Jack the moment he stepped upon the threshold. Bill made a pretense of not noticing his bitter enemy, but quietly grasped his pistol and kept talking, unconcernedly, as before. Strawhan thought his opportunity had come, and that Bill was off his guard, but the moment Strawhan attempted to level his pistol, Bill wheeled and shot him dead, the ball from his weapon entering Strawhan's right eye, felling him without a groan. Bill then turned back to the counter of the bar, and asked everybody in the saloon to take a drink, never giving the slightest heed to the body of the man which lay on the floor dead, with his face smothered in a pool of blood. Everyone drank. The coroner was sent for and the crowd gave their testimony. Bill was acquitted the same day, and serenaded by the authorities at night. Whitney escaped death at Strawhan's hands, but was killed by a Texan named Ben Thompson, in 1873.

Shortly after the event just related, Bill Mulvey, a notorious rough and desperado from St. Joseph, Mo., struck Hays City, and got on what we term in the West, "a great big tear." He paraded the streets with a revolver in each hand, howling like an enraged tiger, and thirsting for someone's blood. He was met by the squire and constable, both of whom endeavored to make him keep the peace, but their efforts were so far futile that he turned upon them and drove both out of the town. Wild Bill, who chanced to be in a saloon in another part of the place, where he was unconscious of the disturbance, was notified, and at once started to arrest Mulvey. Approaching his man quietly, in a most amiable tone he told Mulvey that he should have to arrest him for disturbing the peace. Mulvey had his pistols in his hands at the time, and in an instant they were leveled at Wild Bill's head, with the injunction, "March before me." Bill fully appreciated the danger of his position, but his remarkable self-possession and coolness never deserted him. Before turning to march in front of Mulvey, Bill raised his left hand, and with a look of dissatisfaction, said: "Boys, don't hit him." This remark had the desired effect, for as Bill had not shown his pistol, Mulvey turned to see who Bill had spoken to, and to protect his rear. In the twinkle of an eye, Bill whipped out his pistol and shot Mulvey dead, the ball entering the victim's head just behind the ear.

The West was thus relieved of another desperate character, and Wild Bill received a vote of thanks from the citizens for his conduct.

* * *

Bill's fortunate escape from death in his fight with the McCandlas gang at Rock Creek was no more remarkable than one of his fights at Hays City which occurred in 1870. During this year, the 7th U. S. Cavalry was stationed at that post, and many of the soldiers, partaking of the desperate nature which distinguished the place, gave the authorities great trouble. Bill's duties as city marshal caused an antagonism which finally culminated in a most desperate fight with fifteen of the soldiers, the particulars of which are as follows: On the day in question, several of the soldiers became very drunk, among them a large sergeant who had a particular aversion to Bill on account of his having arrested, at diverse times, several of the members of his company. The sergeant was in Paddy Welch's saloon with several of his men, indulging in a noisy carousal. Welch sent for Bill to remove the crowd, but when he arrived the sergeant insisted on fighting Bill in the street. He confessed that he was no match for Bill in a duel, but dared him to meet him in fistic encounter. To this proposition Bill consented, and taking out his two revolvers he passed them to Welch, and the two combatants, followed by the crowd inside, stepped out of the saloon and into the street. Although the sergeant was much the larger man, he was no equal for Bill, and in a moment after the fight began the sergeant was knocked down, and Bill was administering to him a most severe thrashing. The soldiers, fourteen in number, seeing their sergeant at great disadvantage, and in danger of never getting back to camp with a sound body, rushed in to his assistance, some with clubs, and others with stones, seemingly determined to kill Bill. Paddy Welch was near at hand, and seeing the desperate position he occupied, ran into the crowd and succeeded in placing the two revolvers in his hands. In another moment he discharged a shot which killed one of the soldiers, and would have done more terrible execution but for the crowd that was on him, which prevented him from using his hands.

When the first soldier fell dead there was a hasty dispersion of the others, but only to get their pistols, which were near at hand, and to renew the attack. For a few minutes there was rapid firing, and three more of the soldiers fell, one of them dead, and the other two mortally wounded. The odds were too great for Bill, and though he was struck with seven bullets, he managed to escape from the crowd and get out of town. Night coming on very soon after the fight was over enabled Bill to cross Smoky river and secrete himself several miles from the town, where he remained lying in a buffalo wallow for two days, caring for his wounds. He was hit three times in the arms, once in the side and three times in the legs. None of the wounds were serious, but he was compelled to tear up his shirt and drawers for bandages to stop the flow of blood.

On the following day after the fight, Gen. Sheridan ordered a detachment of cavalry to go in pursuit of Bill, and, using his own words, "to take him dead or alive," but, although the pursuit was entered into earnestly, they never found the object of their search.

After getting able to travel, which was on the third day, Bill managed to drag his sore and hungry body down to Bill Williams's ranch, where he was tenderly cared for. No one can imagine the suffering he endured during the two days he lay in the buffalo wallow. His wounds, though but flesh injuries, gave him excruciating pain. He drew his boots, which were filled with blood, and was unable to put them on again. He lost his hat during the fight, and, after tearing up his underclothes, he literally had no protection from the chill and damp of the night. When he attempted to rise from the ground, the agony he suffered was as intense as mortal could bear; but notwithstanding the pain he endured, the excessive hunger which began to oppress and weaken him, compelled him to make the effort to reach Williams's ranch, which he succeeded in doing, as before stated.

After remaining at the ranch a few days, Bill sent for his friend Whitney, then sheriff of Ellsworth county, he having succeeded Capt. Kingsbury, and by him Bill was taken to Ellsworth. But the constant dread of detection made it advisable for Bill to leave Ellsworth, which he did in a few days, by the kindly assistance of Jim Bomon, a conductor of a freight train on the Kansas Pacific railroad, who locked him in a box car and brought him to Junction City. At this place Bill received proper surgical attention and soon recovered.

* * *

The removal of the Seventh Cavalry from Hays City gave Bill immunity from danger from that quarter, and though he did not return to that place, he accepted the office of city marshal of Abilene, a town one hundred miles east of Hays City, and frequently visited the latter place on business.

Abilene was the point from which all the cattle from Texas for the Eastern markets were shipped. Immense droves were daily brought into the place, and with the cattle came the drovers, a large majority of whom were Texan desperadoes. The town bristled with business, and crimes and drunkenness became so common that by general consent Abilene was called the Gomorrah of the West. Gamblers and bad women, drunken cut-throats and pimps, overshadowed all other society, and the carnival of iniquity never ceased. The civil officers were plastic to the touch of the ruffians, and the town was ruled by intimidation.

When Bill assumed charge of the office of marshal, the law and order class had hopes for a radical change, and yet they were very doubtful of the ability of one man to curb the reckless and lawless spirit of so many vicious desperadoes—men who were familiar with the pistol and did not hesitate to murder and plunder, and who took pleasure in "stampeding" the place.

In two days after Bill entered upon the discharge of his duties, occasion presented for a manifestation of his pluck. Phil. Cole, a gambler, and one of the most dangerous men in the West, in company with his pal, whose name cannot now be recalled, concluded to run the town after their own fashion for at least one day. They began by smashing windows, promiscuously, insulting women, discharging their pistols, and other like conduct. Bill met them while they were in the midst of their deviltry, and undertook their arrest. He knew Phil. Cole by reputation, and was prepared for the fight he expected. Cole told Bill that his arrest depended upon who was the better man, and at once drew his pistol. McWilliams, Bill's deputy, stepped up and tried to pacify Cole, and at the same time to secure his pistol, but Cole was anxious for a fight and fired at Bill, but missed his mark. Bill returned the fire, but at the moment he pulled the trigger of his pistol, Cole, in his struggle, threw McWilliams in front of him and the bullet from the pistol struck the faithful deputy, killing him almost instantly. Cole's pal, who, until this time, seemed a mute spectator of the affray, then drew his pistol, and also fired at Bill, the bullet passing through Bill's hat, and before Cole or his mate could fire again, Bill had put a bullet through the head of each, and the fight was ended. The death of McWilliams was most sincerely deplored by everyone, but by none as it was by Bill, and in years afterward he could not have the sad event recalled to mind without crying like a child.

The killing of Cole was a most fortunate event for the better class of citizens of Abilene, because it at once improved the morals of the place. The men who had for years before rioted at their pleasure, defied the law and badgered decency, began to feel that to continue in the same course would be to risk their lives. Nevertheless, the death of Phil. Cole only diminished the lawless excesses—it did not entirely prevent them. Bill never had another occasion to kill anyone in Abilene, but his club fell heavily on many heads determined on vicious acts. His enemies among the Texas cattle men multiplied rapidly, and he realized that there was not a moment that he could safely turn his back to any of them. A cattle king of Texas, whose name we do not choose to mention, as he is still living, was arrested by Bill for violent conduct on the street during a spree, and, as he strenuously resisted, Bill was forced to use his club. The man paid his fine on the following day, but before leaving town he declared that he would get even with Bill before many months elapsed.

* * *

The large and wealthy cattle raiser referred to, directly after returning to Texas, selected eight desperate characters—men who he knew would not hesitate to commit any crime for the sake of money—and offered them the sum of five thousand dollars in gold if they would kill Wild Bill and secure his heart. The proposition was made at a pre-arranged meeting, which took place in an old barn on the premises of the cattle raiser, at which each of the employed assassins was required to take an oath not to divulge the name of the man who hired them under any circumstances, except in the event of the refusal of the employer to pay over the sum agreed upon directly upon the delivery to him of Wild Bill's heart. It was a terrible contract in the eyes of civilization, but an excellent one in the estimation of those a party to it.

In a few days after the arrangement was concluded, the sum of fifty dollars was placed in the hands of each of the hired assassins as forfeit money, to pay expenses of the trip to Abilene, and the eight villains then started out upon their mission.

After reaching Abilene, as was customary among the Texans who visited the place, the party got on a big drunk, and, while in this condition, one of the number explained the nature of his trip to an acquaintance who, by chance, was a secret friend of Bill's. The information was very soon imparted to Bill, and the villains were foiled in the following manner: Bill decided to go to Topeka by the train, and to have the assassins made acquainted with his purpose. He knew they would follow him, because they would consider it safer to

kill their man by luring him onto the platform of a train, where a knife thrust would finish their work without the knowledge of the other passengers, than to attack him in the boundaries of his official jurisdiction among his friends. Accordingly, Bill got on the evening train going east, and saw the eight villains get into the coach in the rear of the one he entered. Bill wisely concluded that no attempt would be made upon his life until a late hour, when the passengers would generally be asleep, and quietly kept his seat until about eleven o'clock, when the train was passing a dark and deep cut a few miles west of Topeka. He concluded now was the time to act; so, drawing his two revolvers, he entered the car where the eight would-be murderers sat. In an instant all was attention, but confusion soon followed, for Bill raised his pistols and commanded the assassins to file out of the car before him. They saw at once that hesitation meant death, and without attempting the purpose for which they came, every one of them hastily arose and did as Bill commanded, leaping from the rapidly-moving train apparently without a thought of the danger in so doing. Three of them were so badly hurt in the fall that their companions had to carry them off, and one of the most notorious of the party died two days afterwards of his injuries. The parting injunction which Bill gave them forced them to abandon the idea of getting his heart. Said he: "If any of you gray-backed hell-hounds ever cross my track again, I'll make blood-pudding out of your infernal carcasses." Bill would undoubtedly have attacked the men had it not been for the presence of so many passengers, some of whom would certainly have been killed in the conflict.

About one year after the killing of Phil Cole at Abilene, Wild Bill had occasion to visit Wichita, Kansas, on some private business. He made the trip on horseback, there being no other mode of travel between the two places. Bill was acquainted with no one in Wichita, and habit caused him to make his first stop in the place before a saloon, where he hitched his horse and went in. There was no one in the saloon at the time of his entrance; so Bill took a seat expecting the proprietor had just stepped out and would be back in a short time. While he was sitting beside a table reading a newspaper, a stranger stepped in and enquired:

"Is your name Wild Bill?"

"That is what they call me," responded Bill.

"Then take that," said the stranger, drawing a pistol and shooting at Bill. The muzzle of the pistol was so close that the flash burned Bill's face and the bullet struck him at the base of the hair on the left side of his forehead and cut out a furrow of flesh and hair. Bill fell unconscious, but the saloon-keeper coming in a moment after the shot was fired, threw some water in his face and consciousness was soon restored.

The stranger jumped on his horse after discharging the shot and rode off furiously towards the south.

It was hardly ten minutes after the shooting before Bill had recovered sufficiently from the stunning effects of the shot to mount his horse and start in pursuit of his unknown assailant.

Bill was mounted on an excellent horse, and as he had no difficulty in ascertaining the route taken by the stranger, the ride was a fast and furious one. The pursued and pursuer, after a running ride of thirty miles, came in sight of each other, and a desperate fight was now prepared for. The stranger supposed he had killed Bill and was being pursued by some officer of justice; but Bill was urged on by his excessive hunger for revenge, and it soon came—terrible enough. When about fifty yards apart, Bill discharged his pistol at the stranger, but the ball struck and disabled the horse. There was then an exchange of shots and the stranger lay dead on the ground with a bullet in his brain. Not satisfied with killing the man, Bill stooped over the prostrate body and drawing a bowie-knife from its sheath, he cut a slice out of the stranger's head which he considered would correspond with the wound in his own. This bloody trophy Bill carried with him for years afterwards—a dried piece of flesh and hair.

The stranger proved to be a cousin of Phil Cole, the gambler, and from facts gathered afterwards, it was shown that he had long sought an opportunity to avenge his cousin's death. The revenge was, however, visited upon the head of the avenger.

* * *

Bill served the time for which he was chosen as marshal of Abilene, and in the spring of 1872 removed to Kansas City. It was at this place the writer—then connected with the daily *Journal*—met him and formed an intimate acquaintance, which afforded abundant opportunity to learn his real character as a man. Bill was frequently importuned for the particulars of his marvelous adventures, and permission to write his life, but he always positively refused. The last time this request was made, he returned the following reply: "Well,

Buel, I expect my life has been a little interesting, and it might please some people to read about my adventures, but I don't want a word written about me until after I'm dead. I never fought any man for notoriety, and am sorry that I've got the name I have. Since Ned Buntline made a hero out of such material as Bill Cody (Buffalo Bill,) I've thought it time to drop out of sight. I took Cody when he was left alone in the world, a young lad, and partially raised him. Well, I don't want to say anything against the boy, but his pluck wouldn't go at par. I've kept a little diary of all my exploits, and when I'm dead I'll be glad if it falls into your hands, and from it you may be able to write something interesting. When I die it will be just as you now see me, and sickness will not be the cause. For more than ten years I've been constantly expecting to be killed, and it is certain to come before a great while longer."

During this conversation Bill appeared to be unusually sad, and when he referred to his death it was with a seriousness which indicated that he had been notified of his tragic end by some terrible presentiment.

He was an expert poker-player, and followed no other calling while in Kansas City. The place was fairly filled with gamblers, and up to 1875 the voice of the keno caller could be heard in nearly every other building on Main street, between Missouri avenue and Fourth street. The Marble block, and houses on the west side of the square, were particularly the haunts of gamblers. Murders and rows were not infrequent, but Bill kept out of all difficulties. He was both feared and respected. His carriage was that of a peaceable gentleman, and during the three years he made Kansas City his home, he was a party to but one row, and that was of minor consequence. This difficulty occurred in the St. Nicholas Hotel barroom, owned by Joe Siegmund, now the proprietor of a hotel in Malvern, Arkansas. A foppish fellow, half-drunk, being told that the party drinking at the bar was Wild Bill, went up to him, and, in a most provoking manner, asked Bill if he was the desperado who had been killing men indiscriminately out West. The impertinent inquiry called forth from Bill an equally insulting reply. The fellow, evidently bent on a row, then began to talk of shooting, and his ability "to lick any border ruffian that ever lived." Bill walked up to him slowly, and as the senseless fop was attempting to draw a pistol, he caught him by one ear and slapped his face until the fellow howled for mercy.

* * *

In the fall of 1874, Bill met Mrs. Lake, the widow of William Lake, proprietor of Lake's circus, who was killed by Jack Keenan at Granby, Missouri in 1873. The meeting was purely accidental, but the consequences were matrimonial. A courtship followed, and in the early part of 1875 the two were married by a justice of the peace in Kansas City. Within a few months after the marriage Bill became afflicted with sore eyes, from which he suffered intensely, and for the period of nine months was unable to distinguish daylight from darkness. Dr. Thorne, previously noticed as one of Bill's confidants, was his physician, and succeeded in restoring his sight, but his eyes never regained their former strength, and the vision remained impaired. In the winter of 1875–76, a separation occurred between Bill and his wife, the causes of which we deem it improper to relate. Suffice it to say that those best qualified to decide, claim that no blame attaches to Bill for the termination of his marital relation. No divorce, we believe, was ever applied for by either party, but they never met after the spring of 1876.

* * *

In February, 1876, Wild Bill entered into an engagement with Ned Buntline (Judson), the novelist who created Buffalo Bill and his exploits, to appear as a leading character in a border play he had written for the stage. The troupe was made up in New York, and the principal actors were Wild Bill, Buffalo Bill, and Texas Jack. The business was a most disagreeable one for Wild Bill, who entered into the engagement solely under the pressure of pecuniary needs. The authorities of Kansas City had so vigorously prosecuted the gamblers that the professionals were compelled to abandon their games, and thus Bill became, to use his own expression, "severely money-bound." Buntline, with a vivid imagination running at all times through carnage and lawlessness, employed his best ability in getting up the posters heralding the appearance of his troupe. Wild Bill was posted in large, blood-red letters as having killed thirty-six men, and the most desperate man that ever set foot on the plains. His nature arose with revolt at such a publicity of his character, and after playing the role of a border bandit for two months, he peremptorily refused to appear on the stage any longer.

* * *

After leaving the Buntline troupe, Wild Bill came to St. Louis for the purpose of organizing an expedition to the Black Hills. The gold fever was at its height, and St. Louis, like all other Western cities, was very much excited over the auriferous discoveries. Bill remained in St. Louis about three weeks, at the end of which time he had succeeded in organizing a party of nearly one hundred men, which was increased to one hundred and fifty by additions received at Kansas City. The party arrived at the Black Hills in the latter part of June, Bill going to Deadwood, and the others distributing themselves among the hills, where they established ranches and began their quest for gold.

Deadwood was a gay place when Bill entered its limits, and the life led by its mixed citizens was exactly suited to his disposition. Every other house was a saloon, and if ever there was a gambler's paradise, it was there. The female portion of Deadwood's population was limited, but the few who were there were so active and boisterous as to compensate for ten times the same number of ordinary women. Bill was in his element, although he had no disposition to take a part in the wild orgies of the drunken, maudlin crowd which infested every nook and corner of the place. He liked the freedom the society permitted, but indulged himself only in gambling and an occasional drink.

Bill made many friends in Deadwood, and it was not known that he had any enemies in the Black Hills, but while he was surrounded by friends, he should never have forgotten the fact that his enemies were almost like the leaves of the forest. They were always plotting his destruction and laying snares along his path. The end came at last, just as Bill had himself often predicted.

* * *

On the 2nd day of August, 1876, Wild Bill was in Lewis & Mann's saloon, playing a game of poker with Capt. Massey, a Missouri river pilot, Charley Rich, and Cool Mann, one of the proprietors of the saloon. The game had been in progress nearly three hours, when at about 4:00 p.m., a man was seen to enter the door and pass up to the bar. Bill was sitting on a stool with the back of his head towards and about five feet from the bar. When the man entered, Bill had just picked up the cards dealt him, and was looking at his "hand," and therefore took no notice of the newcomer. The man, who proved to be Jack McCall, alias Bill Sutherland, after approaching the bar, turned, and drawing a large navy revolver, placed the muzzle within two inches of Bill's head and fired. The bullet entered the base of the brain, tore through the head, and made its exit at the right cheek, between the upper and lower jaw-bones, breaking off several teeth and carrying away a large piece of the cerebellum through the wound. The bullet struck Capt. Massey, who sat opposite Bill, in the right arm and broke the bone. At the instant the pistol was discharged, the cards fell from Bill's hands and he dropped sideways off the stool without uttering a sound. His companions were so horrified that several moments elapsed before it was discovered that Capt. Massey was wounded.

The assassin turned upon the crowd and compelled them to file out of the saloon before him. After reaching the street he defied arrest, but at five o'clock he gave himself up and asked for an immediate trial. Deadwood was, at that time, so primitive that it had no city officers, and there was no one legally competent to take charge of or try the prisoner. During the same evening, however, a coroner was chosen, who impaneled a jury and returned a verdict to the effect that J. B. Hickok (Wild Bill) came to his death from a wound resulting from a shot fired from a pistol by John McCall, alias Bill Sutherland.

Having proceeded thus far, it was determined to elect a judge, sheriff, and prosecuting attorney to try McCall on the following day. The lessee of McDaniel's theatre offered the use of the theatre for the purposes of the trial, which was arranged to take place at nine o'clock on the following morning. Three men were sent out in different directions to notify the miners in the neighborhood of the murder, and to request their attendance at the trial.

Promptly at the time appointed, the improvised court convened, and Joseph Brown, who had been chosen sheriff, produced the prisoner. F. J. Kuykendall, the *pro tempore* judge, then addressed the crowd in a very appropriate manner, reminding those present that the court was purely a self-constituted one, but that in the discharge of his duty he would be governed by justice, and trust to them for a ratification of his acts. His remarks were greeted with hand-clappings of approval. The prisoner was then led forward and conducted to a seat on the stage to the right of the judge.

Never did a more forbidding countenance face a court than that of Jack McCall; his head, which was covered with a thick crop of chestnut hair, was very narrow as to the parts occupied by the intellectual portion of the brain, while the animal development was exceedingly large. A small, sandy moustache covered a sensual mouth, and the coarse double-chin was partially hid by a stiff goatee. The nose was what is commonly called "snub;" he had cross eyes and a florid complexion, which completed a more repulsive picture than Dore could conceive. He was clad in a blue flannel shirt, brown overalls, heavy shoes, and, as he sat in a stooping position, with his arms folded across his breast, he evidently assumed a nonchalance and bravado which were foreign to his feelings, and betrayed by the spasmodic heavings of his heart.

The selection of a jury consumed all the forenoon, as it was next to impossible to select a man who had not formed or expressed an opinion concerning the murder, although but few who were in the panel had heard of the tragedy until a few hours before. A hundred names were selected, written upon separate scraps of paper, and placed in a hat. They were then well shaken, and the committee appointed for the purpose drew from the hat one name at a time. The party answering to the name then came forward and was examined by the judge touching his fitness to serve as an impartial juror. Ninety-two names were called from the panel before the jury was made up. The jurors being sworn, they took their seats, and testimony for the prosecution was begun.

The first witness called was Charles Rich, who said that he was in the saloon kept by Lewis & Mann on the afternoon of the 2nd, and was seated at a table playing a game of poker with Wild Bill and several others, when the prisoner, whom he identified, came into the room, walked deliberately up to Wild Bill, placed a pistol to the back of the deceased, and fired, saying: "Take that!" Bill fell from the stool upon which he had been seated without uttering a word.

Samuel Young testified that he was engaged in the saloon; that he had just delivered $15 worth of pocket checks to the deceased, and was returning to his place behind the bar when he heard the report of a pistol shot; turning around, he saw the prisoner at the back of Wild Bill with a pistol in his hand which he had just discharged; heard him say, "Take that!"

Carl Mann was one of the proprietors of the saloon in which Wild Bill was killed; was in the poker game; noticed a commotion; saw the prisoner (whom he identified) shoot Wild Bill.

The defense called for the first witness, P. H. Smith, who said he had been in the employ of McCall four months; that he was not a man of quarrelsome disposition; that he had always considered him a man of good character; that he (the witness) had been introduced to Wild Bill in Cheyenne, and drank with him; that the deceased had a bad reputation, and had been the terror of every place in which he had resided.

H. H. Pickens said that he had known defendant four years, and believed him to be a quiet and peaceable man. Wild Bill's reputation as a "shootist" was very hard; he was quick in using the pistol and never missed his man, and had killed quite a number of persons in different parts of the country.

Ira Ford had known the defendant about one year; "like a great many others, he would go upon a spree like the rest of the boys." Wild Bill had the reputation of being a brave man, who could and would shoot quicker than any man in the Western country, and who always "got away" with his antagonist.

The defense called several others, the tenor of whose evidence was but a repetition of the foregoing. No attempt was made to show that Wild Bill had ever seen the prisoner.

The prisoner was called upon to make a statement. He came down from the stage into the auditorium of the theatre, and with his right hand in the bosom of his shirt, his head thrown back, in a harsh, loud, and repulsive voice, with a bulldog sort of bravado, said: "Well, men, I have but a few words to say. Wild Bill threatened to kill me if I crossed his path. I am not sorry for what I have done. I would do the same thing over again." The prisoner then returned to his place on the stage.

The prosecution then adduced testimony to prove that Wild Bill was a much abused man; that he never imposed on any one, and that in every instance where he had slain men he had done so either in the discharge of his duty as an officer of the law or in self-defense.

The case having been placed in the hands of the jury, the theatre was cleared, with the understanding that the verdict should be made known in the saloon where the murder was committed. The prisoner was remanded to the house where he had been imprisoned during the night. At nine o'clock the following verdict was read to the prisoner:

Deadwood City, Aug. 3, 1876—We, the jurors, find the prisoner, Mr. John McCall, not guilty.

The prisoner was at once liberated, and several of the model jurymen who had played their parts in this burlesque upon justice, and who had turned their bloodthirsty tiger loose upon the community indulged in a sickening cheer which grated harshly upon the ears of those who heard it. The first vote taken by the jury resulted in eleven for acquittal and one for conviction, and the single man who desired justice was so intimidated by his fellow-jurors that he was induced to sanction the iniquitous verdict. It was even proposed by one of the jurymen that the prisoner be fined fifteen or twenty dollars and set free.

After the inquest the body of the deceased was placed upon a litter made of two poles and some boards; then a procession was formed, and the remains were carried to Charley Utter's camp, across the creek. Charles Utter, better known as Colorado Charley, had been the intimate friend of the deceased for fifteen years, and with that liberality which is a feature among mountaineers, had always shared his purse with him. Charley was much affected by the death of his friend, and incensed at the villain who had murdered him. A tepee was pitched at the foot of one of the giant trees which rise so majestically above Charley's camp. Preparations were at once made for the funeral. At the time appointed a number of people gathered at the camp—Charley Utter had gone to a great deal of expense to make the funeral as fine as could be had in that country. Under the tepee, in a handsome coffin, covered with black cloth and richly mounted with silver ornaments, lay Wild Bill, a picture of perfect repose. His long chestnut hair, evenly parted over his marble brow, hung in waving ringlets over the broad shoulders; his face was cleanly shaved excepting the drooping moustache, which shaded a mouth that in death almost seemed to smile, but in life was unusually grave; the arms were folded over the stilled breast, which enclosed a heart that had beat with regular pulsation amid the most startling scenes of blood and violence. The corpse was clad in complete dress-suit of black broadcloth, new underclothing, and white linen shirt; beside him in the coffin lay his trusty rifle, which the deceased prized above all other things, and which was to be buried with him in compliance with an often expressed desire.

Upon a large stump at the head of the grave the following inscription was deeply cut:

"A brave man; the victim of an assassin—J. B. Hickok (Wild Bill,) aged 48 years; murdered by Jack McCall, Aug. 2, 1876."

Chapter

THE TEXAS RANGERS, HOW THE LAW GOT INTO THE CHAPARRAL

By Fredric Remington

"You have heard about the Texas Rangers?" said the Deacon to me one night in the San Antonio Club. "Yes? Well, come up to my rooms, and I will introduce you to one of the old originals—dates 'way back in the 'thirties'—there aren't many of them left now—and if we can get him to talk, he will tell you stories that will make your eyes hang out on your shirt front."

We entered the Deacon's cozy bachelor apartments, where I was introduced to Colonel "Rip" Ford, of the old-time Texas Rangers. I found him
a very old man, with a wealth of snow-white hair and beard—bent, but not
withered. As he sunk on his stiffened limbs into the armchair, we disposed
ourselves quietly and almost reverentially, while we lighted cigars. We began
the approaches by which we hoped to loosen the history of a wild past from
one of the very few tongues which can still wag on the days when the Texans,
the Comanches, and the Mexicans chased one another over the plains of Texas,
and shot and stabbed to find who should inherit the land.

Through the veil of tobacco smoke the ancient warrior spoke his sentences
slowly, at intervals, as his mind gradually separated and arranged the details
of countless fights. His head bowed in thought; anon it rose sharply at recol-
lections, and as he breathed, the shouts and lamentations of crushed men—the
yells and shots—the thunder of horses' hoofs—the full fury of the desert com-
bats came to the pricking ears of the Deacon and me.

We saw through the smoke the brave young faces of the hosts which
poured into Texas to war with the enemies of their race. They were clad in
loose hunting-frocks, leather leggings, and broad black hats; had powder horns
and shot-pouches hung about them; were armed with bowie knives, Mississippi
rifles, and horse pistols; rode Spanish ponies, and were impelled by Destiny to
conquer, like their remote ancestors, "the godless hosts of Pagan" who "came
swimming o'er the Northern Sea."

"Rip" Ford had not yet acquired his front name in 1836, when he enlisted in
the famous Captain Jack Hayes's company of Rangers, which was fighting the
Mexicans in those days, and also trying incidentally to keep from being eaten
up by the Comanches.

Said the old Colonel: "A merchant from our country journeyed to New
York, and Colonel Colt, who was a friend of his, gave him two five-shooters—
pistols they were, and little things. The merchant in turn presented them to
Captain Jack Hayes. The captain liked them so well that he did not rest till
every man jack of us had two apiece.

"Directly," mused the ancient one, with a smile of pleasant recollection,
"we had a fight with the Comanches—up here above San Antonio. Hayes
had fifteen men with him—he was doubling about the country for Indians.
He found 'sign,' and after cutting their trail several times he could see that
they were following him. Directly the Indians overtook the Rangers—there

were seventy-five Indians. Captain Hayes—bless his memory!—said, 'They are fixin' to charge us, boys, and we must charge them.' There were never better men in this world than Hayes had with him," went on the Colonel with pardonable pride; "and mind you, he never made a fight without winning.

"We charged, and in the fracas killed thirty-five Indians—only two of our men were wounded—so you see the five-shooters were pretty good weapons. Of course they wa'n't any account compared with these modern ones, because they were too small, but they did those things. Just after that Colonel Colt was induced to make bigger ones for us, some of which were half as long as your arm.

"Hayes? Oh, he was a surveyor, and used to go out beyond the frontiers about his work. The Indians used to jump him pretty regular; but he always whipped them, and so he was available for a Ranger captain. About then—let's see," and here the old head bobbed up from his chest, where it had sunk in thought—"there was a commerce with Mexico just sprung up, but this was later—it only shows what that man Hayes used to do. The bandits used to waylay the traders, and they got very bad in the country. Captain Hayes went after them—he struck them near Lavade, and found the Mexicans had more than twice as many men as he did; but he caught them napping, charged them afoot—killed twenty-five of them, and got all their horses."

"I suppose, Colonel, you have been charged by a Mexican lancer?" I inquired.

"Oh yes, many times," he answered.

"What did you generally do?"

"Well, you see, in those days I reckoned to be able to hit a man every time with a six-shooter at one hundred and twenty-five yards," explained the old gentleman—which no doubt meant many dead lancers.

"Then you do not think much of a lance as a weapon?" I pursued.

"No; there is but one weapon. The six-shooter when properly handled is the only weapon—mind you, sir, I say *properly*," and here the old eyes blinked rapidly over the great art as he knew its practice.

"Then, of course, the rifle has its use. Under Captain Jack Hayes sixty of us made a raid once after the celebrated priest-leader of the Mexicans—Padre Jarante—which same was a devil of a fellow. We were very sleepy—had been two nights without sleep. At San Juan every man stripped his horse, fed, and went to sleep. We had passed Padre Jarante in the night without kno-wing it. At about twelve o'clock next day there was a terrible outcry—I was awakened by shooting. The Padre was upon us. Five men outlying stood the charge, and went under. We gathered, and the Padre charged three times. The third time he was knocked from his horse and killed. Then Captain Jack Hayes awoke, and we got in a big *casa*. The men took to the roof. As the Mexicans passed we emptied a great many saddles. As I got to the top of the *casa* I found two men quarrelling." (Here the Colonel chuckled.) "I asked what the matter was, and they were both claiming to have killed a certain Mexican who was lying dead some way off. One said he had hit him in the head, and the other said he had hit him in the breast. I advised peace until after the fight. Well—after the shooting was over and the Padre's men had had enough, we went out to the particular Mexican who was dead, and, sure enough, he was shot in the head and in the breast; so they laughed and made peace. About this time one of the spies came in and reported six hundred Mexicans coming. We made an examination of our ammunition, and found that we couldn't afford to fight six hundred Mexicans with sixty men, so we pulled out. This was in the Mexican war, and only goes to show that Cap-tain Hayes's men could shoot all the Mexicans that could get to them if the ammunition would hold out."

"What was the most desperate fight you can remember, Colonel?"

The old man hesitated; this required a particular point of view—it was quality, not quantity, wanted now; and, to be sure, he was a connoisseur. After much study by the Colonel, during which the world lost many thrilling tales, the one which survived occurred in 1851.

"My lieutenant, Ed Burleson, was ordered to carry to San Antonio an Indian prisoner we had taken and turned over to the commanding officer at Fort McIntosh. On his return, while nearing the Nueces River, he spied a couple of Indians. Taking seven men, he ordered the balance to continue along the road. The two Indians proved to be fourteen, and they charged Burleson up to the teeth. Dismounting his men, he poured it into them from his Colt's six-shooting rifles. They killed or wounded all the Indians except two, some of them dying so near the Rangers that they could put their hands on their boots. All but one of Burleson's men were wounded—himself shot in the head with an arrow. One man had four 'dogwood switches' [Arrows] in his body, one of which was in his bowels. This man told me that every time he

76

raised his gun to fire, the Indians would stick an arrow in him, but he said he didn't care a cent. One Indian was lying right up close, and while dying tried to shoot an arrow, but his strength failed so fast that the arrow only barely left the bowstring. One of the Rangers in that fight was a curious fellow—when young he had been captured by Indians, and had lived with them so long that he had Indian habits. In that fight he kept jumping around when loading, so as to be a bad target, the same as an Indian would under the circumstances, and he told Burleson he wished he had his boots off, so he could get around good"—and here the Colonel paused quizzically. "Would you call that a good fight?"

The Deacon and I put the seal of our approval on the affair, and the Colonel rambled ahead.

"In 1858 I was commanding the frontier battalion of State troops on the whole frontier, and had my camp on the Deer Fork of the Brazos. The Comanches kept raiding the settlements. They would come down quietly, working well into the white lines, and then go back a-running—driving stolen stock and killing and burning. I thought I would give them some of their own medicine. I concluded to give them a fight. I took two wagons, one hundred Rangers, and one hundred and thirteen Tahuahuacan Indians, who were friendlies. We struck a good Indian trail on a stream which led up to the Canadian. We followed it till it got hot. I camped my outfit in such a manner as to conceal my force, and sent out my scouts, who saw the Indians hunt buffalo through spyglasses. That night we moved. I sent Indians to locate the camp. They returned before day, and reported that the Indians were just a few miles ahead, whereat we moved forward. At daybreak, I remember, I was standing in the bull-wagon road leading to Santa Fe and could see the Canadian River in our front—with eighty lodges just beyond. Counting four men of fighting age to a lodge, that made a possible three hundred and twenty Indians. Just at sunup an Indian came across the river on a pony. Our Indians down below raised a yell—they always get excited. The Indian heard them—it was very still then. The Indian retreated slowly, and began to ride in a circle. From where I was I could hear him puff like a deer—he was blowing the bullets away from himself—he was a medicine-man. I heard five shots from the Jagers with which my Indians were armed. The painted pony of the medicine-man jumped ten feet in the air, it seemed to me, and fell over on his rider—then five more Jagers went off, and he was dead. I ordered the Tahuahuacans out in front, and kept the Rangers

out of sight, because I wanted to charge home and kind of surprise them. Pretty soon I got ready, and gave the word. We charged. At the river we struck some boggy ground and floundered around considerable, but we got through. We raised the Texas yell, and away we went. I never expect again to hear such a noise—I never want to hear it—what with the whoops of the warriors—the screaming of the women and children—our boys yelling—the shooting, and the horses just a-mixin' up and a-stampedin' around," and the Colonel bobbed his head slowly as he continued.

"One of my men didn't know a buck from a squaw. There was an Indian woman on a pony with five children. He shot the pony—it seemed like you couldn't see that pony for little Indians. We went through the camp, and the Indians pulled out—spreading fanlike, and we a-running them. After a long chase I concluded to come back. I saw lots of Indians around in the hills. When I got back, I found Captain Ross had formed my men in line. 'What time in the morning is it?' I asked. 'Morning, hell!' says he—it's one o'clock!' And so it was. Directly I saw an Indian coming down a hill near by, and then more Indians and more Indians—till it seemed like they wa'n't ever going to get through coming. We had struck a bigger outfit than the first one. That first Indian he bantered my men to come out single-handed and fight him. One after another, he wounded five of my Indians. I ordered my Indians to engage them, and kind of get them down in the flat, where I could charge. After some running and shooting they did this, and I turned the Rangers loose. We drove them. The last stand they made they killed one of my Indians, wounded a Ranger, but left seven of their dead in a pile. It was now nearly nightfall, and I discovered that my horses were broken down after fighting all day. I found it hard to restrain my men, they had got so heated up; but I gradually withdrew to where the fight commenced. The Indian camp was plundered. In it we found painted buffalo-robes with beads a hand deep around the edges—the finest robes I have ever seen—and heaps of goods plundered from the Santa Fe traders. On the way back I noticed a dead chief, and was for a moment astonished to find pieces of flesh cut out of him; upon looking at a Tahuahuacan warrior I saw a pair of dead hands tied behind his saddle. That night they had a cannibal feast. You see, the Tahuahuacans say that the first one of their race was brought into the world by a wolf. 'How am I to live?' said the Tahuahuacan. 'The same as we do,' said the wolf; and when they were with me, that is just about how they lived. I reckon it's necessary to tell you about the old woman who was found in our lines. She was looking at the sun and making incantations, a-cussing us out generally and elevating her voice. She said the Comanches would get even for this day's work. I directed my Indians to let her alone, but I was informed afterwards that that is just what they didn't do."

At this point the Colonel's cigar went out, and directly he followed; but this is the manner in which he told of deeds which I know would fare better at the hands of one used to phrasing and capable also of more points of view than the Colonel was used to taking. The outlines of the thing are strong, however, because the Deacon and I understood that fights were what the old Colonel had dealt in during his active life, much as other men do in stocks and bonds or wheat and corn. He had been a successful operator, and only recalled pleasantly the bull quotations. This type of Ranger is all but gone. A few may yet be found in outlying ranches. One of the most celebrated resides near San Antonio—"Big-foot Wallace" by name. He says he doesn't mind being called "Big-foot," because he is six feet two in height, and is entitled to big feet. His face is done off in a nest of white hair and beard, and is patriarchal in character. In 1836 he came out from Virginia to "take toll" of the Mexicans for killing some relatives of his in the Fannin Massacre, and he considers that he has squared his accounts; but they had him on the debit side for a while. Being captured in the Meir expedition, he walked as a prisoner to the city of Mexico, and did public work for that country with a ball-and-chain attachment for two years. The prisoners overpowered the guards and escaped on one occasion, but were overtaken by Mexican cavalry while dying of thirst in a desert. Santa Anna ordered their "decimation," which meant that every tenth man was shot, their lot being determined by the drawing of a black bean from an earthen pot containing a certain proportion of white ones. "Big-foot" drew a white one. He was also a member of Captain Hayes's company, afterwards a captain of Rangers, and a noted Indian-fighter. Later he carried the mails from San Antonio to El Paso through a howling wilderness, but always brought it safely through—if safely can be called lying thirteen days by a water hole in the desert, waiting for a broken leg to mend, and living meanwhile on one prairie wolf, which he managed to shoot. Wallace was a professional hunter, who fought Indians and hated "greasers"; he belongs to the past, and has been "outspanned" under a civilization in which he has no place, and is today living in poverty.

The civil war left Texas under changed conditions. That and the Mexican wars had determined its boundaries, however, and it rapidly filled up with new elements of population. Broken soldiers, outlaws, poor immigrants living in bull-wagons, poured in. "Gone to Texas" had a sinister significance in the late sixties. When the railroad got to Abilene, Kansas, the cow-men of Texas found a market for their stock, and began trailing their herds up through the Indian country.

Bands of outlaws organized under the leadership of desperadoes like Wes Hardin and King Fisher. They rounded up cattle regardless of their owners' rights, and resisted interference with force. The poor man pointed to his brand in the stolen herd and protested. He was shot. The big owners were unable to protect themselves from loss. The property right was established by the six-shooter, and honest men were forced to the wall. In 1876 the property-holding classes went to the Legislature, got it to appropriate a hundred thousand dollars a year for two years, and the Ranger force was reorganized to carry the law into the chaparral. At this time many judges were in league with bandits; sheriffs were elected by the outlaws, and the electors were cattle-stealers.

The Rangers were sworn to uphold the laws of Texas and the United States. They were deputy sheriffs, United States marshals—in fact, were often vested with any and every power, even to the extent of ignoring disreputable sheriffs. At times they were judge, jury, and executioner when the difficulties demanded extremes. When a band of outlaws was located, detectives or spies were sent among them, who openly joined the desperadoes, and gathered evidence to put the Rangers on their trail. Then, in the wilderness, with only the soaring buzzard or prowling coyote to look on, the Ranger and the outlaw met to fight with tigerish ferocity to the death. Shot, and lying prone, they fired until the palsied arm could no longer raise the six-shooter, and justice was satisfied as their bullets sped. The captains had the selection of their men, and the right to dishonorably discharge at will. Only men of irreproachable character, who were fine riders and dead-shots, were taken. The spirit of adventure filled the ranks with the most prominent young men in the State, and to have been a Ranger is a badge of distinction in Texas to this day. The display of anything but a perfect willingness to die under any and all circumstances was fatal to a Ranger, and in course of time they got the *moral* on the bad man. Each one furnished his own horse and arms, while the State gave him ammunition, "grub," one dollar a day, and extra expenses. The enlistment was for twelve months. A list of fugitive Texas criminals was placed in his hands, with which he was expected to familiarize himself. Then, in small parties, they packed the bedding on their mule, they hung the handcuffs and leather thongs about its neck, saddled their riding-ponies, and threaded their way into the chaparral.

On an evening I had the pleasure of meeting two more distinguished Ranger officers—more modern types—Captains Lea Hall and Joseph Shely; both of them big, forceful men, and loath to talk about themselves. It was difficult to associate the quiet gentlemen who sat smoking in the Deacon's rooms with what men say; for the tales of their prowess in Texas always ends, "and that don't count Mexicans, either." The bandit never laid down his gun but with his life; so the "la ley de huga" [Mexican law of shooting escaped or resisting prisoners] was in force in the chaparral, and the good people of Texas were satisfied with a very short account of a Ranger's fight.

The most distinguished predecessor of these two men was a Captain McNally, who was so bent on carrying his raids to an issue that he paid no heed to national boundary-lines. He followed a band of Mexican bandits to the town of La Cueva, below Ringgold, once, and, surrounding it, demanded the surrender of the cattle which they had stolen. He had but ten men, and yet this redoubtable warrior surrounded a town full of bandits and Mexican soldiers. The Mexican soldiers attacked the Rangers, and forced them back under the river-banks, but during the fight the *jefe politico* was killed. The Rangers were in a fair way to be overcome by the Mexicans, when Lieutenant Clendenin turned a Gatling loose from the American side and covered their position. A parley ensued, but McNally refused to go back without the cattle, which the Mexicans had finally to surrender.

At another time McNally received word through spies of an intended raid of Mexican cattle-thieves under the leadership of Cammelo Lerma. At Resaca de la Palma, McNally struck the depredators with but sixteen men. They had seventeen men and five hundred head of stolen cattle. In a running fight for miles McNally's men killed sixteen bandits, while only one escaped. A young Ranger by the name of Smith was shot dead by Cammelo Lerma as he dismounted to look at the dying bandit. The dead bodies were piled in ox-carts and dumped in the public square at Brownsville. McNally also captured King Fisher's band in an old log house in Dimmit County, but they were not convicted.

Showing the nature of Ranger work, an incident which occurred to my acquaintance, Captain Lea Hall, will illustrate. In De Witt County there was a feud. One dark night sixteen masked men took a sick man, one Dr. Brazel, and two of his boys, from their beds, and, despite the imploring mother and daughter, hanged the doctor and one son to a tree. The other boy escaped in the green corn. Nothing was done to punish the crime, as the lynchers were men of property and influence in the country. No man dared speak above his breath about the affair.

Captain Hall, by secret-service men, discovered the perpetrators, and also that they were to be gathered at a wedding on a certain night. He surrounded the house and demanded their surrender, at the same time saying that he did not want to kill the women and children. Word returned that they would kill him and all his Rangers. Hall told them to allow their women and children to depart, which was done; then, springing on the gallery of the house, he shouted, "Now, gentlemen, you can go to killing Rangers; but if you don't surrender, the Rangers will go to killing you." This was too frank a willingness for midnight assassins, and they gave up.

Spies had informed him that robbers intended sacking Campbell's store in Wolfe City. Hall and his men lay behind the counters to receive them on the designated night. They were allowed to enter, when Hall's men, rising, opened fire—the robbers replying. Smoke filled the room, which was fairly illuminated by the flashes of the guns—but the robbers were all killed, much to the disgust of the lawyers, no doubt, though I could never hear that honest people mourned.

The man Hall was himself a gentleman of the romantic Southern soldier type, and he entertained the highest ideals, with which it would be extremely unsafe to trifle, if I may judge. Captain Shely, our other visitor, was a herculean, black-eyed man, fairly fizzing with nervous energy. He is also exceedingly shrewd, as befits the greater concreteness of the modern Texas law, albeit he too has trailed bandits in the chaparral, and rushed in on their camp-fires at night, as two big bullet-holes in his skin will attest. He it was who arrested Polk, the defaulting treasurer of Tennessee. He rode a Spanish pony sixty-two miles in six hours, and arrested Polk, his guide, and two private detectives, whom Polk had bribed to set him over the Rio Grande. When the land of Texas was bought up and fenced with wire, the old settlers who had used the land did not readily recognize the new regime. They raised the rallying-cry of "free grass and free water"—said they had fought the Indians off, and the land belonged to them. Taking nippers, they rode by night and cut down miles of fencing. Shely took the keys of a county jail from the frightened sheriff, made arrests by the score, and lodged them in the big new jail. The country-side rose in arms, surrounded the building, and threatened to tear it down. The big Ranger was not deterred by this outburst, but quietly went out into the mob, and with mock politeness delivered himself as follows:

"Do not tear down the jail, gentlemen—you have been taxed for years to build this fine structure—it is yours—do not tear it down. I will open the doors wide—you can all come in—do not tear down the jail; but there are twelve Rangers in there, with orders to kill as long as they can see. Come right in, gentlemen—but come fixed."

The mob was overcome by his civility.

Texas is today the only State in the Union where pistol-carrying is attended with great chances of arrest and fine. The law is supreme even in the lonely *jacails* out in the rolling waste of chaparral, and it was made so by the tireless riding, the deadly shooting, and the indomitable courage of the Texas Rangers.

CHAPTER VI.

BILLY, THE KID

Adapted from *The Authentic Life of Billy, the Kid*

By Pat Garrett

William H. Bonney was born in the city of New York, November 23, 1859. But little is known of his father, as he died when Billy was very young, and he had little recollection of him. In 1862 the family, consisting of the father, mother, and two boys, of whom Billy was the eldest, emigrated to Coffeyville, Kansas. Soon after settling there the father died, and the mother with her two boys removed to Colorado, where she married a man named Antrim, who removed to Santa Fe, New Mexico, shortly after the marriage. Billy was then four or five years of age. Antrim remained at and near Santa Fe for some years, or until Billy was about eight years of age.

It was here that the boy exhibited a spirit of reckless daring, yet generous and tender feeling, which rendered him the darling of his young companions in his gentler moods, and their terror when the angry fit was on him. It was here that he became adept at cards and noted among his comrades as successfully aping the genteel vices of his elders.

84

It has been said that at this tender age he was convicted of larceny in Santa Fe, but as a careful examination of the court records of that city fail to support the rumor, and as Billy, during all his after life, was never charged with a little meanness or petty crime, the statement is to be doubted.

About the year 1868, when Billy was eight or nine years of age, Antrim again removed and took up his residence at Silver City, in Grant County, New Mexico. From this date to 1871, or until Billy was twelve years old, he exhibited no characteristics prophesying his desperate and disastrous future. Bold, daring, and reckless, he was open-handed, generous-hearted, frank, and manly. He was a favorite with all classes and ages, especially was he loved and admired by the old and decrepit, and the young and helpless. To such he was a champion, a defender, a benefactor, a right arm. He was never seen to accost a lady, especially an elderly one, but with his hat in his hand, and did her attire or appearance evidence poverty, it was a poem to see the eager, sympathetic, deprecating look in Billy's sunny face, as he proffered assistance or afforded information. A little child never lacked a lift across a gutter, or the assistance of a strong arm to carry a heavy burden when Billy was in sight.

To those who knew his mother, his courteous, kindly, and benevolent spirit was no mystery. She was evidently of Irish descent. Her husband called her Kathleen. She was about the medium height, straight, and graceful in form, with regular features, light blue eyes, and luxuriant golden hair. She was not a beauty, but what the world calls a fine-looking woman. She kept boarders in Silver City, and her charity and goodness of heart were proverbial. Many a hungry "tenderfoot" has had cause to bless the fortune which led him to her door.

Billy loved his mother. He loved and honored her more than anything else on earth. Yet his home was not a happy one to him. He has often declared that the tyranny and cruelty of his stepfather drove him from home and a mother's influence, and that Antrim was responsible for his going to the bad. However this may be, after the death of his mother, some four years since, the stepfather would have been unfortunate had he come in contact with his eldest stepson.

Billy's educational advantages were limited, as were those of all of the youth of this border country. He attended public school, but acquired more information at his mother's knee than from the village pedagogue. With great natural intelligence and an active brain, he became a fair scholar. He wrote a fair letter, was a tolerable arithmetician, but beyond this he did not aspire.

The best and brightest side of Billy's character has been portrayed above. The shield had another side never exhibited to his best friends—the weak and helpless. His temper was fearful, and in his angry moods he was dangerous. He was not loud or swaggering, or boisterous. He never threatened. He had no bark, or, if he did, the bite came first. He never took advantage of an antagonist, but barring size and weight, would, when aggrieved, fight any man in Silver City. His misfortune was, he could not and would not stay whipped. When oversized and worsted in a fight, he sought such arms as he could buy, borrow, beg, or steal, and used them, upon more than one occasion, with murderous intent.

During the latter portion of Billy's residence in Silver City, he was the constant companion of Jesse Evans, a mere boy, but as daring and dangerous as many an older and more experienced desperado. He was older than Billy and constituted himself a sort of preceptor to our hero. These two were destined to jointly participate in many dangerous adventures, many narrow escapes, and several bloody affrays in the next few years, and, fast friends as they now were, the time was soon to come when they would be arrayed in opposition to one another, each thirsting for the other's blood, and neither shrinking from the conflict. They parted at Silver City, but only to meet again many times during Billy's short and bloody career.

When young Bonney was about twelve years of age, he first imbrued his hand in human blood. This affair, it may be said, was the turning point in his life, outlawed him, and gave him over a victim of his worser impulses and passions.

As Billy's mother was passing a knot of idlers on the street, a filthy loafer in the crowd made an insulting remark about her. Billy heard it and quick as thought, with blazing eyes, he planted a stinging blow on the blackguard's mouth, then springing to the street, stooped for a rock. The brute made a rush for him, but as he passed Ed. Moulton, a well-known citizen of Silver City, he received a stunning blow on the ear which felled him, whilst Billy was caught and restrained. However, the punishment inflicted on the offender by no means satisfied Billy. Burning for revenge, he visited a miner's cabin, procured a Sharp's rifle, and started in search of his intended victim. By good fortune, Moulton saw him with the gun, and, with some difficulty, persuaded him to return it.

Some three weeks subsequent to this adventure, Moulton, who was a wonderfully powerful and active man, skilled in the art of self-defense, and with something of the prize-fighter in his composition, became involved in a rough-and-tumble barroom fight, at Joe Dyer's saloon. He had two shoulder-strikers to contend with and was getting the best of both of them, when Billy's "antipathy"—the man who had been the recipient of one of Moulton's "lifters," standing by, thought he saw an opportunity to take cowardly revenge on Moulton, and rushed upon him with a heavy barroom chair upraised. Billy saw the motion, and like lightning darted beneath the chair—once, twice, thrice, his arm rose and fell—then, rushing through the crowd, his right hand above his head, grasping a pocket-knife, its blade dripping with gore, he went out into the night, an outcast and a wanderer, a murderer, self-baptized in human blood. He went out like banished Cain, yet less fortunate than the first murderer, there was no curse pronounced against his slayer. His hand was now against every man, and every man's hand against him. Alas! for Billy.

* * *

And now we trace our fugitive to Arizona. His deeds of desperate crime in that Territory are familiar to old residents there but it is impossible to follow them in detail, or to give exact dates. It is probable that many of his lawless achievements have escaped both written history and tradition. Records of the courts, at the Indian agency and military posts, and reports from officers and citizens give all the information which can be obtained and cover his most prominent exploits. These reports tally correctly with Billy's disconnected recitals, as given to his companions, in after years, to pass away an idle hour.

After the fateful night when Billy first imbrued his hands in blood and fled his home, he wandered for three days and nights without meeting a human being except one Mexican sheepherder. He talked Spanish as fluently as any Mexican of them all, and secured from this boy a small stock of provisions, consisting of tortillas and mutton. He was on foot, and trying to make his way to the Arizona line. Becoming bewildered, he made a circuit and returned to the vicinity of McKnight's ranch, where he took his initiatory in horse-stealing.

The next we hear of Billy, some three weeks after his departure from Silver City, he arrived at Fort (then Camp) Bowie, Arizona, with a companion, both mounted on one sore-backed pony, equipped with a pack-saddle and rope bridle, without a quarter of a dollar between them, nor a mouthful of provision in the commissary.

Billy's partner doubtless had a name, but he was so given to changing it that it was impossible to fix on the right one. Billy always called him "Alias."

With a fellow of Billy's energy and peculiar ideas as to the rights of property, this condition of impoverishment could not continue. After recuperating his enervated physique at the Fort, he and his companion, on foot (having disposed of their pony), with one condemned rifle and one pistol, borrowed from soldiers, started out on Billy's first unlawful raid.

As is generally known, Fort Bowie is in Pima County, Arizona, and on the Chiracahua Apache Indian Reservation. These Indians were peaceable and quiet at this time, and there was no danger in trusting one's self amongst them. Billy and his companion fell in with a party of three of these Indians, some eight or ten miles southwest of Fort Bowie in the passes of the mountains. A majority of the different tribes of Apaches speak Spanish, and Billy was immediately at home with these. His object was to procure a mount for himself and his companion. He tried arguments, wheedling, promises to pay, and every other plan his prolific brain could suggest—all in vain. These Indians' confidence in white man's reliability had been severely shaken in the person of Indian Agent Clum.

Billy gave a vague account of the result of this enterprise, yet uncompromising as it sounds, it leaves little to surmise. Said he:

"It was a ground hog case. Here were twelve good ponies, four or five saddles, a good supply of blankets, and five pony loads of pelts. Here were three blood-thirsty savages, reveling in all this luxury and refusing succor to two free-born, white American citizens, foot sore and hungry. The plunder had to change hands—there was no alternative—and as one live Indian could place a hundred United States troops on our trail in two hours, and as a dead Indian would be likely to take some other route, our resolves were taken. In three minutes there were three "good Injuns" lying around there, careless like, and, with ponies and plunder, we skipped. There was no fight. It was about the softest thing I ever struck."

The movements of these two youthful brigands for a few days subsequent to the killing of these Indians are lost sight of. It is known that they disposed of superfluous ponies, equipage, and furs to immigrants from Texas, more than a hundred miles distant from Fort Bowie, and that they returned to the reservation splendidly mounted and armed, with money in their pockets. They were on the best of terms with government officials and citizens at Fort Bowie, Apache Pass, San Simon, San Carlos, and all the settlements in that vicinity, and spent a good deal of their time at Tucson, where Billy's skill as a monte dealer and card player generally kept the two boys in luxuriant style and gave them enviable prestige among the sporting fraternity, which was then a powerful and influential element in Arizona.

If anything was known by the authorities, of the Indian killing episode, nothing was done about it. No one regretted the loss of these Indians, and no money could be made by prosecuting the offenders.

The quiet life Billy led in the plazas palled upon his senses, and, with his partner, he again took the road, or rather the mountain trails. There was always a dash of humor in Billy's most tragical adventures. Meeting a band of eight or ten Indians in the vicinity of San Simon, the two young fellows proposed and instituted a horserace. Billy was riding a very superior animal, but made the race and bets on the inferior one ridden by his partner, against the best horse the Indians had. He also insisted that his partner should hold the stakes, consisting of money and revolvers.

Billy was to ride. Mounting his partner's horse, the word was given, and three, instead of two, horses shot out from the starting point. The interloper was Billy's partner, on Billy's horse. He could not restrain the fiery animal, which flew the track, took the bit in his teeth, and never slackened his headlong speed until he reached a deserted cattle ranch, many miles away from the improvised racetrack.

Billy lost the race, but who was the winner? His partner with all the stakes, was macadamizing the rocky trails, far beyond their ken, and far beyond successful pursuit. It required all Billy's Spanish eloquence, all his persuasive powers of speech and gesture, all his sweetest, most appealing expressions of infantile innocence, to convince the untutored and unreasoning savages that he, himself, was not only the greatest loser of them all, but that he was the victim of the perfidy of a traitor—to them a heinous crime. Had not he, Billy, taken all the bets, and lost them all? Whilst their loss was divided between a half-dozen, he had lost his horse, his arms, his money, his friends, and his confidence in humanity, with nothing to show for it but an old plug of a pony that evidently could not win a race against a lame burro.

When did youth and good looks, with well simulated injured innocence, backed by eloquence of tongue and hand-spiced with grief and righteous anger, fail to affect, even an Apache. With words of condolence and encouragement from his sympathizing victims, Billy rode sadly away. Two days thereafter, a hundred miles from thence, Billy might have been seen solemnly dividing spoils with his fugitive friend.

The last and darkest deed of which Billy was guilty in Arizona was the killing of a soldier blacksmith at Fort Bowie. The date and particulars of this killing are not upon record, and Billy was always reticent in regard to it. There are many conflicting rumors in regard thereto. Billy's defenders justify him on the ground that the victim was a bully, refused to yield up money fairly won from him, by Billy, in a game of cards, and precipitated his fate by attempting to inflict physical chastisement on a beardless boy. One thing is sure, this deed exiled Billy from Arizona, and he is next heard of in the State of Sonora, Republic of Mexico.

* * *

In Sonora, Billy's knowledge of the Spanish language, and his skill in all games of cards practiced by the Mexican people, at once established for him a reputation as a first class gambler and high-toned gentleman. All that is known of his career in Sonora is gathered from his own relation of casual events, without detail or dates. He went there alone, but soon established a coalition with a young Mexican gambler, named Melquiades Segura, which lasted during his stay in the Republic.

There is but one fatal encounter, of which we have official evidence, charged against Billy during his sojourn in Sonora, and this necessitated his speedy and permanent change of base. This was the killing of Don Jose Martinez, a monte dealer, over a gaming table. Martinez had, for some weeks, persistently followed a course of bullying and insult towards Billy, frequently refusing to pay him money fairly won at his game. Billy's entrance to the clubroom was a signal for Martinez to open his money drawer, take out a six shooter, lay it on the table beside him, and commence a tirade of abuse directed against "Gringos" generally, and Billy in particular.

There could be but one termination to this difficulty. Billy settled his affairs in the plaza, he and Segura saddled their horses, and about nine o'clock at night rode into a placita having two outlets, hard by the clubroom. Leaving Segura with the horses, Billy visited the gambling house.

The insult came as was expected. Billy's pistol was in the scabbard. Martinez had his on the table and under his hand. Before putting his hand on his pistol the warning came from Billy's lips, in steady tones: "Jose, do you fight as bravely with that pistol as you do with your mouth?" and his hand fell on the butt of his pistol. And here Billy exhibited that lightning rapidity, iron nerve, and marvelous skill with a pistol, which gave him such advantage over antagonists, and rendered his name a terror, even to adepts in pistol practice.

Martinez was no coward but he counted too much on his advantage. The two pistols exploded as one, and Martinez fell back in his seat, dead, shot through the eye. Billy slapped his left hand to his right ear, as though he were reaching for a belligerent mosquito. He said, afterwards, that it felt as though some one had caught three or four hairs and jerked them out.

Before it was fairly realized that Martinez was dead, two horsemen were rushing across the cienega which lies between the plaza and the mountains, and Billy had shaken the dust of Sonora from his feet, forever.

A party of about twenty Mexicans started immediately in pursuit, which they held steadily for more than ten days. They found the horses ridden from the plaza by Billy and Segura, but horses were plenty to persons of such persuasive manners as the fugitives. The chase was fruitless and the pursuers returned to Sonora.

The family of Martinez offered a large reward for the apprehension and return of Billy to Sonora, and a lesser one for Segura. Several attempts were subsequently made, by emissaries of the family, to inveigle Billy back there. The bait was too thin.

* * *

After their flight from Sonora, Billy and Segura made their way to the city of Chihuahua, where their usual good luck at cards deserted them. Billy appeared, unconsciously, to make enemies of the gambling fraternity there. Perhaps a little envy of his skill, his powers, and his inimitable nonchalant style had something to do with it.

His difficulties culminated one night. Billy had won a considerable sum of money at a monte table when the dealer closed his bank and sneeringly informed Billy that he did not have money enough in his bank to pay his losses, whilst he was, at that moment, raking doubloons and double doubloons into a buckskin sack—money enough to pay Billy a dozen times over, leering at Billy the meanwhile.

Billy made no reply, but he and Segura left the house. That monte dealer never reached home with his sack of gold, and his peon, who was carrying the sack, now lives on the Rio Grande, in New Mexico, in comparatively affluent circumstances.

Billy and his partner were seen no more, publicly, on the streets of Chihuahua City, but three other prosperous monte dealers were mysteriously "held up," at night, as they were returning home from the clubrooms, and each was relieved of his wealth. It was afterwards remarked that each of these men had offended Billy or Segura. The gamblers speculated at large upon the mysterious disappearance of the dealer who had so openly and defiantly robbed Billy, and they and his family mourn him as dead. Perhaps they do so with cause.

The two adventurers concluded that Chihuahua was not the heaven they were seeking, and vanished. It may be in place to remark that for some months thereafter, the boys settled their little bills along their sinuous route, in Spanish gold, by drafts on a buck-skin sack, highly wrought in gold and silver thread and lace, in the highest style of Mexican art.

As to the monte dealer who so suddenly disappeared, although Billy never disclosed the particulars of the affair, recent advices from Chihuahua give the assurance that the places which knew him there have known him no more since that eventful night.

* * *

After leaving Chihuahua, Billy and Segura went to the Rio Grande, where they parted company, but only for a short time. Up to the month of December, 1876, Billy's career was erratic, and it is impossible to follow his adventures consecutively; many of them are, doubtless, lost to history. He fell in again with his old companion, Jesse Evans, and all that is known of Billy's exploits during the ensuing few months is gained by his own and Jesse's disconnected narrations.

This youthful pair made themselves well known in Western Texas, Northern and Eastern Mexico, and along the Rio Grande in New Mexico by a hundred deeds of daring crime. Young Jesse had already won for himself the reputation of a brave but unscrupulous desperado, and in courage and skill with deadly weapons, he and Billy were fairly matched. They were, at this time, of nearly the same size. Jesse was, probably, a year or two the oldest, whilst Billy was, slightly, the tallest, and a little heavier. Billy was seventeen years of age in November, 1876, and was nearly as large as at the day of his death. A light brown beard was beginning to show up on his lip and cheeks; his hair was of a darker brown, glossy, and luxuriant; his eyes were a deep blue, dotted with spots of a hazel hue, and were very bright, expressive, and intelligent. His face was oval in form, the most noticeable feature being two projecting upper front teeth, which knowing newspaper correspondents, who never saw the man nor the scenes of his adventures, describe as "fangs which gave to his features an intensely cruel and murderous expression." Nothing can be further from the truth. That these teeth were a prominent feature in his countenance is true; that when he engaged in conversation, or smiled they were noticeable is true; but they did not give to his always pleasing expression a cruel look, nor suggest either murder or treachery. All who ever knew Billy will testify that his polite, cordial, and gentlemanly bearing invited confidence and promised protection—the first of which he never betrayed, and the latter he was never known to withhold. Those who knew him best will tell you that in his most savage and dangerous moods his face always wore a smile. He ate and laughed, drank and laughed, rode and laughed, talked and laughed, fought and laughed, and killed and laughed. No loud and boisterous guffaw, but a pleasant smile or a soft and musical "ripple of the voice." Those who knew him watched his eyes for an exhibition of anger. Had his biographers stated that the expression of his eyes—to one who could read them—in angry mood was cruel and murderous, they would have shown a more perfect knowledge of the man. One could scarcely believe that those blazing, baleful orbs and that laughing face could be controlled by the same spirit.

Billy was, at this time, about five feet seven and one half inches high, straight as a dart, weighed about one hundred and thirty-five pounds, and was as light, active, and graceful as a panther. His form was well-knit, compact, and wonderfully muscular. It was his delight, when he had a misunderstanding with one larger and more powerful than himself, but who feared him on account of his skill with weapons, to unbuckle his belt, drop his arms, and say: "Come on old fellow: I've got no advantage now. Let's fight it out, knuckles and skull." He usually won his fights; if he got the worst of it, he bore no malice.

There were no bounds to his generosity. Friends, strangers, and even his enemies, were welcome to his money, his horse, his clothes, or anything else of which he happened, at the time, to be possessed. The aged, the poor, the sick, the unfortunate and helpless never appealed to Billy in vain for succor.

There is an impression among some people that Billy was excessively gross, profane, and beastly in his habits, conversation, and demeanor. The opposite is the case. A majority of the "too tooist," "uttermost, utterly utter," "curled darlings" of society might take example by Billy's courteous and gentlemanly demeanor, to their own great improvement and the relief of disgusted sensible men. It would be strange, with Billy's particular surroundings, if he did not indulge in profanity. He did; but his oaths were expressed in the most elegant phraseology, and, if purity of conversation were the test, hundreds of the prominent citizens of New Mexico would be taken for desperadoes sooner than young Bonney.

Billy was, when circumstances permitted, scrupulously neat and elegant in dress. Some newspaper correspondents have clothed him in fantastic Italian brigand or Mexican guerrilla style, with some hundreds of dollars worth of gold lace, etc., ornamenting his dress; but they did not so apparel him with his consent. His attire was, usually, of black: a black frock coat, dark pants and vest, a neat boot to his small, shapely foot, and (his only noticeable peculiarity in dress) usually, a Mexican sombrero. He wore this for convenience, not for show. They are very broad-brimmed, protecting the face from the sun, wind, and dust, and very durable. They are expensive, but Billy never owned one which cost hundreds of dollars. Some silly fellow, with a surplus of money and paucity of brains, may have loaded his hat with a thousand dollars worth of medals, gold lace, and thread, but Billy was not of those.

Billy and Jesse put in the few months they spent together by indulging in a hundred lawless raids—sometimes committing depredations in Mexico and fleeing across the Rio Grande into Texas or New Mexico, and vice versa, until hundreds of ranchmen in both republics were on the look out for them, and in many conflicts, on either side of the river, they escaped capture, and consequent certain death, almost by miracle. There was no mountain so high, no precipice so steep, no torrent so fierce, no river so swift, no cave so deep, but these two would essay it in their daring rides for liberty. More than one bold pursuer bit the dust in these encounters, and a price was offered for the bodies of the outlaws, dead or alive.

The Mescalero Apache Indians, from the Fort Stanton, New Mexico, Reservation, used to make frequent raids into Old Mexico, and often attacked emigrants along the Rio Grande. On one occasion, a party from Texas, consisting of three men and their families, on their way to Arizona, came across Billy and Jesse in the vicinity of the Rio Miembres. They took dinner together and the Texans volunteered much advice to the two unsophisticated boys, representing the danger they braved by travelling unprotected through an Indian country, and proposing that they should pursue their journey in company. They represented themselves as old and experienced Indian fighters. The boys declined awaiting the slow motion of ox wagons, and after dinner, rode on.

About the middle of the afternoon, the boys discovered a band of Indians moving along the foothills on the south, in an easterly direction. They speculated on the chances of their new friends, the emigrants, falling in with these Indians, until, from signs of a horse's footprints, they became convinced that an Indian messenger had preceded them from the east, and putting that and that together, it was evident to them that the band of Indians they had seen were bent on no other mission than to attack the emigrants.

With one impulse the young knights wheeled their horses and struck across the prairie to the foothills to try and cut the Indian trail. This they succeeded in doing, and found that the party consisted of fourteen warriors, who were directing their course so as to surely intercept the emigrants, or strike them in camp. The weary horses caught the spirit of their brave riders, and over rocks and hills, through canyons and tule break, the steady measured thud of their hoofs alone broke the silence.

"Can we make it, Billy?" queried Jesse. "Will our horses hold out?"

"The question isn't, will we? but how soon?" replied Billy. "It's a ground hog case. We've got to get there. Think of those white-headed young ones, Jesse, and whoop up. When my horse's four legs let up, I've got two of my own."

Just at dusk the brave boys rounded a point in the road and came in full view of the emigrant's camp. In time—just in time. At this very moment the terrible yell of the Apache broke upon their ears, and the savage band charged the camp from a pass on the south. The gallant horses which had carried the boys so bravely were reeling in their tracks. Throwing themselves out of the saddles, the young heroes grasped their Winchesters and on a run, with a yell as blood-curdling as any red devil of them all could utter, they threw themselves amongst the yelling fiends. There was astonishment and terror in the tone which answered the boys' war cry, and the confusion amongst the reds increased as one after another of their number went down under the unerring aim of the two rifles. Jesse had stumbled and fallen into a narrow arroyo, overgrown with tall grass and weeds. Raising himself to his knees, he found that his fall was a streak of great good luck. As he afterwards remarked, he could not have made a better entrenchment if he had worked a week. Calling Billy, he plied his Winchester rapidly. When Billy saw the favorable position Jesse had involuntarily fallen into, he bounded into it; but just as he dropped to his knees a ball from an Indian rifle shattered the stock of his Winchester and the broken wood inflicted a painful wound on Billy's hand. His gun useless, he fought with his six-shooter-fuming and cursing his luck.

The boys could not see what was going on in the camp, as a wagon intervened; but soon Billy heard the scream of a child as if in death-agony, and the simultaneous shriek of a woman. Leaping from his entrenchment, he called to Jesse to stay there and cover his attack, whilst he sprang away, pistol in one hand and a small Spanish dagger in the other, directly towards the camp. At this moment the Indians essayed to drive them from their defense. Billy met them more than halfway and fought his way through a half-dozen of them. He had emptied his revolver, and had no time to load it. Clubbing his pistol he rushed on, and, dodging a blow from a burly Indian, he darted under a wagon and fell on a prairie axe.

Billy afterwards said he believed that his howl of delight frightened those Indians so that he and Jesse won the fight. He emerged on the other side of the wagon. A glance showed him the three men and all the women and children but one woman and one little girl, ensconced behind the other two wagons, and partly protected by a jutting rock. One woman and the little girl were lying, apparently lifeless, on the ground. With yell on yell Billy fell among the reds with his axe. He never missed hearing every crack of Jesse' rifle, and in three minutes there was not a live Indian in sight. Billy's face, hands, and clothing, the wagons, the camp furniture, and the grass were bespattered with blood and brains.

Turning to the campers, the boys discovered that the little girl had received a fracture of the skull in an attempt, by an Indian brave, to brain her, and the mother had fainted. All three of the men were wounded. One was shot through the abdomen and in the shoulder. It is doubtful if he survived. The other two were but slightly hurt. Billy had the heel of his boot battered, his gun shot to pieces, and received a wound in the hand. Jesse lost his hat. He said he knew when it was shot off his head, but where it went to he could not surmise.

* * *

After parting with the emigrants, Billy and Jesse changed their course and returned to the Rio Grande. Here they fell in with a party of young fellows, well known to Jesse, who urged them to join company and go over to the Rio Pecos, offering them employment which they guaranteed would prove remunerative. Among this party of "cow boys," were James McDaniels, William Morton, and Frank Baker, all well known from the Rio Grande to the Rio Pecos. Our two adventurers readily agreed to join fortunes with this party, and Jesse did do so; but Billy received information, a day or two before they were ready to start, that his old partner Segura was in the vicinity of Isleta and San Elizario, Texas, and contemplated going up the Rio Grande to Mesilla and Las Cruces. Billy at once decided to await his coming, but promised his companions that he would surely meet them in a short time, either at Mesilla or in Lincoln County.

It was here, at Mesilla, and by Jim McDaniels, that Billy was dubbed "The Kid," on account of his youthful appearance, and under this "nom de guerre" he was known during all his after eventful life, and by which appellation he will be known in the future pages of this history.

The Kid's new-found friends, with Jesse, left for Lincoln County, and he waited, impatiently, the arrival of Segura. He made frequent short trips from Mesilla, and, on his return from one of them, he led back his noted gray horse which carried him in and out of many a "tight place" during the ensuing two years.

It was early in the fall of 1876 when The Kid made his famous trip of eighty-one miles in a little more than six hours, riding the gray the entire distance. The cause and necessity for this journey is explained as follows:

Segura had been detected, or suspected, of some lawless act at San Elizario, was arrested and locked up in the jail of that town. There was strong prejudice against him there, by citizens of his own native city, and threats of mob violence were whispered about. Segura, by promises of rich reward, secured the services of an intelligent Mexican boy and started him up the Rio Grande in search of The Kid, in whose cool judgment and dauntless courage he placed implicit reliance. He had received a communication from The Kid, and was about to join him when arrested.

Faithful to his employer, the messenger sought The Kid at Mesilla, Las Cruces, and vicinity, at last finding him at a ranch on the west side of the Rio Grande, about six miles north of Mesilla and nearly opposite the town of Doña Ana. The distance to San Elizario from this ranch was: To Mesilla, six miles, to Fletch Jackson's (called the Cottonwoods), twenty-three miles, to El Paso, Texas, twenty-seven miles, and to San Elizario, twenty-five miles, footing up eighty-one miles. The ride, doubtless, exceeded that distance, as The Kid took a circuitous route to avoid observation, which he covered in a little more than six hours, as above stated.

He mounted on the willing gray, at about six o'clock in the evening, leaving the messenger to await his return.

He remarked to the boy that he would be on his way back, with Segura, by twelve o'clock that night. The boy was skeptic, but The Kid patted his horse's neck. "If I am a judge of horseflesh," said he, "this fellow will make the trip," and away he sped.

Avoiding Mesilla, the horseman held down the west bank of the river, about eighteen miles to the little plaza of Chamberino, where, regardless of fords, he rushed into the ever treacherous current of the Rio Grande.

More than once the muddy waters overwhelmed horse and rider. For thirty minutes or more, The Kid and his trusted gray battled with the angry waves, but skill, and strength, and pluck prevailed, horse and rider emerged, dripping, from the stream, full five hundred yards below the spot where they had braved the flood.

And now they rushed on, past the Cottonwood, past that pillar which marks the corner where join Mexico, New Mexico, and Texas, past Hart's Mills, until The Kid drew rein in front of Ben Dow-ell's saloon, in El Paso, then Franklin, Texas.

It was now a quarter past ten o'clock, and the gray had covered fifty-six miles. The bold rider took time to swallow a glass of Peter Den's whiskey and feed his horse a handful of crackers. In ten minutes, or in less, he was again speeding on his way, with twenty-five miles between him and his captive friend.

About twelve o'clock, perhaps a few minutes past, one of the Mexicans who were guarding Segura at the lock-up in San Elizario was aroused by a hammering voice calling in choice Spanish to open up. "*Quien es?*" (Who's that?) inquired the guard.

"Turn out," replied The Kid. "We have two American prisoners here."

Down rattled the chain, and the guard stood in the doorway. The Kid caught him gently by the sleeve and drew him towards the corner of the building. As they walked, the shining barrel of a revolver dazzled the vision of the jailer, and he was notified in a low, steady, and distinct tone of voice that one note of alarm would be the signal for funeral preliminaries. The guard was convinced, and quickly yielded up his pistol and the keys. The Kid received the pistol, deliberately drew the cartridges, and threw it on top of the jail. He gave instructions to the jailer and followed him into the hall. The door of the room in which Segura was confined was quickly opened, and the occupant cautioned to silence. The Kid stood at the door, cocked revolver in hand, and, in low tones, conversed with Segura, occasionally addressing a stern mandate to the affrighted guard to hasten, as he bungled with the prisoner's irons.

All this was accomplished in the time it takes to relate it. With the assistance of Segura the two guards were speedily shackled together, fastened to a post, gagged, the prison doors locked, and the keys rested with the guard's revolver on top of the house. The Kid declared himself worn out with riding, mounted his old partner on the gray, then taking a swinging gait, which kept the horse in a lope, they soon left the San Elizario jail and its inmates far behind.

Taking a well-known ford, they crossed the Rio Grande, and in a little more than an hour were sleeping at the ranch of a Mexican confederate. This friend hid the plucky horse on the bank of the river, mounted a mustang, and took the direction of San Elizario to watch the denouement, when the state of affairs should be revealed to the public.

Before daylight, the faithful friend stood again before his cabin with The Kid's horse and a fresh, hardy mustang, saddled and bridled. He roused the sleepers. Quickly a cup of coffee, a tortilla, and a scrag of dried mutton were swallowed, and again, across the prairie, sped the fugitives.

Two hours later, a party of not less than thirty men, armed and mounted, rode up to the ranch. The proprietor, with many a male-diction, in pure Castellano, launched against "gringos ladrones," related his tale of robbery and insult, how his best horse had been stolen, his wife insulted, and his house ransacked for plunder. He described the villains accurately, and put the pursuers on their trail. He saw them depart and returned sadly to his home, to mourn, in the bosom of his family, over the wickedness of the world, and to count a handful of coin which The Kid had dropped in making his hasty exit.

The pursuers followed the trail surely, but it only led them a wild goose chase across the prairie, a few miles, then making a detour, made straight for the bank of the Rio Grande again. It was plain to see where they entered the stream, but the baffled huntsmen never knew where they emerged.

The Kid and his companion reached the ranch where the Mexican boy awaited them about noon the next day. This messenger was rewarded with a handful of uncounted coin and dismissed.

And thus, from one locality after another, was The Kid banished by his bloody deeds and violations of law. Yet, not so utterly banished. It was his delight to drop down, occasionally, on some of his old haunts, in an unexpected hour, on his gallant gray, pistol in hand, jeer those officers of the law, whose boasts had slain him a hundred times, to watch their trembling limbs and pallid lips, as they blindly rushed to shelter.

One instant's glance around he threw,
From saddle-bow his pistol drew,
Grimly determined was his look;
His charger with his spurs he struck,
All scattered backward as he came,
For all knew—
And feared "Billy, The Kid."

His look was hardly "grim," but through his insinuating smile, and from his blazing eyes, enough of "determination" and devilish daring gleamed to clear the streets, though twenty such officers were on duty.

* * *

"The Lincoln County War," in which The Kid was now about to take a part, had been brewing since the summer of 1876, and commenced in earnest in the spring of 1877. It continued for nearly two years, and the robberies and murders consequent thereon would fill a volume. The majority of these outrages were not committed by the principals or participants in the war proper, but the unsettled state of the country caused by these disturbances called the lawless element, horse and cattle thieves, footpads, murderers, escaped convicts, and outlaws from all the frontier states and territories; Lincoln and surrounding counties offered a rich and comparatively safe field for their nefarious operations.

It is not the intention, here, to discuss the merits of the embroglio—to censure or uphold either one faction or the other, but merely to detail such events of the war as the hero of these adventures took part in.

The principals in this difficulty were, on one side, John S. Chisum, called "The Cattle King of New Mexico," with Alex A. McSween and John H. Tunstall as important allies. On the other side were the firm of Murphy & Dolan, merchants at Lincoln, the county seat, and extensive cattle-owners, backed by nearly every small cattle-owner in the Pecos Valley. This latter faction was supported by Hon. T. B. Catron, United States attorney for the Territory, a resident and eminent lawyer of Santa Fe, and a considerable cattle-owner in the Valley.

John S. Chisum's herds ranged up and down the Rio Pecos, from Fort Sumner way below the line of Texas, a distance of over two hundred miles, and were estimated to number from forty thousand to eighty thousand head of full-blood, graded, and Texas cattle. A. A. McSween was a successful lawyer at Lincoln, retained by Chisum, besides having other pecuniary interests with him. John H. Tunstall was an Englishman, who only came to this country in 1876. He had ample means at his command, and formed a co-partnership with McSween at Lincoln, the firm erecting two fine buildings and establishing a mercantile house and the "Lincoln County Bank," there. Tunstall was a liberal, public-spirited citizen, and seemed destined to become a valuable acquisition to the reliable business men of our country. He, also, in partnership with McSween, had invested considerably in cattle.

This bloody war originated about as follows: The smaller cattle-owners in Pecos Valley charged Chisum with monopolizing, as a right, all this vast range of grazing country—that his great avalanche of hoofs and horns engulfed and swept away their smaller herds, without hope of recovery or compensation—that the big serpent of this modern Moses, swallowed up the lesser serpents of these magicians. They maintained that at each "round-up" Chisum's vast herd carried with them hundreds of head of cattle belonging to others.

On Chisum's part he claimed that these smaller proprietors had combined together to round-up and drive away from the range—selling them at various military posts and elsewhere throughout the country—cattle which were his property and bearing his mark and brand under the system of reprisals. Collisions between the herders in the employ of the opposing factions were of frequent occurrence, and, as above stated, in the winter and spring of 1877 the war commenced in earnest. Robbery, murder, and bloody encounters ceased to excite either horror or wonder.

Under this state of affairs it was not so requisite that the employees of these stockmen should be experienced vaqueros as that they should possess courage and the will to fight the battles of their employers, even to the death. The reckless daring, unerring marksmanship, and unrivalled horsemanship of The Kid rendered his services a priceless acquisition to the ranks of the faction which could secure them. As related, he was enlisted by McDaniels, Morton, and Baker, who were adherents to the Murphy-Dolan cause.

Throughout the summer and a portion of the fall of 1877, The Kid faithfully followed the fortunes of the party to which he had attached himself. His time was spent on the cattle-ranges of the Pecos Valley, and on the trail, with occasional visits to the plazas, where, with his companions, he indulged, without restraint, in such dissipations as the limited facilities of the little *tendejón* afforded. His encounters with those of the opposite party were frequent, and his dauntless courage and skill had won for him name and fame, which admiration, or fear, or both, forced his friends, as well as his enemies, to respect.

But the Kid was not satisfied. Whether conscientious scruples oppressed his mind, whether he pined for a more exciting existence, or whether policy dictated his resolve, he determined to desert his employers, his companions, and the cause in which he was engaged and in which he had wrought yeoman's service. He met John H. Tunstall, a leading factor of the opposition. Whether The Kid sought this interview, or Tunstall sought him, or befell by chance is not known. At all events, our hero expressed to Tunstall his regret for the course he had pursued against him and offered him his future services. Tunstall immediately put him under wages and sent him to the Rio Feliz, where he had a herd of cattle.

The Kid rode back to camp and boldly announced to his confederates that he was about to forsake them, and that when they should meet again, "those hands, so frankly interchanged," may dye "with gore the green."

Dark and lowering glances gleamed out from beneath contracted brows at this communication, and The Kid half-dreaded and half-hoped a bloody ending to the interview. Angry expostulation, eager argument, and impassioned entreaty all failed to shake his purpose. Perhaps the presence and intervention of his old and tried friend Jesse Evans stayed the threatened explosion. Argued Jesse:

"Boys, we have slept, drank, feasted, starved, and fought cheek by jowl with The Kid; he has trusted himself alone amongst us, coming like a man to notify us of his intention; he didn't sneak off like a cur, and leave us to find out, when we heard the crack of his Winchester, that he was fighting against us. Let him go. Our time will come. We shall meet him again, perhaps in fair fight." Then, under his breath, "And he'll make some of you brave fellows squeak." Silently and sullenly the party acquiesced, except Frank Baker, who insinuated in a surly tone that now was the time for the fight to come off.

"Yes, you d——d cowardly dog!" replied The Kid. "Right now, when you are nine to one; but don't take me to be fast asleep because I look sleepy. Come you, Baker, as you are stinking for a fight; you never killed a man you did not shoot in the back; come and fight a man that's looking at you."

Red lightning flashed from The Kid's eyes as he glared on cowering Baker, who answered not a word. With this banter on his lips, our hero slowly wheeled his horse and rode leisurely away, casting one long regretful glance at Jesse, with whom he was loath to part.

* * *

After pledging allegiance to Tunstall, The Kid plodded along for some months in the monotonous groove fashioned for the "cow boy." In his bearing one would never detect the dare-devilism which had heretofore characterized him. He frequently came in contact with his employer and entertained for him strong friendship and deep respect, which was fully reciprocated by Tunstall. He was also ever a welcome guest at the residence of McSween. Both Tunstall and McSween were staunch friends to The Kid, and he was faithful to them to the last. His life passed on uneventfully. Deeds of violence and bloodshed were of frequent occurrence on the Pecos and in other portions of the country, but all was quiet on the Rio Feliz. The Kid had seemed to lose his taste for blood.

He was passive, industrious, and, seemingly, content. It was the lull before the storm.

In the month of February, 1878, William S. Morton (said to have had authority as deputy sheriff), with a posse of men composed of cow boys from the Rio Pecos, started out to attach some horses which Tunstall and McSween claimed. Tunstall was on the ground with some of his employees. On the approach of Morton and his party, Tunstall's men all deserted him—ran away. Morton afterwards claimed that Tunstall fired on him and his posse; at all events, Morton and party fired on Tunstall, killing both him and his horse. One Tom Hill, who was afterwards killed whilst robbing a sheep outfit, rode up as Tunstall was lying on his face, gasping, placed his rifle to the back of his head, fired, and scattered his brains over the ground.

This murder occurred on the 18th day of February, 1878. Before night The Kid was apprised of his friend's death. His rage was fearful. Breathing vengeance, he quitted his herd, mounted his horse, and from that day to the hour of his death his track was blazed with rapine and blood. The Kid rode to Lincoln and sought McSween. Here he learned that R. M. Bruer had been sworn in as special constable, was armed with a warrant, and was about to start, with a posse, to arrest the murderers of Tunstall. The Kid joined this party, and they proceeded to the Rio Pecos.

On the 6th day of March, Bruer and his posse "jumped up" a party of five men below the lower crossing of Rio Penasco and about six miles from the Rio Pecos. They fled and the officer's party pursued. They separated, and The Kid, recognizing Morton and Baker in two of the fugitives who rode in company, took their trail and was followed by his companions. For fully five miles the desperate flight and pursuit was prolonged. The Kid's Winchester belched fire continually, and his followers were not idle; but distance and the motion of running horses disconcerted their aim, and the fugitives were unharmed. Suddenly, however, their horses stumbled, reeled, and fell, almost at the same instant. Perhaps they were wounded; no one paused to see. A friendly sink-hole in the prairie, close at hand, served the fleeing pair as a breastwork, from which they could have "stood off" twice the force behind them. And yet the pursuers had the best of it, as the pursued had but two alternatives—to surrender or starve.

After considerable parley, Morton said that if the posse would pledge their word and honor to conduct himself and his companion, Baker, to Lincoln in safety, they would surrender. The Kid strongly opposed giving this pledge. He believed that two of the murderers of Tunstall were in his power, and he thirsted for their blood. He was overruled, the pledge was given, the prisoners were disarmed and taken to Chisum's ranch. The Kid rode in the advance, and, as he mounted, was heard to mutter: "My time will come."

On the 9th day of March, 1878, the officer, with posse and prisoners, left Chisum's for Lincoln. The party numbered thirteen men. The two prisoners, special constable R. M. Bruer, J. G. Skurlock, Chas. Bowdre, The Kid, Henry Brown, Frank McNab, Fred Wayt, Sam Smith, Jim French, John Middleton and——McClosky. They stopped at Roswell, five miles from Chisum's, to give Morton the opportunity to mail a letter at the post-office there. This letter he registered to a cousin, Hon. H. H. Marshall, Richmond, Va. A copy of this letter is in the hands of the author, as well as a letter subsequently addressed to the postmaster by Marshall. Morton descended from the best blood of Virginia, and left many relatives and friends to mourn his loss.

Morton and the whole party were well known to the postmaster, M. A. Upson, and Morton requested him, should any important event transpire, to write to his cousin and inform him of the facts connected therewith. Upson asked him if he apprehended danger to himself on the trip. He replied that he did not, as the posse had pledged themselves to deliver them safely to the authorities at Lincoln, but, in case this pledge was violated, he wished his people to be informed. McClosky, of the officer's posse, was standing by and rejoined: "Billy, if harm comes to you two, they will have to kill me first."

The Kid had nothing to say. He appeared distrait and sullen, evidently "digesting the venom of his spleen." After a short stay the cortege went on their way. The prisoners were mounted on two inferior horses. This was the last ever seen of these two unfortunates, alive, except by the officer and his posse. It was nearly ten o'clock in the morning when they left the post-office. About four o'clock in the evening, Martin Chavez, of Picacho, arrived at Roswell from above, and reported that the trail of the party left the direct road to Lincoln, and turned off in the direction of Agua Negra. This was an unfrequented route to the base of Sierra de la Capitana, and the information at once settled all doubts in the minds of the hearers as to the fate of Morton and Baker.

On the 11th, Frank McNab, one of the posse, returned to Roswell and entered the post-office. Said Upson: "Hallo! McNab; I thought you were in Lincoln by this time. Any news?"

"Yes," replied he, "Morton killed McClosky, one of our men, made a break to escape, and we had to kill them."

"Where did Morton get weapons?" queried Upson.

"He snatched McClosky's pistol out of its scabbard, killed him with it, and ran, firing back as he went. We had to kill them, or some of us would have been hurt," explained McNab.

This tale was too attenuated. Listeners did not believe it. The truth of the matter, as narrated by The Kid, and in which rendering he was supported by several of his comrades, was as follows:

It had been resolved by two or three of the guards to murder Morton and Baker before they reached Lincoln. It has been stated by newspaper correspondents that The Kid killed McClosky. This report is false. He was not one of the conspirators, nor did he kill McClosky. He cursed Bruer, in no measured terms for giving a pledge of safety to the prisoners, but said, as it had been given, there was no way but to keep their word.

He further expressed his intention to kill them both, and said his time would come to fulfill his threat, but he would not murder an unarmed man.

McCloskey and Middleton constantly rode behind the prisoners, as if to protect them; the others brought up the rear, except The Kid and Bowdre, who were considerably in advance. About twenty or thirty miles from Roswell, near the Black Water Holes, McNab and Brown rode up to McClosky and Middleton. McNab placed his revolver to McClosky's head and said: "You are the son-of-a-bitch that's got to die before harm can come to these fellows, are you?" and fired as he spoke. McClosky rolled from his horse a corpse. The terrified, unarmed prisoners fled as fast as their sorry horses could carry them, pursued by the whole party and a shower of harmless lead. At the sound of the first shot, The Kid wheeled his horse. All was confusion. He could not take in the situation. He heard firearms, and it flashed across his mind that, perhaps, the prisoners had, in some accountable manner, got possession of weapons. He saw his mortal enemies attempting to escape, and as he sank his spurs in his horse's sides, he shouted to them to halt. They held their course, with bullets whistling around them. A few bounds of the infuriated gray carried him to the front of the pursuers—twice only, his revolver spoke, and a life sped at each report. Thus died McClosky, and thus perished Morton and Baker. The Kid dismounted, turned Morton's face up to the sky, and gazed down on his old companion long and in silence.

He asked no questions, and the party rode on to Lincoln, except McNab, who returned to Chisum's ranch. They left the bodies where they fell. They were buried by some Mexican sheepherders.

* * *

Returning to Lincoln, The Kid attached himself to the fortunes of McSween, who was every day becoming more deeply involved in the events of the war. He was a peaceably disposed man, but the murder of his partner aroused all the belligerent passion within him. The Kid still adhered to Bruer's official posse, as hunger for vengeance was, by no means, satiated, and Bruer was still on the trail of Tunstall's murderers.

One of the actors in that tragedy was an ex-soldier named Roberts. The Kid heard that he could be found in the vicinity of the Mescalero Apache Indian Agency, at South Fork, some forty miles south of Lincoln. Roberts was a splendid shot, an experienced horseman, and as brave as skillful. Bruer and party were soon on their way to attempt his arrest. The Kid knew that he would never be taken alive by this party, with the fate of Morton and Baker, at their hands, so fresh in his memory; and this to The Kid, was a strong incentive to urge the expedition. It was life he wanted, not prisoners.

As the party approached the building from the east, Roberts came galloping up from the west. The Kid espied him, and bringing his Winchester to rest on his thigh, he spurred directly towards him as Bruer demanded a surrender. Roberts' only reply was to The Kid's movements. Like lightning his Winchester was at his shoulder and a ball sang past The Kid's ear. Quick as his foe, The Kid's aim was more accurate, and the ball went crashing through Roberts' body, inflicting a mortal wound. Hurt to the death, this brave fellow was not conquered, but lived to wreak deadly vengeance on the hunters. Amidst a shower of bullets he dismounted and took refuge in an outhouse, from whence, whilst his brief life lasted, he dealt death with his rifle. He barricaded the door of his weak citadel with a mattress and some bed-clothing, which he found therein, and from this defense he fought his last fight. His bullets whistled about the places of concealment, where lurked his foes. Wherever a head, a leg, or an arm protruded, it was a target for his rifle. Charley Bowdre was severely wounded in the side, a belt of cartridges around his body saving his life. Here Dick Bruer met his death. Dr. Blazer's sawmill is directly across the street from Roberts' hiding place. In front of the mill were lying numerous huge saw-boys. Unseen by Roberts, Bruer had crept behind these, to try and get a shot at him. But no sooner did Bruer raise his head to take an observation than the quick eye of Roberts detected him—but one of Bruer's eyes was exposed—it was enough—a bullet from a Winchester found entrance there, and Bruer rolled over dead behind the boy.

The brave fellow's time was short, but to his last gasp his eye was strained to catch sight of another target for his aim, and he died with his trusty rifle in his grasp.

To The Kid, the killing of Roberts was neither cause for exultation, nor "one for grief." He had further bloody work to do. He swore he would not rest nor stay his murderous hand so long as one of Tunstall's slayers lived.

Bruer dead, the command of the squad, by common consent, was conferred upon The Kid. He had little use for the position, however, as throwing around his deeds the protection of law, which he held in disdain. What he wanted was two or three "free riders" who, without fear or compunction, would take their lives in their hands and follow where he led.

On their return to Lincoln, the posse was disbanded, but most of those composing it joined fortunes with The Kid as their accepted leader. With emissaries riding over the country in every direction, he bided his time and opportunity. He spent most of his time in Lincoln and frequently met adherents of the other faction, which meetings were ever the signal for an affray. J. B. Matthews, well known throughout the Territory as "Billy" Matthews, held The Kid in mortal aversion. He was not with the posse who killed Tunstall, but denounced, in no measured terms, the killers of Morton, Baker, and Roberts. He was an intimate friend of popular Jimmy Dolan of the firm of Murphy & Dolan, and a strong supporter of their cause. "Billy" was brave as any red-handed killer of them all. He was in Lincoln plaza on the 28th day of March, and, by chance, unarmed. He came suddenly face to face with The Kid, who immediately "cut down" on him with his Winchester. "Billy" darted into a doorway, which The Kid shot into slivers about his head. Matthews had his revenge, though, as will hereafter appear.

At this time William Brady was sheriff of Lincoln County. Major Brady was an excellent citizen and a brave and honest man. He was a good officer, too, and endeavored to do his duty with impartiality. The objections made against Sheriff Brady were that he was strongly prejudiced in favor of the Murphy-Dolan faction—those gentlemen being his warm personal friends, and that he was lax in the discharge of his duty through fear of giving offence to one party or the other.

Sheriff Brady held warrants for The Kid and his associates, charging them with the murders of Morton, Baker, and Roberts. The Kid and his accomplices had evaded arrest by dodging Brady on the plaza and standing guard in the field. They resolved to end this necessity for vigilance, and by a crime which would disgrace the record of an Apache. The Kid was a monomaniac on the subject of revenge for the death of Tunstall. No deed so dark and damning but he would achieve it to sweep obstacles from the path which led to its accomplishment. Brady with his writs barred the way, and his fate was sealed.

On the 1st day of April, 1878, Sheriff Brady, accompanied by George Hindman and J. B. Matthews, started from Murphy & Dolan's store, Lincoln, to go to the court house, and there announce that no court would be held at the stated April term. In those days of anarchy a man was seldom seen in the plaza or streets of Lincoln without a gun on his shoulder. The sheriff and his attendants each bore a rifle. Tunstall & McSween's store stood about halfway between the two above named points. In the rear of the Tunstall & McSween building is a corral, the east side of which projects beyond the house and commands a view of the street, where the sheriff must pass. The Kid and his companions had cut grooves in the top of the adobe wall in which to rest their guns. As the sheriff came in sight a volley of bullets were poured upon them from the corral, and Brady and Hindman fell, whilst Matthews took shelter behind some old houses on the south side of the street. Brady was killed outright, being riddled with balls. Hindman was mortally wounded, but lived a few moments.

Ike Stockton, who was for so long a terror in Rio Arriba County, this Territory, and in Southern Colorado, and who was recently killed at Durango, kept a saloon in Lincoln plaza at the time the above recited event occurred, and was supposed to be a secret ally of The Kid and gang. He was a witness to the killing of Brady, and, at this moment approached the fallen men. Hindman called faintly for water. The Rio Bonito was close at hand, Stockton brought water to the wounded man in his hat. As he raised his head he discovered Matthews in his concealment. At this moment The Kid and his fellows leaped the corral wall and approached with the expressed intention of taking possession of the arms of Brady and Hindman. Ike knew that as soon as they came in view of Matthews, he would fire on them, and he was equally sure that were he to divulge Matthews presence, he would, himself, become a target. So he "fenced" a little, trying to persuade The Kid that he had not better disturb the arms, or to defer it a while. The Kid was, however, determined, and as he stooped and raised Brady's gun from the ground, a ball from Matthews' rifle dashed it from his hand and plowed a furrow through his side, inflicting a painful though not dangerous wound. For once The Kid was baffled. To approach Matthews' defense was to court death, and it was equally dangerous to persevere in his attempt to possess himself with Brady and Hindman's arms.

Discretion prevailed and the party retired to the house of McSween. Hindman lived but a few moments.

This murder was a most dastardly crime on the part of The Kid, and lost him many friends who had, theretofore, excused and screened him.

* * *

The Kid and his desperate gang were now outlawed in Lincoln, yet they haunted the plaza by stealth and always found a sure and safe place of concealment at McSween's. The laws were not administered, and they often dared to enter the plaza in broad day, defying their enemies and entertained by their friends.

For some space Lincoln County had no sheriff. Few were bold enough to attempt the duties of the office. At length, George W. Peppin consented to receive a temporary appointment. He appointed, in his turn, a score of deputies, and during his tenure of office, robbery, murder, arson, and every crime in the calendar united and held high carnival in their midst. The Kid was not idle. Wherever a bold heart, cool judgment, skillful hand, or reckless spirit was required in the interests of his faction, The Kid was in the van.

San Patricio, a small Mexican plaza on the Rio Ruidoso, some seven miles from Lincoln by a trail across the mountain, was a favorite resort for The Kid and his band. Most of the Mexicans there were friendly to him, and kept him well informed as to any movement which might jeopardize his liberty.

Jose Miguel Sedillo, a faithful ally of The Kid, brought him information, one day in June about daylight, that Jesse Evans with a party from below were prowling about, probably with the intention of stealing a bunch of horses belonging to Chisum and McSween, and which were in charge of The Kid and party.

Without waiting for breakfast, The Kid started with five men, all who were with him at that time. They were Charley Bowdre, Henry Brown, J. G. Skurlock, John Middleton, and Tom O. Foliard. This latter was a young Texan, bold and unscrupulous, who followed the fortunes of The Kid from the day they first met, literally to the death. At this time he had only been with the gang a few days.

Taking Brown with him, The Kid ascended a ridge on the west of the Ruidoso, and followed it up, towards the Bruer ranch, where he had left the horses.

He sent Bowdre, in charge of the other three, with instructions to follow the river up on the east bank.

After riding some three miles The Kid heard firing in the direction where Bowdre and his men should be. The shots were scattering, as though a skirmish was in progress. He dismounted and sent Brown on to circle a hill on the left, whilst himself led his gray down the steep declivity towards the river and road and in the direction of the shooting. With much difficulty he reached the foot of the mountain, crossed the river, and was laboriously climbing a steep ascent on the east when the clatter of a single horse's feet arrested his attention, and, in a moment he descried Brown, through a gap of the hills, riding furiously towards the north, and, at that moment a fusillade of firearms saluted his ears. He mounted and then came a most wonderful ride of less than a mile; it was not remarkable for speed, but the wonder is how he made it at all. Through crevices of rock it would seem a coyote could scarce creep, over ragged precipices, through brush, and cactus, he made his devious, headlong way, until, leaving the spur of hills he had with such difficulty traversed, another similar elevation lay in front of him, between the two a gorge some half mile across; and, at the foot of the opposite hill, the scene of conflict was in view. Jesse, with a band of eight men, had attacked Bowdre's party; they were fighting and skirmishing amongst the rocks and undergrowth at the foothills, and were so mixed, confused, and hidden, that The Kid could scarce distinguish friends from foes. He spied Bowdre, however, in the hands of the enemy, among whom he recognized Jess, and, with one of his well-known war cries, to cheer his friends, he dashed madly through the gorge.

Bowdre's relation of previous events shows how Evans and men attacked him about two miles from the hills. Having an inferior force, he made a run for the foot-hills and took a stand there amongst the rock and brush. Several shots were fired during the chase. Evans made a detour of the hill to avoid the range of Bowdre's guns, and the skirmish commenced. Bowdre became separated from his men. He saw Brown as he rode to the rescue and sought ambush on the east of the hill. Evans also saw Brown, and sent a shower of lead after him, which was the volley that reached the ears of The Kid and brought him to the scene. Thinking to join Brown, who had not recognized him, Bowdre broke from cover on a run, but fell into the hands of Jesse and four of his men. He was powerless against numbers, and his only hope was to stand Evans off until assistance arrived. How he prayed for the appearance of The Kid as he shot anxious glances around. No shot was fired. Evans and party covered him with their revolvers, and Jesse's merry blue eyes danced with boyish glee, albeit a little devil lurked about the corners, as he bantered his prisoner:

"Where's your pard, Charley? I expected to meet him this morning. I'm hungry and thought I'd flay and roast The Kid for breakfast. We all want to hear him bleat."

Bowdre choked back the retort which rose to his lips. He was dismounted and his gun taken from the scabbard, where he had replaced it when surprised, but his captors made no motion to relieve him of his revolver. Bowdre stood with his hand resting on his horse's haunch. Three of Evans' men were dismounted, and two of their horses stood heads and tails, each bridle rein thrown over the other's saddle horn. At this moment it was that The Kid's well-known yell rang out like the cry of a panther. The Evans crowd seemed paralyzed, and Bowdre remarked: "There comes your breakfast, Jess." All gazed wonderingly at the apparition of a gray horse, saddled and bridled, dashing across the valley, with no semblance of a rider save a leg thrown across the saddle and a head and arm protruding from beneath the horse's neck, but, at the end of this arm the barrel of a pistol glistened in the sunlight. Quicker than it can be told, there scarce seemed space to breathe 'till the gray dashed among the amazed gazers.

The Kid's voice rang out: "Mount, Charley, mount." He straightened himself in the saddle and drew rein, but before he could check his headlong speed, the powerful gray had breasted the two horses which were hitched together, threw them heavily and one mounted man lost his seat, and fell beneath his horse. Triumph in his eye, Bowdre had seized his gun, unnoticed, and mounted, ranging himself beside The Kid.

This meeting was a sight not soon to be forgotten by those who witnessed it. These two young beardless desperadoes, neither of them yet twenty-one years of age—boyish in appearance, but experienced in crime—of nearly equal size, each had earned a reputation for desperate daring by desperate deeds, which had made their names a terror wherever they were known. They had slept together on the prairies, by camp fires, in Mexican pueblos, and on the mountain tops; they had fought the bloody Mescaleros and Chiricahuas side by side; they had shared their last dollar and their last chunk of dried deer meat, and had been partners in many other reckless and less creditable adventures, since their earliest boyhood.

No one would have thought, from their smiling faces, that these two were mortal foes. Their attitudes were seemingly careless and unconstrained, as they sat their chafing horses, each with a revolver, at full-cock, in his right hand, resting on his thigh. Though their eyes twinkled with seeming mirth, they were on the alert. Not for an instant did each take his eye from the other's face. As their restless horses champed the bit, advanced, retreated, or wheeled, that steady gaze was never averted. It seemed their horses understood the situation and were eager for the strife.

And thus, for a moment, they gazed. There was a little sternness in The Kid's eye, despite its inevitable smile. Jesse, at length, laughingly broke the silence.

"Well, Billy, this is a hell of a way to introduce yourself to a private picnic party. What do you want anyhow?"

"How are you, Jess?" answered The Kid. "It's a long time since we met. Come over to Miguel Sedillo's and take breakfast with me; I've been wanting to have a talk with you for a long time, but I'm powerful hungry."

"I, too, have been wanting to see you, but not exactly in this shape," responded Jess. "I understood you are hunting the men who killed that Englishman, and I wanted to say to you that neither I nor any of my men were there. You know if I was I would not deny it to you nor any other man."

"I know you wasn't there, Jess," replied The Kid. "If you had been, the ball would have been opened without words."

"Well, then," asked Jess, "what do you jump us up in this style for? Why you'd scare a fellow half to death that didn't know you as well as I do."

"O, ask your prisoner here, Charley," said The Kid, "he'll tell you all about it. You won't go to breakfast with me then? Well, I'm gone. One word, Jess, before I go. There's a party from Seven Rivers lurking about here; they are badly stuck after a bunch of horses which I have been in charge of. The horses are right over the hills there, at Bruer's old ranch. If you meet that crowd, please say to them that they are welcome to the horses, but I shall be there when they receive them, and shall insist that they take Old Gray and some other horses along, as well as me and a few choice friends. Come, put up your pistol, Jess, and rest your hand."

With these words The Kid slowly raised his pistol-hand from his thigh, and Jesse as deliberately raised his. The dancing eyes of Jesse were fixed on The Kid, and the darker, pleasant, yet a little sterner eyes of The Kid held Jesse's intently. Simultaneously the muzzles of their pistols were lowered, neither for an instant pointing in the direction of the other, then, with the spontaneous movement of trained soldiers, were dropped into their scabbards. As they raised their hands and rested them on the horns of their saddles, seven breasts heaved a sigh of relief.

"I have some more men scattered about here," remarked Jesse.

"And so have I," replied The Kid. "Now, Jesse, you ride down the arroyo," pointing east, "and I will ride to the top of the hills," pointing west. "I'll get my men together in a moment, and I suppose you can herd yours. No treachery, Jess. If I hear a shot, I shall know which side it comes from. Old Gray does not care in which direction he carries me, and he can run."

With these words, The Kid reined his horse towards the Rio Ruidoso, and without turning his head, rode leisurely away. Bowdre sat a moment and watched Evans, whose eyes followed The Kid. Jess, at last, wheeled, his horse, ejaculated: "By G—d, he's a cool one," called to his followers and dashed down the arroyo. Bowdre rejoined The Kid, and in twenty minutes the party of six were reunited and were trotting merrily, with sharpened appetites, to breakfast.

Thus ended this bloodless encounter. It was incomprehensible to their followers that these two leaders could meet without bloodshed; but, per chance, the memory of old times came over them and curbed their bold spirits.

* * *

During all this time Sheriff Peppin was not idle, but could do little towards restoring peace in the distracted county. In selecting his deputies, he had chosen some brave and reliable business men, upon whom he could depend. Among these was Marion Turner, of the firm of Turner and Jones, merchants at Roswell. Turner had been for years, off and on, in the employ of Chisum, by whom he was trusted, and who valued his services highly. He had been a staunch adherent of Chisum at the commencement of his struggle and up to May, 1878, when he seceded, for what he probably deemed sufficient cause, and became his old employer's bitterest enemy. Turner had control of the sheriff's operations in the valley of the Rio Pecos, and soon raised a posse of between thirty and forty men, composed principally of cattle-owners and cow boys, few of whom knew the taste of fear.

One morning Turner received information that The Kid had left his quarters and started up the Pecos towards Fort Sumner. He had several warrants against The Kid for murder, and he now swore to either arrest him, kill him, or die in the attempt. With his full force he took the trail. After riding some twenty miles he pronounced this movement of The Kid's to be a blind, and turning west, he left the trail and took a short, straight-out to Lincoln. The result proved his sound judgment, as The Kid and band were there, safely barricaded in the elegant and spacious residence of McSween, prepared to stand a siege and defend their position to the last. Sheriff Peppin with a few recruits joined Turner at the "Big House," as it was called, of Murphy and Dolan, a short distance from McSween's. Turner, however, was the ruling genius of the enterprise. For three days spasmodic firing was kept up from both sides, but no harm was done.

On the morning of July 19th, 1878, Turner expressed his intention of going to the house of McSween and demanding the surrender of The Kid and others against whom he held warrants. This project was denounced as foolhardy, and it was predicted that he would be shot down before he got within speaking distance. Nothing daunted, he persisted in his design and called for volunteers to accompany him. His partner, John A. Jones, than whom a braver man never lived in New Mexico, at once proffered to attend him, and his example was followed by eight or ten others.

The advancing party saw the portholes which pierced the sides of the building, and, to their surprise, they were allowed to walk up to the walls and ensconce themselves between these openings with-out being hailed, or receiving a hint that their presence was suspected by those within. The explanation of this circumstance was that the besieged were at that moment holding a council of war in a room in the rear, where the whole garrison was assembled. The result of this discussion was, The Kid had sworn that he would never be taken alive; his ruling spirit had swayed the more timid, and it was resolved to drive off the assailants, or die at their posts. McSween appeared to be inert, expressing no opinion, or desire. As they returned to their posts, they were astonished to find the front yard occupied by their foes. The Kid hailed the intruders, when Turner promptly notified him that he held warrants for the arrest of Wm. H. Bonney, and others of his companions, amongst them Alex A. McSween.

115

The Kid replied: "We, too, have warrants for you and all your gang, which we will serve on you, hot, from the muzzles of our guns." In short, The Kid and all his confederates refused to make terms, and Turner retired in safety. Not so, however, his attendants. Their position, once gained, they did not propose to relinquish. And now the fight commenced in earnest.

At this juncture, Lieut. Col. Dudley, of the Ninth Cavalry, arrived from Fort Stanton, nine miles distant, with one company of infantry and one of artillery. Planting his cannon in a depression of the road, between the belligerent parties, he proclaimed that he would turn his guns loose on the first of the two who fired over the heads of his command. Yet the fight went on, and the big guns were silent.

Turner was confident, and said he would have The Kid out of there if he had to burn the house over his head.

The Kid, on his part, was sanguine—he said he could stand the besiegers off, and was as gay as if he were at a wedding. Both knew that the struggle must be a bloody one, and neither anticipated an easy victory.

Turner's men took possession of all the surrounding buildings, from which desultory firing was kept up. Doors, windows, and other woodwork, were slivered by flying bullets, and earth flew from adobe walls. This fusillade from the besiegers was aimed to cover the operations of those allies within the yard, who were laboring to fire the building—working kindlings under door and window sills and wherever woodwork was exposed. A portion of The Kid's party had gained the roof, and from behind the parapets, harassed the foe. Turner sent a dozen men to the hills which overlook the plaza, and their heavy, long-range guns soon dislodged them. A magnificent piano in one of the front rooms was hit several times by these marksmen in the hilltops, and at each stroke sent forth discordant sounds.

The truth is Mrs. McSween and three lady friends left the house before the fight commenced. It is also true that she requested permission to return for some purpose, the firing ceased—she went bravely in—returned almost immediately, and the firing was resumed.

About noon the flames burst forth from the front doors and windows, and the fate of the building was sealed. All efforts of the inmates to extinguish them were fruitless, and the assailants shouted their joy. Soon the whole front of the house was deserted by its defenders, and Jack Long, having procured a little coal oil, less than a gallon, made his way into a room not yet on fire, carefully saturated the furniture with the oil, fired it, and made his escape. An adobe building burns very slowly, and this was a large one, containing eleven rooms. Yet the flames were slowly and surely driving the inmates back. The besiegers called on them to surrender every few minutes. The only reply was curses and defiance.

And now, as night sets in the defenders have but one room, a kitchen at the back of the house, that is tenable, and this would furnish shelter but a short time. The question of surrender was discussed and vetoed by The Kid with [scorn]. Bloody, half naked, begrimed with smoke and dust, his reckless spirit was untamed. Fiercely he threw himself in the doorway, the only means of escape, and swore that he would brain and drag back into the burning building the first that made a motion to pass that door. "Hold," said he, "until the fire breaks through upon us, then all as one man, break through this door, take the underbrush on the Rio Bonito, and from there to the hills. We'll have an even chance with them in the bottom." This ipse dixit settled it. The Rio Bonito was not more than fifty yards from the back of the house.

And now one affrighted Mexican, unheeding The Kid's threat, precipitated the bloody finale. He called out to stop shooting and they would surrender. A blow from The Kid's revolver, and the presumptuous fellow lay bruised and senseless on the floor. The Kid had not time to execute all his threat. So soon as the Mexican's voice was heard on the outside, the firing ceased. Robert W. Beckwith, a cattle owner of Seven Rivers, with John Jones passed round the corner of the main building in full view of the kitchen doorway. No sooner did Beckwith appear than a shot from the house inflicted a wound on his hand. He saw The Kid and McSween in the door, and shouting "McSween! McSween," opened fire on them. The Kid shot but once, and Beckwith fell dead, the ball entering near the eye. The Kid called to "come on," and leaping over Beckwith's prostrate body, pistol in hand, he fought his way through a score of enemies, step by step he fought, until reaching the brink of the river he plunged across, and was hid from sight by weeds and brush. He was followed by all his band who had life and strength to flee, and several of those left a bloody trail behind. McSween less fortunate than The Kid, fell dead in the yard, refusing to surrender or to flee. He was pierced with nine bullets. Tom O. Foliard, the new recruit, was the last one who left the yard, and showed his pluck by stopping to pick up a friend, Morris. Discovering that he was dead, he dropped him, and amidst a shower of lead made his escape unharmed.

It was now ten o'clock at night. The fight for the present, was ended, the building was in ashes, there were seven mutilated corpses lying about, and several on both sides nursed desperate wounds.

Turner's party lost but one man killed, besides Beckwith. The Kid's party had killed McSween, Harvey Morris, and three Mexicans. Turner's party numbered about forty men, and The Kid's nineteen, aside from McSween.

* * *

After the disastrous events, detailed in the last chapter, The Kid gathered together such of his gang as were fit and took to the mountains south of Lincoln. From thence they made frequent raids, stealing horses and mules from the vicinity of Dowlin's Mill, the Indian agency, Tularosa, and the Pecos Valley, varying the monotony by occasionally taking in a few ponies from the Mescaleros. They became bold in their operations, approaching the agency without fear.

On the 5th day of August, 1878, they rode up in full sight of the agency, and were coolly appropriating some horses, when the book keeper, named Bernstein, mounted on a horse and said he would go and stop them. He was warned of his danger by persons who knew The Kid and gang, but, unheeding, he rode boldly up and commanded them to desist. The only reply was from The Kid's Winchester, and poor Bernstein answered for his temerity with his life. This gentleman was a Jew, well known in the Territory. He had been in the employ of Spiegelberg Bros. and Murphy & Dolan previous to his connection with the agency, and was an excellent business man and accomplished gentleman.

Sheriff Peppin, with his cohorts, had retired from active service after the bloody nineteenth of July, and law was a dead letter in the county. Immediately after the killing of Bernstein, The Kid, accompanied by Foliard, Fred Wayt, Middleton, and Brown, went to Fort Sumner, San Miguel County, eighty-one miles north of Roswell on the Rio Pecos. Here they established a rendezvous, to which they clung to the last chapter of this history. Bowdre and Skurlock were both married. Their Mexican wives were devoted to them and followed their fortunes faithfully. These two, Bowdre and Skurlock, remained in Lincoln County for a time, but, in the absence of their chief, avoided publicity. The Kid and friends, in the meantime, applied themselves industriously to the pursuit of pleasures. They worshipped, religiously, at the shrines of Bacchus and Venus, but only for a brief space. They had arrived at Sumner on the 18th day of August. About the first of September, this party of five started for Lincoln, for the purpose of assisting Bowdre and Skurlock to remove their families to Sumner.

On the tenth of September, The Kid, with three of his party, again left Sumner for Lincoln County—this time bent on plunder. Chas. Fritz, Esq., living on his ranch eight miles east of Lincoln, on the Rio Bonito, was a steady friend of Murphy & Dolan's during all the troubles, and his hospitable dwelling was always open to their friends. Hence, The Kid and his ilk bore him no good will. They made a descent on his ranch and got away with eighteen or twenty horses, most of them valuable ones. With their booty they returned to Sumner and secreted the stock near by.

There was at Fort Sumner at this time, a buffalo-hunter who had just returned from the plains named John Long, or John Mont, or John Longmont. He was a six-footer, a splendid shot, and coveted the reputation of a "bad man." He was a boisterous bully.

A day or two after The Kid returned from his raid on Fritz, Long, in a drunken frenzy, was shooting his revolver promiscuously up and down the street of Sumner, and the terrified citizens had mostly retired from sight. The Kid issued from a store and, to avoid the bullets, sprang behind a tree-box. Here was an opportunity for Long, to whom The Kid was unknown, to exhibit his magnanimity.

"Come out, buddy," said he. "Don't be afraid, I won't hurt you."

"The h—l you won't!" replied The Kid. "There's no danger of your hurting anybody, unless you do it accidentally. They say you always kill your men by accident."

This retort hit Long hard, as he had killed a man at Fort Griffin, Texas, a short time previously, and saved himself from a furious mob by pleading that it was an accident. He eyed The Kid viciously and queried:

"Where are you from, buddy?"

"I'm from every place on earth but this," responded The Kid, and Long walked sullenly away.

On the following day Long, with several companions, was indulging in a big drunk in a little tendejon kept by a Jew. Long was, as usual, the biggest, the loudest, and the drunkest of the crowd. The Kid entered, in company with young Charley Paine, and the two passed to the back of the store. Long hailed them:

"Where are you going? You d—d little son-of-a-b—h," said he.

The Kid wheeled quickly and walked up to him, with something glistening in his eye which wise men are wont to "let their wisdom fear," and said:

"Who did you address that remark to, sir?"

"O!" answered Long, with a sickly smile, "I was just joking with that other fellow."

"Be very careful," replied The Kid, "how you joke fellows in whose company I happen to be. You will notice that I am the 'littlest' of the two. I am too stupid to understand or appreciate your style of jokes, and if you ever drop another one that hits the ground as close to me as that last, I'll crack your crust; do you understand?"

Long made no reply. He was completely cowed. The Kid gazed sternly at him a moment, and walked carelessly away. The big fighter annoyed him no more. He was killed shortly afterwards at a ranch on the plains by a Mexican named Trujillo.

The Kid remained at Sumner but a few days, when he, Foliard, Bowdre, Wayt, Brown, and Middleton, took the horses stolen from Fritz and started up the Rio Pecos with the intention of adding to their herd before they drove them away. They raided Grzelachowski's ranch, at Alamo Gordo, and other ranches at Juan de Dios and the vicinity of Puerta de Luna, forty miles north of Fort Sumner, and increased their stock of animals to thirty-five or forty head.

Pretty well "heeled," they took a course nearly due east, and in the direction of the Pan Handle of Texas. At Theackey's ranch Bowdre sold out his interest in the stolen stock to his companions, and rejoined Skurlock, at Sumner, where he was employed by Peter Maxwell, to herd cattle. The Kid with the remaining four went on to Atascosa, on the Canadian, leaving Fort Bascom on their left and passing through the plaza of Trujillo.

After the outlaws were gone, the citizens about Puerta de Luna aroused themselves, and one Fred Rothe, then a resident of Las Colonias, now of Anton Chico, raised a party of eight or ten Mexicans, rode to Fort Sumner to enlist more men, failed to increase his force, followed the trail of the stolen stock to Hubbell Springs, about twenty-five miles, got a good look at both thieves and plunder, but, not being on speaking terms with The Kid, and too modest to accost him, and without firing a shot, returned to the river.

The Kid and his band quickly disposed of their ill-gotten plunder, and almost as quickly exhausted the proceeds at monte table and saloons.

The Kid and Foliard returned to Fort Sumner and joined Bowdre and Skurlock. Bowdre continued in the employ of Maxwell, but was interested in all the illegal traffic of his friend. The Kid must have some object upon which to concentrate his energies. Tunstall during his life had been not only his friend but also his banker. He was dead, and amply revenged. Then McSween had supplied the place of Tunstall in his friendship and interest. McSween, also, was dead. There was left but John S. Chisum, of the trio, in whose service he had worked, fought, and killed. But Chisum failed to respond to his petitions for assistance—or remuneration, as The Kid chose to term it—and he conceived for Chisum a mortal hatred, which he tried to flatter himself was justified by his refusal to countenance him in his lawless career, but which was, doubtless, merely feigned as an excuse to plunder Chisum's vast herds of cattle and horses. So upon his return from the Canadian, his energies were all enlisted in cattle "speculations," Chisum, per force, furnishing the capital.

In December, 1878, The Kid and Foliard again visited Lincoln. George Kimbreel had been elected sheriff in November, and held warrants for both of them. They were arrested and placed in the old jail, from whence they easily made their escape and returned to Fort Sumner, where they continued their cattle raids, living in clover; and The Kid by his pleasing manners and open-handed generosity made himself almost universally popular.

Lincoln, with a properly exercised authority, would have been a dangerous locality for The Kid, but he flickered like a moth around the flame. To his daring spirit it was fun to ride through the plaza and salute citizens and officers with a cheerful *buenos dias*.

In the month of February, 1879, The Kid again met Jesse Evans, and in the plaza, at Lincoln. James J. Dolan was about delivering a herd of cattle to the agents of Thomas B. Catron. Dolan had reached a point near Lincoln with his herd, and visited the plaza with two of his employees—Jesse Evans and Wm. Campbell. That night the three, in company with Edgar A. Waltz, agent and brother-in-law of Catron, and J. B. Matthews, met The Kid and Foliard in the street. The meeting was by appointment, and after a few sharp words, ended in a reconciliation—all pledging themselves to bury the hatchet, and cease their, now, causeless strife. At the commencement of the interviews, Jesse said to The Kid: "Billy, I ought to kill you for murdering Bob Beckwith." The Kid replied: "You can't start your lead pump any too quick to suit me, Jess. I have a hundred causes to kill you." Dolan and Matthews interfered as peacemakers, and the threatened row was quelled.

The parties, so reconciled, adjourned to a saloon and drowned old animosities in whisky. Late in the night a lawyer named Chapman arrived in the plaza from Las Vegas. He had been employed by Mrs. McSween to settle up the estate of her deceased husband. It was charged that Chapman was busily engaged in blowing the embers of a dead struggle, and he had made enemies. As he was passing The Kid and party, who had just issued from the saloon, Campbell, who was chock full of bad whiskey and fight, accosted him and told him he wanted to see him dance. Chapman replied indignantly. But few words passed when Campbell shot him dead. The Kid and Jesse were thus witnesses to one killing in which they did not take a hand. The misfortune of this affair was that two innocent parties were arrested, with the guilty one, for this crime. Dolan and Matthews were indicted, tried, and triumphantly acquitted. Campbell was arrested, placed in the guardhouse at Fort Stanton, made his escape and fled the country. The Kid and Jess parted that night never to meet again.

* * *

Leaving Lincoln after his interview with Evans, The Kid returned to Fort Sumner, and, securing some new recruits to his service, he inaugurated a system of plunder which baffled all resistance; and a stock-owner's only course to secure immunity from loss, was to conciliate The Kid and court his friendship. The property of those he claimed as friends he held sacred.

There was an attraction in the very danger which attended The Kid's presence in Lincoln. Again in March, 1879, he, with Foliard, took a trip to that plaza. Upon this occasion they made a showing to comply with the law, and on their arrival, laid away their guns and revolvers. They were again arrested on the old warrants, and placed under guard in the house of Don Juan Patron, and handcuffed; but otherwise their confinement was not irksome. They were guarded by Deputy Sheriff T. B. Longworth, and The Kid had pledged his word to him that he would make no attempt to escape. Longworth knew him well and trusted him. They did not betray this trust until they were again placed in jail. They led a gay life at the house of Patron. Plenty to eat and drink, the best of cigars, and a game of poker with any one, friend or stranger, who chanced to visit them.

On the 21st day of March, 1879, Longworth received orders to place the two prisoners in jail—a horribly dismal hole, unfit for a dog-kennel. The Kid said,—"Tom, I've sworn I would never go inside that hole again alive."

"I don't see," said Tom, "how either you or I can help it. I don't want to put you there, I don't want to put any one there; but that's orders, and I have nothing to do but to obey. You don't want to make trouble for me?"

The Kid walked gloomily up to the jail door and, stopping, said to Longworth,—"Tom, I'm going in here because I won't have any trouble with you, but I'd give all I've got if the son-of-a-b—h that gave the order was in your boots."

He passed into the hall, his cell was pointed out to him, the door of unpainted pine was standing open, he took a pencil from his pocket and wrote on it:

William Bonney was incarcerated first time, December, 22, 1878; Second time, March, 21, 1879, and hope I never will be again. W. H. Bonney.

This inscription still stands, and was copied by the author in August, 1881.

It is suspected that the sheriff knew the prisoners' stay in jail would be short, and he was tired of feeding them. At all events they left when they got ready, and The Kid prowled about the plaza for two or three weeks, frequently passing up and down in broad day, with a Winchester in his hand, cursing the sheriff to his heart's content.

In April they returned to Fort Sumner, and resumed depredations on loose stock, and followed the business industriously throughout the summer and fall. In October of 1879, The Kid, with Foliard, Bowdre, Skurlock, and two Mexicans, rounded up and drove away from Bosque Grande, twenty-eight miles north of Roswell, one hundred and eighteen head of cattle, the property of Chisum. They drove them to Yerby's ranch—in his absence—branded them, and turned them loose on the range. This ranch is north of Sumner. They said that Chisum owed them $600 each for services rendered during the war. They afterwards drove these cattle to Grzelachowski's ranch, at Alamo Gordo, and sold them to Colorado beef-buyers, telling them that they were employed in settling up Chisum's business. Chisum followed the cattle up, recovered them, and drove them back to his range—but The Kid had the money.

123

In January, 1880, a fellow named Joe Grant arrived at Fort Sumner, and was straightaway cheek by jowl with The Kid and his companions. It afterwards transpired that Grant had heard a good deal of The Kid and aspired to win a reputation as a "Holy Terror," as he termed it, by killing the New Mexico desperado. That he had killed his man, and was a "bad one," there is no doubt. He disclosed a good deal of his disposition, if not his intention, one day in Sumner, by remarking: "I like to pick these fighters and lay them out on their own dung hill. They say The Kid is a bad citizen, but I am his loadin' any jump in the road." The Kid heard this, but kept his own counsel, drinking and carousing with Grant every day. Whilst Grant was swaggering and boasting, The Kid was in his usual jovial humor, but no movement of his companion escaped his wary eye.

James Chisum, brother of John S., with three men, had been to Canyon Cueva, near Juan de Dios, north of Fort Sumner, and there recovered a bunch of cattle which had been stolen from their range, it was said, by The Kid. He returned as far as Sumner, arriving there one day about the middle of January, and camped within a mile of the plaza. His party were young Herbert, Jack Finan, and William Hutchison, known on the range as "Buffalo Bill." The Kid, Barney Mason, and Charley Thomas rode out to Chisum's camp and demanded to look through his herd for the XIX brand. They did so, but found none.

The Kid then good-naturedly insisted that Chisum and his men should go to Bob. Hargrove's saloon and take a drink. There they found Joe Grant, viciously drunk. As the party entered, he snatched a fine ivory-handled pistol from Finan's scabbard, and put his own in place of it. The Kid had his eye on him, and remarking "That's a beauty, Joe," took the pistol from his hand and revolved the chambers. It was his design to extract some of the cartridges, but he found only three in it, and deftly whirling the chambers until the next action would be a failure, he returned it to Grant, who flourished it about and at last said to The Kid:

"Pard, I'll kill a man quicker'n you will for the whisky."

"What do you want to kill anybody for?" answered The Kid. "Put up your pistol and let's drink."

During this conversation, Grant had passed behind the counter, and was knocking decanters and glasses about with the pistol. Thus, with the counter between him and the crowd, and revolver in hand, it seemed he had "the drop" on any one in the room whom he might want. The Kid remarked:

"Let me help you break up housekeeping, Pard," and drawing his pistol, also went to knocking the glassware about. Grant continued:

"I want to kill John Chisum, any how, the d—d old———," and he eyed James Chisum with a wicked glare.

"You've got the wrong pig by the ear, Joe," said The Kid. "That's not John Chisum."

"That's a lie," shouted Grant. "I know better," and, turning his pistol full on The Kid, who was smiling sarcastically, he pulled the trigger, but the empty chamber refused to respond; with an oath he again raised the hammer, when a ball from The Kid's revolver crashed through his brains, and he fell behind the counter. The Kid threw the shell from his pistol and said:

"Unfortunate fool; I've been there too often to let a fellow of your calibre overhaul my baggage. Wonder if he's a specimen of Texas desperadoes."

Shortly after the killing of Grant, The Kid made a trip below, remaining for some weeks in the vicinity of Roswell. Verando, three miles from that place, was his headquarters. He was "flush" and spent money freely. The Chisum ranch was but about seven miles from Verando, and those who knew him best suspected that The Kid harbored the intention of waylaying Chisum and urging a fight with him. He kept himself pretty full of whisky, and upon one occasion, at Verando, he was sitting in front of the saloon where a covey of snow-birds were hopping about. He drew his revolver and remarked: "Suppose, boys, old John Chisum was a pretty little bird, which he is not, and suppose that pretty little bird sitting in that straw was him; now if I was to shoot that little bird, and hit him anywhere except in the head, it would be murder;" and with the words, he fired. A bystander picked up the dead bird, and its head was shot off. "No murder!" cried The Kid. "Let's give old John another chance," and another bird's head disappeared. He killed several in this manner, until at last he hit one in the breast. "I've murdered old John at last," said he, "let's go and take a drink."

CHAPTER VII.

PAT GARRETT, SHERIFF

Adapted from *The Authentic Life of Billy, The Kid*

By Pat Garrett

In the month of October, 1880, just previous to the events narrated in the last chapter, the author of this history first became personally and actively engaged in the task of pursuing and assisting to bring to justice The Kid, and others of his ilk, in an official capacity. The reader will perceive how awkward it would appear to speak of myself in the third person, so at the risk of being deemed egotistical, I shall use the first person in the future pages of this work.

In October, Azariah F. Wild, a detective in the employ of the Treasury Department, hailing from New Orleans, La., visited New Mexico to glean some information in regard to the circulation of counterfeit money, some of which had certainly been passed in Lincoln County. Mr. Wild sent for me to go to Lincoln and confer with and assist him in working up these cases. I met him there, and in the course of our interview, I suggested that it would be policy to employ a reliable man to join the gang and ferret out the facts. Wild at once adopted the plan, giving me authority to act in the matter according to my judgment.

I returned to my home, near Roswell, and immediately sent to Fort Sumner for Barney Mason, whom I had tried and knew I could trust. Mason came to me at once, and before I could name the matter to him, he told me that he had stopped at Bosque Grande, twenty-eight miles above, at the ranch of Dan Dedrick, and that Dan had read to him a letter from W. H. West, partner of his brother Sam. Dedrick, in the stable business at White Oaks. The gist of the letter was that West had $30,000 in counterfeit greenbacks, that his plan was to take this money to Mexico, there buy cattle with it, and drive them back across the line. He wanted to secure the services of a reliable assistant whose business would be to accompany him, West, to Mexico, make sham purchases of the cattle as fast as they were bought, receiving bills of sale therefore, so that, in case of detection, the stock would be found in legal possession of an apparently innocent party—and the latter suggested Barney Mason as just the man to assume the role of scapegoat in these nefarious traffickings.

Mason was considerably surprised when he knew that this was the very business on which I had sent for him. Accompanied by Mason, I returned to Lincoln, and Wild, after giving Mason full instructions, and finding that he comprehended them, employed him, at a stipulated salary, per them and expenses, to go to White Oaks and fall in with any proposition which might be made to him by West, Dedrick, or any other parties.

Mason left Lincoln for White Oaks, November 20. The night he arrived there, he went to West and Dedrick's stable to look after his horse. Let it be understood that there are three brothers of the Dedrick's—Dan who lived at Bosque Grande at this time, but is now a partner of Sam at Socorro, is the oldest. Sam at that time was a partner of West, at White Oaks, and Mose, the youngest, who was floating promiscuously over the country, stealing horses, mules, and cattle, is now on the wing, having jumped a bail bond.

As Mason entered West and Dedrick's corral, he met The Kid, Dave Rudabaugh, and Billy Wilson. Rudabaugh had killed a jailer at Las Vegas in 1879 whilst attempting to liberate a friend named Webb. He was on the dodge, and had associated himself with The Kid. Billy Wilson had sold some White Oaks property to W. H. West and received in payment $400 in counterfeit money. This he had spent (as is alleged), and flourished around promiscuously. He, also, was on the dodge. There was no graver charge at that time against Wilson; but the murder of Carlyle, a few days subsequent, as related in the last chapter, renders him liable to indictment for complicity in that crime.

Mason was well known to the three outlaws, and had always been on friendly terms with them. They addressed him in their usual good-natured manner, The Kid asking him what brought him there. Mason's reply intimated that a chance to "take in" a band of horses near by was the cause of his presence. The Kid "smelled a rat," had an interview with his friends and Dedrick, and wanted to kill Mason right there, of which design Mason was ignorant until afterwards. Dedrick vetoed the plans at once—he knew it would be dangerous to him and to his business.

J. W. Bell, afterwards my deputy, was known by Mason to be a friend of mine, so he sought him and advised him of the presence of The Kid and party at the corral. Bell raised a posse of citizens and then went alone to the stable. He interviewed West, who assured him that those he sought were not there. He then inquired about their horses, and West declared that they had no horses there. That statement was false, as West and Dedrick slipped the horses out to the gang during the night.

Mason remained at White Oaks several days, but, owing to the intense excitement caused by the presence of The Kid, and his pursuit by the citizens, he did not deem it a fitting time to broach the subject of his visit to West. I had told him to be sure and see me before he started to Mexico and to come to Roswell in a few days at all hazards. He reached my house on the 25th.

In the meantime I was daily hearing of the depredations of The Kid and gang in the vicinity of White Oaks. I had heard that they were afoot, and guessed that they would go to Dan Dedrick, at Bosque Grande, for horses. I sent word to my neighbors, requesting them to meet me at Roswell, five miles from my house, after dark. I imparted my plans to Mason and he volunteered to accompany me. We left home in the evening. When near Roswell we saw a man riding one horse and leading another. He was going south, in the direction of Chisum's ranch. We went on to Roswell, and found that this wayfarer had avoided that place, and concluded he was dodging. Knowing that The Kid's party had become separated, we thought he might be a straggler from that band, trying to get out of the country.

Mason knew all The Kid's party, so taking him with me, we pursued and caught up with the fugitive near Chisum's ranch. Mason at once recognized him as Cook, who had fled from the fight at Coyote Springs. We disarmed him, took him back to Roswell, and put him in irons. Capt. J. C. Lea had Cook in charge for some three or four weeks, then sent him to jail at Lincoln, from whence he made his escape.

My neighbors had responded to my call, and, about nine o'clock that night, I started up the Rio Pecos with a posse, consisting of the following named citizens: Messrs. Lawton, Mitchell, Mason, Cook, Whetstone, Wildy, McKinney, Phillips, Hudson, Olinger, Roberts, and Alberding. At daybreak we surrounded Dedrick's ranch, at Bosque Grande twenty-eight miles north of Roswell. Here we found two escaped prisoners from the Las Vegas jail. One was Webb, who had been sentenced to hang for the killing of a man named Killeher, at Las Vegas, and had taken an appeal. The other was Davis, who was awaiting trial for stealing mules. These two had made their escape, in company with three others, two of whom had been killed whilst resisting re-arrest, and the other had been returned to the jail at Las Vegas. We found no other person whom we wanted; so, causing Webb and Davis to fall into ranks, we proceeded up the Rio Pecos, arriving at Fort Sumner about daylight the morning of the 27th of November. Here I received a letter from Capt. Lea, detailing further depredations of The Kid and band about White Oaks, the killing of Carlyle, etc. I gained some further information from a buck-board driver, and determined to leave the two prisoners, Webb and Davis, under guard at Sumner, and pursue the outlaws. I went to A. H. Smith, a citizen of Sumner, and made inquiries. He assured me that The Kid and his two companions had not yet returned from the vicinity of White Oaks, but that Foliard, Bowdre, and Pickett were at Cañaditas, about twenty miles, north of east, from Fort Sumner, where Bowdre was in the employ of T. G. Yerby.

Stopping at Fort Sumner only long enough to get breakfast, I left four of my men in charge of the prisoners and, with the balance, started for Las Cañaditas. Olinger and myself were both commissioned as deputy United States marshals, and held United States warrants for The Kid and Bowdre for the killing of Roberts on an Indian reservation.

* * *

The Country between Fort Sumner and Las Cañaditas, was well known to me, and, in order to approach the ranch unobserved, we took across the prairie, designing to make observations from the surrounding hills through our field glasses. When yet some eight miles distant from the ranch, we discovered a horse-man riding in that direction, evidently coming from another ranch about twelve miles from Fort Sumner, and bound for Las Cañaditas. He was a long distance from us, but with the assistance of excellent field glasses we recognized Tom O. Foliard. There was a pass through the hills, unknown to all our party except myself, which would surely intercept him if we could get through in time. This was a "hard road to travel." It was overgrown with weeds and brush and encumbered with loose rock, rendering it almost impassable. With much difficulty we made through the path and came out on the beaten road within three hundred yards of Foliard, who had not before suspected our presence. He was equal to the situation. Soon as he saw us the splendid animal he rode sprang away under whip and spur, and his Winchester pumped lead fast and furious as he ran. We pursued, but, instead of riding on to him, as I had anticipated, he left us like the wind. He fired twenty-six shots, as he afterwards declared. I fired but three times. There were but Lawton and Mitchell with me, as the others had fallen behind in the almost inaccessible ravine. These two used their rifles industriously. No harm was done by this fusillade on either side, except that Foliard's horse was wounded in the thigh. He made a splendid run and a brave horseback fight, reaching the ranch and giving the alarm in time, as when we reached there the birds had flown to the hills.

We were not sure whether Foliard had succeeded in reaching the ranch, and if he had, presumed the party might remain and give us a fight. So we approached with caution. Lawton, Mason, McKinney, and Roberts, only, were with me, as I had sent Mitchell back to bring up the rear. I proposed to divide what force we had and charge on the house. I was overruled. My companions advised to await the rest of the posse. When we did walk up to the ranch, unopposed, our precautions appeared rather ludicrous to us, as we only found

Bowdre's wife and another Mexican woman, who hailed our advent with "terror-born lamentations." Our labor, however, was not without its reward, as we captured a pair of mules stolen from a stage company on the Rio Grande by Mose Dedrick, and by him turned over to The Kid. We also secured four stolen horses.

We returned to Fort Sumner, stayed one night, and relieving guard over the prisoners, started for The Kid's stronghold, Los Portales, where he was wont to harbor his stolen stock. This is sixty miles east of Fort Sumner and is the veritable castle so graphically described by newspaper correspondents; its approaches impassable except to the initiated—inaccessible and impregnable to foes. Here is where romance has surrounded the young brigand with more than oriental luxury, blest him with the loves of female beauties whose charm would shame the fairest tenant of an eastern seraglio, and clothed him in gorgeous splendor. It seems cruel to rob this fairy castle of its magnificence, to steal the romance from so artfully woven a tale; but the naked facts are: Los Portales is but a small cave in a quarry of rock, not more than fifteen feet high, lying out and obstructing the view across a beautiful level prairie, and bubbling up, near the rocks, are two springs of cool clear water, furnishing an ample supply for at least one thousand head of cattle. There is no building nor corral. All signs of habitation are a snubbing post, some rough working utensils and a pile of blankets. "Just that and nothing more."

The Kid had about sixty head of cattle in the vicinity of Los Portales, all but eight of which were stolen from John Newcomb at Agua Azul. We found only two cows and calves and a yearling, and heard afterwards that The Kid had moved his stock to another spring about fifteen miles east. We had brought no provisions with us and found only some musty flour and a little salt in the cave. We killed the yearling and banqueted on beef straight while there. The next day we circled the camp, found no more stock, and, after an absence of four days, returned to Fort Sumner.

On our return trip we took dinner at Wilcox's ranch, twelve miles from the Fort. Wilcox told me that Bowdre was very anxious to have an interview with me. He wanted to see if he could get bonds in case he came in and gave himself up. I left word with Wilcox for Bowdre to meet me at the forks of the road, two miles from Sumner, at two o'clock the following day. He kept the appointment, and I showed him a letter from Capt. J. C. Lea, of Roswell, wherein it was promised that if he, Bowdre, would change his evil life and forsake his disreputable associates, every effort would be made by good citizens to procure his release on bail and give him an opportunity to redeem himself.

Bowdre did not seem to place much faith in these promises, and evidently thought I was playing a game to get him in my power. He, however, promised to cease all commerce with The Kid and his gang. He said he could not help but feed them when they came to his ranch, but that he would not harbor them more than he could help. I told him if he did not quit them or surrender, he would be pretty sure to get captured or killed, as we were after the gang and would sleep on their trail until we took them in, dead or alive. And thus we parted.

On my arrival at Fort Sumner I dismissed the posse, except Mason, and they returned to Roswell. I hired C. B. Hoadley to convey the prisoners to Las Vegas. On my arrival at Sumner with them from below, I had written to Desiderio Romero, sheriff of San Miguel County, advising him that I had them under guard at Fort Sumner and requesting him to come after them. I had heard nothing from him, and concluded to take them to Las Vegas myself, and get them off my hands. The day we were to start, Juan Roibal and two other Mexicans came into Sumner from Puerto de Luna to inquire about the horses of Grzelachowski stolen by The Kid. They returned as far as Gayheart's ranch with us, assisting Mason and myself to guard the prisoners. At Gayheart's they took the direct route to Puerto de Luna, and, after some delay, we started by the right-hand road. We were only three or four miles on our way when a messenger from Roibal intercepted us with information that a sheriff's posse, from Las Vegas, were at Puerto de Luna on their way to Fort Sumner after the prisoners.

This changed my route and I took the other road. We met the Las Vegas posse about eight miles from Puerto de Luna. They were led by two deputy sheriffs, Francisco Romero and a Dutchman—and he was a Dutchman. They had arrived at Puerto de Luna with three men, in a spring wagon, and had there swelled the party of five to twenty or twenty-five, all Mexicans, except the irrepressible Dutchman. Discarding the wagon, they were all mounted, and came down upon my little party like a whirlwind of lunatics—their steeds prancing and curveting—with loud boasts and swaggering airs—one would have drought they had taken a contract to fight the battle of Valverde over again, and that an army of ten thousand rebels opposed them instead of two manacled prisoners.

At Puerto de Luna the deputies receipted to me for the prisoners, and, as I was turning them over, Webb accosted me and said he had but ten dollars in the world, but would give me that if I would accompany him to Las Vegas; that he thought it was my duty to do so, as I had arrested him, and he never would have surrendered to such a mob as this. I replied that if he looked at it in that light, and feared for his safety—I would go on, but, of course, refused his money.

The deputies took the prisoners to have them ironed. I was sitting in the store of A. Grzelachowski, when Juanito Maes, a noted desperado, thief, and murderer, approached me, threw up his hands and said he had heard I wanted him and had come to surrender. I replied that I did not know him, had no warrant for him, and did not want him. As Maes left me a Mexican named Mariano Leiva, the big bully of the town, entered, his hand on a pistol in his pocket, walked up to me, and said he would like to see any d—d Gringo arrest him. I told him to go away and not annoy me. He went out on the porch, where he continued in a tirade of abuse, all directed against me.

I finally went out and told him that I had no papers for him and no business with him, that whenever I did have he would not be put to the trouble of hunting me, that I would be sure to find him. With an oath, he raised his left arm in a threatening manner, his right hand still on his pistol. I slapped him off the porch. He landed on his feet, drew his pistol and fired without effect. My pistol went off prematurely, the ball striking at his feet—the second shot went through his shoulder, when he turned and ran, firing back as he went, way wide of the mark.

I entered the store and got my Winchester. In a few moments Deputy Romero came in and informed me that I was his prisoner. I brushed him aside and told him I did not propose to submit, asking him the cause of my arrest. He said it was for shooting at Leiva, and reached for my gun. I told him I had no intention of evading the law, but he could not disarm me; that I did not know what sort of mob I had struck; that one man had already deliberately shot at me, and I proposed to keep my arms and protect myself. Mason had come in, and now picked up his rifle and said: "Shall I cut the son-of-a in two, Pat?" I told him not to shoot, that I did not mind the barking of these curs. My friend, Grzelachowski, interfered in my defense and the bold deputy retired. I went to an Alcalde the next morning, had an examination, and was discharged.

Deputy Romero had written to the sheriff at Las Vegas that he had arrested the two prisoners, and was on his way up with them, and, also, had Barney Mason, one of The Kid's gang, in charge. The sheriff immediately started his brother, with five or six men, to meet us at Major Hay's ranch. They came in all the paraphernalia of war; if possible, a more ludicrously bombastic mob than the one inaugurated at Puerto de Luna. Threats and oaths and shouts made a pandemonium there. The Romero who had just joined us swore that he had once arrested The Kid at Anton Chico (which was a lie, notwithstanding he proved it by his posse), that he wanted no weapons to arrest The Kid—all he wanted was to get his eyes on him. And yet it is pretty sure that this poodle would have ridden all night to avoid sleeping within ten miles of an old camp of The Kid's.

Rudabaugh once remarked that it only required lightning bugs and corn-cobs to stampede officers of Las Vegas or Puerto de Luna.

Before we reached Hay's ranch, I had heard that Frank Stewart, agent for cattle-owners on the Canadian, with a numerous party, was at or near Anton Chico, and was on the trail of The Kid and his band; that he wanted to recover some stock stolen by them, but would much rather have the beeves. On this information I had started Mason to Anton Chico with a message for Stewart. The Las Vegas deputies offered objections to his leaving the posse, as they had, by some process of reasoning, got it in their heads that Mason was their prisoner, although they had no warrant for him and had not arrested him. I paid no attention to their senseless gabble, except to tell them that Mason would be in Las Vegas nearly as soon as we would, and if they wanted him then, they could arrest him. I pointed him out to the sheriff, a few days afterwards, in Las Vegas, but they had changed their minds and did not want him.

A few miles from Las Vegas, this delectable posse stopped at a wayside tendejon to hoist in a cargo of aguardiente; I seized the opportunity to escape their objectionable society, and rode on, alone, into the town. I was ashamed to be seen with the noisy, gabbling, boasting, senseless, undignified mob, whose deportment would have disgusted The Kid and his band of thieves.

As Mason and myself had left the direct road from Fort Sumner to Las Vegas to meet the officers at Puerta de Luna, we missed The Kid, Rudabaugh, and Wilson, who were then on their way to Las Cañaditas, as heretofore rela-ted. I had understood that Frank Stewart, the agent of Panhandle stockmen, was going below to hunt The Kid, and my message, sent to him at Anton Chico by Mason, mentioned in the last chapter, was to the effect that I wanted to see him before he started. He came, with Mason, and met me at Las Vegas, but had sent his party on to White Oaks.

Stewart had planned to search in the vicinity of White Oaks, and, should he miss the gang there, to cut across the mountains, strike the Rio Pecos below, and follow it up. I opposed this course, as giving the outlaws time to leave the country or seek a safe hiding place. Stewart was convinced that his plan would not work, and, about 1:00 p.m., on the 14th day of December, 1880, Stewart, Mason, and myself left Las Vegas to overtake Stewart's posse and turn them back. We stopped at Hay's ranch, eighteen miles from Las Vegas, got supper, and continued our ride. About one o'clock at night we fell in with some Mexican freighters, camped by the roadside, and slept until daylight. We rode hard until about nine o'clock on the morning of the 15th, when we hove in sight of Stewart's party.

Whilst eating a hearty breakfast, Stewart, who wanted to sound the disposition of his men but did not wish to confide all our plans to them, said:

"Boys, there is a bunch of steers down near Fort Sumner, which I am anxious to round up and take in."

They all dropped on the class of property he was after, and a few of them weakened when they understood that a conflict with The Kid and his desperate band was, probably, impending, whilst others were more than willing to take a hand.

At last Stewart said: "Do as you please, boys, but there is no time to talk. Those who are going with me, get ready at once. I want no man who hesitates."

In a moment, Lon Chambers, Lee Halls, Jim East, "Poker Tom," "The Animal," and "Tenderfoot Bob" were in the saddle ready to accompany us.

We took a southwesterly direction, aiming to strike the Rio Pecos at Puerto de Luna. We made about forty-five miles that day and pulled up at a Mexican ranch about nine o'clock at night, some fifteen miles north of Puerto de Luna, where we found entertainment for neither man nor beast. We, however, consoled ourselves with remembrances of buffalo humps we had consumed in days past, and feasted on anticipation of good cheer on the morrow.

On the morning of the 16th, we took the road at daylight. It was intensely cold, and some of our party walked, leading their horses, to save their feet. Between eight and nine o'clock we drew up in front of Grzelachowski's store, were cordially welcomed and hospitably entertained. To rest and save our horses we determined to lay over until the next morning. We spent the day infusing warmth into our chilled clothes and through the medium of mesquite-root fires and internal applications of liquid fuel, and in eating apples and drawing corks. We were entertained by the vaporings of one Francisco Arragon, who was a veritable Don Quixote—with his mouth.

Over and over again, he took in The Kid and all his band—each time in questionable Spanish. His weapons were eloquence, fluency, and well-emphasized oaths, inspired by frequent potations of a mixed character. This great brave did not take to me kindly, but lavished all his surplus affection, attention, and maudlin sentiment on Stewart and Mason, and threw before them the aegis of his prowess and infallibility. At last he invited my two companions to accompany him to his house, "just across the street," where he promised to regale them with rock and rye, ad infinitum. Little persuasion was necessary to start my friends. The rock and rye was produced, and after two or three libations, Don Francisco opened his combat with the windmills. It was his philosophy that, as they were run by wind, they must he fought by wind and he launched whole tornadoes against invisible foes. It was evidently the object of this hero to impress the wife of his bosom with his bravery, and he succeeded to such an extent that his ravings elicited from her a thousand impassioned entreaties that he would stay his dreadful hand and refrain from annihilating The Kid and all his cohorts, thus endangering his own precious life. This was what Arragon was playing for, and, if she had failed to exhibit distress and alarm he would, doubtless, have hammered her black and blue so soon as he had her alone. And yet her entreaties only redoubled his profane threatenings. He was eager to get at the bloody desperadoes. He wanted me, nor none of my party to accompany him. He, alone, would do all the fighting; would round them up, bring them in, and turn them over to me. He seemed to think Americans were scarce, and he wanted to save them. He was going to get me all the volunteers I wanted in the morning—ten, twenty, or thirty. After fighting this range battle until near night, he concluded to start out immediately, and bring them in right away; that they would take shelter when they saw him coming, but he would tear the walls down over their heads and drag them out by the heels. At last, the trio, Stewart, Mason, and the wife, elicited from him a solemn pledge that he would give The Kid and his followers a few hour's lease of life.

In the morning I thought I would waste a little time and see if I could get this doughty ally along. Stewart begged that he might he allowed to go, just to see how he did it. He said he would he ready at ten o'clock, and mounting his horse he rode furiously up and down the streets and plaza pretending to be enlisting recruits, but secretly dissuading citizens from going. At ten o'clock we asked him if he was ready. He was not, but would be almost immediately.

About two o'clock, the bold Arragon announced that he had no legal right to interfere with the outlaws and declined to accompany us. It was with difficulty I prevented Stewart from roping and dragging him by the horn of his saddle.

We got away from Puerto de Luna about three o'clock in the evening, with but one recruit—Juan Roibal. Of all the cowardly braggarts, not one could be induced to go when the time came. They were willing to ride in any direction but that in which The Kid might be encountered. I must, however, except two young men, Americans, Charlie Rudolph and George Wilson, who did not start with us, having neither horses nor arms; but, ashamed of the pusillanimity of their townsmen, they borrowed horses and arms and overtook us at John Gayheart's ranch, eighteen miles below Puerto de Luna and twenty-five above Fort Sumner. We reached here about nine o'clock in the night of December 17th in a terrible snow storm from the northwest.

At Gayheart's we got a lunch, rested a while, and by twelve o'clock were again in the saddle, with a ride of twenty-five miles before us, which we were determined to make by daylight. I had started a spy, Jose Roihal, brother to Juan, from Puerto de Luna to Fort Sumner the day previous. He was a trustworthy fellow, recommended to me by Grzelachowski. He had ridden straight through to Fort Sumner without stopping, obtained all the information possible, and, on his return, met me at Pablo Beaubien's ranch, a mile above Gayheart's, where he reported.

His appearance at Fort Sumner excited no suspicion. He kept his eyes open and his mouth closed. When necessary to talk he pretended to be a sheepherder looking for strays. It was a sure thing that The Kid, with five adherents, was at Fort Sumner and that he was on the *que vive*. George Farnum, a buckboard driver, had told him that Mason and myself were on the way down, but neither of them knew that we were not alone. They kept horses saddled, and were prepared to "take us in," when we should heave in sight, or to run, as occasion demanded.

After gaining all the information possible, without exciting suspicion, Jose rode leisurely out from Fort Sumner, crossing the river on the west. Foliard and Pickett followed him across the river and asked him who he was, his business, etc. He replied that he was a herder and was hunting stray sheep. His interlocutors seemed satisfied, and allowed him to depart.

The Kid, Foliard, Bowdre, Rudabaugh, Wilson, and Pickett, after their meeting at Las Cañaditas, had gone directly to Fort Sumner, and were there putting in a gay time at cards, drinking, and dancing. The Kid had heard of the capture of mules and other stolen stock at Yerby's ranch, and was terribly angered thereat. The gang had squandered many precious hours in cursing me, and threatening me with bloody death. The Kid had written to Capt. Lea, at Roswell, that if the officers would give him a little time, and let him alone until he could rest up his horses and get ready, he would leave the country for good; but if he was pursued, or harassed, he would inaugurate a bloody war and fight it out to the fatal end.

With this information from our faithful spy, we left Gayheart's ranch about midnight, reaching Fort Sumner just before daylight. I camped the outfit a little above the plaza, took Mason with me, and went prospecting. We understood that the outlaws kept their horses at A. H. Smith's corral when in Sumner, and we first visited him. We found that their horses were not there, then wakened Smith, who told us that they had left after dark the night before. We all turned in at Smith's except Mason, who went to the house of his father-in-law. He returned, however, immediately, and said he had heard that The Kid and gang were in an old deserted building nearby. This report served to excite us, rouse us out of bed, and disappoint us, as there was no one at the house designated. We concluded we would, per force, possess our souls in patience until daylight.

* * *

As soon as any one was stirring in the plaza of Fort Sumner on the morning of the 18th, I left our party, except Mason, in concealment and started out to take observations. I met a Mexican named Iginio Garcia, in my rounds, whom I knew to be a tool of The Kid's, and spoke to him. I warned him not to betray my presence to any of tire gang and not to leave the plaza. He represented that he had urgent business below, but assured me that he would keep my counsel. I consented that he should go, as it did not matter much. If they knew I was there, they would labor under the impression that my only support in an engagement would be Mason and, perhaps, a Mexican or two. The fact of the presence of Stewart and his party, I felt sure had not been betrayed. Garcia lived twelve miles south of Fort Sumner, and started in that direction.

A day or two previous to these events, A. H. Smith had sent Bob. Campbell and Jose Valdez to Bosque Grande, to drive up a bunch of milch cows which he had bought from Dan. Dedrick. Garcia met these two near his home. He knew that Campbell was a friend and accomplice of The Kid and that Valdez was, at least, a friend. He told them that I was at Fort Sumner, and they immediately turned the cows loose and separated; Campbell went to a camp close by, hired a Mexican boy, and sent him to The Kid with a note. The Kid and gang were at Wilcox's ranch, twelve miles east of Sumner. Valdez rode into Sumner, where I met him and inquired if he had seen Garcia. He said he saw him at a distance, but did not speak to him. I asked no further questions, as I was convinced I would get no word of truth from him.

On receipt of Campbell's note, The Kid sent Juan, a stepson of Wilcox, to the Fort to see how the laird lay, with instructions to return and report as soon as possible. Wilcox and his partner, Brazil, were law-abiding citizens and, subsequently, rendered me invaluable assistance in my efforts to capture the gang; but had they been betrayed to The Kid, he would have killed them without compunction. Seeing Juan in the plaza, I suspected his errand, accosted him, and found my surmise was correct. After a little conversation I concluded that I would fully trust him. I made known my business to him; he promised to faithfully follow my instructions, and I believed him. I gleaned from this messenger the following information.

The Kid and all his hand had intended to come to Fort Sumner the following day in a wagon. The Kid had, that morning, received a note from Bob Campbell, by a Mexican boy, wherein Bob related how he and Valdez met Garcia, and that Garcia had notified them of my presence at Sumner. Hence Valdez had lied to me. This note disarranged The Kid's plans, and he had sent Juan in to try to learn something of my movements, number of my force, etc. I asked Juan if he would work with me to deceive the outlaws. He said he would do anything I told him. I left him and went to Valdez. I made him write a note to The Kid saying that I and all my party had gone to Roswell, and there was no danger. I then wrote a note to Wilcox and Brazil, stating that I was at Fort Sumner with thirteen men, that I was on the trail of The Kid and gang, and that I would never let up until I got them, or run them out of the country, and asking them to cooperate with me. So soon as Juan had transacted his business in the plaza, he came to me; I gave him the two notes, warning him not to get them mixed, and started him home.

The Kid and party were impatiently awaiting Juan's return. They scanned Valdez's note eagerly—then shouted their scorn at my timidity; said this news was too good for them; that they had intended to come in after me anyhow; had a good will to follow us; if they could kill me, they would not be further molested; if we had not run away, they would have "shot us up a lot," and set us on foot. Juan was not asleep and, when opportunity served, gave the other note to Wilcox.

I was confident that the gang would be in Fort Sumner that night, and made arrangements to receive them. There was an old hospital building on the eastern boundary of the plaza—the direction from which they would come— the wife of Bowdre occupied a room of the building, and I felt sure they would pay their first visit to her. I took my posse there, placed a guard about the house, and awaited the game.

They came fully two hours before we expected them. We were passing away the time playing cards. There were several Mexicans in the plaza, some of whom, I feared, would convey information to the gang, as I had them with me, in custody. Snow was lying on the ground, increasing the light outside. About eight o'clock a guard cautiously called from the door, "Pat, someone is coming!" "Get your guns, boys," said I. "None but the men we want are riding this time of night."

The Kid, with all his reckless bravery, had a strong infusion of caution in his composition when not excited. He afterwards told me that as they approached the building that night he was riding in front with Foliard. As they bore down close upon us, he said, a strong suspicion arose in his mind that they might be running into unseen danger. "Well," said I, "what did you do?" He replied, "I wanted a chew of tobacco, bad. Wilson had some that was good, and he was in the rear. I went back after tobacco, don't you see?" and his eye twinkled mischievously.

One of the Mexicans followed me out, and we two joined the guard, Lon. Chambers, on one side, and Mason, with the rest of the party, went round the building to intercept them should they aim to pass on into the plaza. The gang were in full sight approaching. In front rode Foliard and Pickett. I was under the porch and close against the wall, partly hidden by some harness hanging, Chambers close behind me, and the Mexican behind him. I whispered:—"That's them." They rode up until Foliard's horse's head was under the porch, when I called, "Halt!" Foliard reached for his pistol—Chambers and I both fired; his horse wheeled and ran at least one hundred and fifty yards. Quick as possible I fired at Pickett. The flash of Chambers's gun disconcerted my aim, and I missed him; but one would have thought, by the way he ran and yelled, that he had a dozen balls in him. When Foliard's horse ran with him, he was uttering cries of mortal agony, and we were convinced that he had received his death. He, however, wheeled his horse and, as he rode slowly back, he said, "Don't shoot, Garrett. I'm killed." Mason called, "Take your medicine old boy, take your medicine," and was going to Foliard. I called to Mason and told him that he was killed, and might want revenge. He could pull a trigger yet, and to be careful how he approached him. I called to Tom to throw up his hands, that I would give him no chance to kill me. He said he was dying and could not throw up his hands, and begged that we would take him off his horse and let him die as easy as possible. Holding our guns down on him we went up, took his gun out of the scabbard, lifted him off his horse, carried him into the house and laid him down, took off his pistol, which was full-cocked, and found that he was shot through the left side, just below the heart, and his coat was cut across the front by a bullet. During this encounter with Foliard and Pickett, the party on the other side had seen The Kid and the rest of the gang, had fired on them and killed Rudabaugh's horse, which, however, ran twelve miles with him, to Wilcox's ranch, before he tired. Soon as Mason and his party fired, these four ran like a bunch of wild Nueces steers. They were completely surprised and demoralized. As soon as The Kid and companions disappeared, Mason came round the building just as Foliard was returning, reeling in his saddle. After we had laid him down inside, he begged me to kill him, said if I was a friend of his I would put him out of his misery. I told him I was no friend to men of his kind who sought to murder me because I tried to do my duty, and that I did not shoot up my friends as he was shot. Just then Mason entered the room again. He changed his tone at once and cried, "Don't shoot any more, for God's sake, I'm already killed." Perhaps he guessed that if he called on Mason to put him out of his misery, he would comply with his request. Mason told him again to "take his medicine." He replied, "It's the best medicine I ever took." He also asked Mason to tell McKinney to write to his grandmother in Texas, and inform her of his death. Once he exclaimed, "O! my God, is it possible I must die?" I said to him, just before he died, "Tom, your time is short." He answered, "The sooner the better: I will be out of pain." He censured no one, but told who were there with him. He died in about three quarters of an hour after he was shot.

Pickett was unhurt, but was nearly scared to death. He went howling over the prairie, yelling bloody murder, and was lost until the next night. He ran his horse down and then took it on foot, reached Wilcox's ranch about dark the next night, and hid in a haystack. He had run his horse full twenty-five miles in a northeast direction, before he gave out, and then walked twelve or fifteen miles to the ranch. Here he remained, crouching in fear and trembling in the haystack, until he saw his companions ride in from the hill.

The gang, now reduced to five, remained at Wilcox's that night. They were depressed and disheartened. After a long consultation, they concluded to send some one to Fort Sumner the following morning to spy out the lay of the land. They relieved guard through the night to prevent surprise and sent Wilcox's partner, Mr. Brazil, to the plaza the next day. They had suspected Wilcox and Brazil of treachery, when they were so effectually surprised at the hospital building, but had been entirely reassured by them since their return.

* * *

Brazil came to me at Fort Sumner on the morning of December 20th. He described the condition of the crestfallen band and told me they had sent him in to take items and report to them. I told him to return and tell them that I was at Sumner with only Mason and three Mexicans, that I was considerably scared up and wanted to go back to Roswell, but feared to leave the plaza. Brazil did not return until the following day. When he was ready to start, I told him if he found the gang at the ranch when he arrived there, to remain. If they had left, or did leave, after his arrival, to come and report to me; that, if he did not come to me sooner, I would start for the ranch at two o'clock in the morning; and, that, if I did not meet him on the road, I would feel sure they were at the ranch.

This faithful friend went home and returned, reaching Sumner about twelve o'clock in the night. There was snow on the ground, it was desperately cold, and Brazil's beard was full of icicles. He reported that The Kid and his four companions had taken supper at Wilcox's, then mounted, and left. We all started for the ranch. I sent Brazil ahead to see whether the gang had returned, whilst, with my posse, I took a circuitous route by Lake Ranch, a mile or two off the road, thinking they might be there. We rounded up the house, found it vacant, and rode on towards Wilcox's. About three miles from there we met Brazil. He said the outlaws had not returned and showed me their trail on the snow. After following this trail a short distance, I was convinced that they had made for Stinking Springs, where was an old deserted house built by Alejandro Perea. When within a half-mile of the house, we halted and held a consultation. I told my companions I was confident we had them trapped, and cautioned them to preserve silence. When within about four hundred yards, we divided our party and left Juan Roibal in charge of the horses. With one-half the force I circled the house. Finding a dry arroyo, we took its bed and were able to approach pretty close. Stewart, with the rest of the posse, found concealment within about two hundred yards of the building on the other side. There were three horses tied to projecting rafters of the house, and, knowing that there were five of the gang, and that they were all mounted when they left Wilcox's, we concluded they had led two horses inside. There was no door; only an opening, where a door had once been. I sent a messenger, who crept around to Stewart, proposing that, as they were surely there, we should stealthily enter the house, cover them with our guns, and hold them until daylight. Stewart demurred. Lee Hall was in favor of the plan. Shivering with cold, we awaited daylight or a movement from the inmates of the house.

I had a perfect description of The Kid's dress, especially his hat. I had told all the posse that, should The Kid make his appearance, it was my intention to kill him, and the rest would surrender. The Kid had sworn that he would never yield himself a prisoner, but would the fighting, with a revolver at each ear, and I knew he would keep his word. I was in a position to command a view of the doorway, and told my men that when I brought up my gun, to all raise and fire.

Before it was fairly daylight, a man appeared at the entrance with a nose bag in his hand, whom I firmly believed to be The Kid. His size and dress, especially the hat, corresponded with his description exactly. I gave the signal by bringing my gun to my shoulder, my men raised, and seven bullets sped on their errand of death. Our victim was Charley Bowdre. Turning, he reeled back into the house. In a moment Wilson's voice was heard. He called to me and said that Bowdre was killed and wanted to come out. I told him to come out with his hands up. As he started, The Kid caught hold of his belt, drew his revolver around in front of him and said, "They have murdered you, Charley, but you can get revenge. Kill some of the sons-of before you die." Bowdre came out, his pistol still hanging in front of him, but with his hands up. He walked towards our ranks until he recognized me, then came straight to me, motioned with his hand towards the house, and strangling with blood, said, "I wish—I wish—I wish—" then, in a whisper, "I'm dying!" I took hold of him, laid him gently on my blankets, and he died almost immediately.

Watching every movement about the house in the increasing light, I shortly saw a motion of one of the ropes by which the horses were tied, and dropped on the fact that they were attempting to lead one of them inside. My first impulse was to shoot the rope in two, but it was shaking so, I feared to miss. I did better—just as the horse was fairly in the opening, I shot him and he fell dead, partially barricading the outlet. To prevent another attempt of this kind, I shot the ropes in two which held the other two horses, and they walked away. They still had two horses in the house, one of them The Kid's favorite mare, celebrated for speed, bottom, and beauty.

I now opened a conversation with the besieged, of whom The Kid was spokesman. I asked him how he was fixed in there.

"Pretty well," answered The Kid, "but we have no wood to get breakfast."

"Come out," said I, "and get some. Be a little sociable."

"Can't do it, Pat," replied he. "Business is too confining. No time to run around."

"Didn't you fellows forget a part of your program yesterday?" said I. "You know you were to come in on us at Fort Sumner, from some other direction, give us a square fight, set us afoot, and drive us down the Pecos."

Brazil told me that when he took the information to The Kid that I only had Mason and three Mexicans with me at Sumner, and was afraid to leave for home, he proposed to come and take me in. Bowdre had objected to the expedition. My banter caused The Kid to drop on the fact that they had been betrayed, and he became reticent.

Our party were becoming very hungry, and, getting together, we arranged to go to Wilcox's ranch for breakfast. I went first, with one-half the men. The distance was only about three miles. When we reached there, Brazil asked me what news I brought. I told him the news was bad, that we had killed the very man we did not want to kill. When he learned that it was Bowdre, he said, "I don't see why you should be sorry for having killed him. After you had the interview with him the other day, and was doing your best to get him out of his troubles, he said to me, as we were riding home, 'I wish you would get that d—d long-legged son-of-a out to meet me once more; I would just kill him and end all this trouble!' Now, how sorry are you?"

I made arrangements with Wilcox to haul out to our camp some provisions, wood, and forage for our horses. I did not know how long the outlaws might hold out, and concluded I would make it as comfortable as possible for myself and the boys. Charley Rudolph had frozen his feet slightly the night previous. On my return, Stewart and the balance of the boys went to breakfast.

About three o'clock the gang turned loose the two horses from the inside. We picked them up, as we had the other two. About four o'clock the wagon arrived from Wilcox's with provisions and wood. We built a rousing fire and went to cooking. The odor of roasting meat was too much for the famished lads, who were without provisions. Craving stomachs overcame brave hearts. Rudahaugh stuck out from the window a handkerchief that had once been white, at the end of a stick, and called to us that they wanted to surrender. I told them that they could all come out with their hands up, if they wanted to. Rudabaugh then came out to our camp and said they would all surrender if I would guarantee them protection from violence. This, of course, I did. Rudabaugh returned to the house, where they held a short consultation. In a few moments they all, The Kid, Wilson, Pickett, and Rudabaugh, came out, were disarmed, got their supper, and we took them to Wilcox's. I sent Brazil, Mason, and Rudolph back to the ranch with a wagon after the body of Bowdre. On their arrival with the corpse at Wilcox's ranch, the cortege started for Fort Sumner, getting there before night. We turned Bowdre's body over to his wife, ironed the prisoners, and by sundown Stewart, Mason,

Jim East, "Poker Tom," and myself, with the prisoners in charge, started for Las Vegas.

The Kid and Rudahaugh were cheerful and gay during the trip. Wilson seemed dejected, and Pickett frightened. The Kid said that, had they succeeded in leading the three horses, or two of them, or one of them, into the house, they would have made a break to get away. He said, also, that he, alone, would have made a target of himself until his mare could have carried him out of range of our guns, or we had killed him, if it had not been for the dead horse barring his way. He said he knew she would not try to pass that, and, if she did, she would have knocked the top of his head off against the lintel of the doorway. Whilst at Fort Sumner, The Kid had made Stewart a present of the mare, remarking that he expected his business would be so confining for the next few months that he would hardly find time for horse-back exercise.

We reached Gayheart's ranch, with our prisoners, about midnight, rested until eight in the morning, and reached Puerto de Luna about two o'clock p.m., on Christmas day. My friend Grzelachowski gave us all a splendid dinner. My ubiquitous Don Quixote Aragon proffered to me, again, his invaluable services and that of his original mob, which I respectfully declined.

With a fresh team, we got away from Puerto de Luna about four o'clock, broke our wagon, borrowed one of Capt. Clarency, and reached Hay's ranch for breakfast. At 2:00 p.m., December 26, we reached Las Vegas and, through a crowd of citizens, made our way to the jail. Our objective point was the Santa Fe jail, as there were United States warrants against all our prisoners except Pickett. Him we intended to leave at Las Vegas. The other three we proposed to go on to Santa Fe with in the morning, although we expected, and so did Rudabaugh, that the authorities at Las Vegas would insist on holding him for the killing of the jailor. We had promised Rudabaugh to take him to Santa Fe, and were determined to do it. So Stewart went and made oath that we were holding this prisoner on a United States warrant; armed with which instrument and our warrant, we intended to hold this prisoner and take him to Santa Fe.

* * *

On the Morning of December 27th, I had fresh irons placed on The Kid, Rudabaugh, and Wilson. Michael Cosgrove, Esq., mail contractor, being well acquainted in Santa Fe, I induced him to accompany me there with the prisoners. I therefore released two of my guards, and started with Cosgrove, Stewart, and Mason.

After breakfast we went to the jail for our prisoners. They turned out The Kid and Wilson to us, who were handcuffed together. We demanded Rudabaugh. They refused to yield him up, saying he had escaped from that jail, and they wanted him for murder. I told them that our right to the prisoner ranked theirs, as I was a deputy United States marshal and had arrested Rudabaugh for an offense against laws of the United States, that I knew nothing of any other offense or arrest, that he was my prisoner, I was responsible for him, and intended to have him. Stewart drew his affidavit on them, and they, at last, turned Rudabaugh out to us.

We had been on the train with our three prisoners but a few minutes when we noticed that a good many Mexicans, scattered through the crowd, were armed with rifles and revolvers and seemed considerably excited. Stewart and I concluded their object was to take Rudabaugh off the train. I asked Stewart if we should make a fight for it; he said we would, of course. I said, "Let's make a good one." We felt sure they intended to mob him, or we might have given him up. Besides, he acknowledged that he was afraid of them, and we were pledged to protect him and take him to Santa Fe.

Stewart guarded one door of the car, and I the other. These armed ruffians crowded about the car, but none of them made a formal demand for Rudabaugh, or stated their business. Deputy Sheriff Romero, brother to the sheriff who had so distinguished himself when I brought Webb to him at Hay's ranch, headed a mob of five, who approached the platform where I was standing, flourishing their revolvers. One of the mob said, "Let's go right in and take him out of there," and they pushed this deputy up on the platform, crowding after him. I merely requested them, in my mildest tones, to get down, and they slid to the ground like a covey of hardhack turtles off the banks of the Pecos. They did not seem at all frightened, but modest and bashful-like. Rudabaugh was excited. The Kid and Wilson seemed unconcerned. I told them not to be uneasy, that we were going to make a fight if they tried to enter the car, and if the fight came off, I would arm them all, and let them take a hand. The Kid's eyes glistened, as he said:—"All right, Pat. All I want is a six-shooter. There is no danger, though. Those fellows won't fight." The mob were weakening and all they wanted was for someone to coax them to desist, so it would not look so much like a square back-down. Some influential Mexicans reasoned a little with them and they subsided. We were detained by them about three-quarters of an hour. I understood, afterwards, that they had presented their guns to the engineer and threatened him if he moved the train. One of the railroad officials threatened them with the law for detaining the United States mail. At last Deputy United States Marshal Mollay mounted the cab and pulled the train out.

I had telegraphed to Deputy United States Marshal Charles Conklin, and found him at the Santa Fe depot, waiting for us. Deputy United States Marshal Tony Neis took The Kid and Wilson from Santa Fe to Mesilla, where The Kid was first tried for the murder of Roberts at the Mescalero Apache Indian agency. He was acquitted. He was again tried, at the same term, for the murder of Sheriff William Brady, and sentenced to be hung on the 13th day of May, 1881, at Lincoln, the county seat of Lincoln County. He was brought from Mesilla by Deputy Marshal Robert Olinger and Deputy Sheriff David Woods, of Dona Ana County, and turned over to me by them at Fort Stanton, nine miles west of Lincoln, April 21, 1881. Lincoln County has never had a jail, until the last few weeks, that would hold a cripple. The county had just purchased the large two-story building, formerly the mercantile house of Murphy & Dolan, for the use of the county as a public building, but no jail had been constructed; hence I was obliged to place a guard over The Kid. I selected Deputy Sheriff J. W. Bell, and Deputy Marshal Robert Olinger, for this duty, and assigned them a guard room in the second story of the county building, separate and apart from other prisoners. This room was at the northeast corner of the building, and one had to pass from a hall, through another large room, to gain the only door to it. There were two windows—one on the north, opening to the street, and the other on the east, opening into a large yard, which ran east a hundred yards, or more, and projected into the street twelve or fourteen feet past the north, or front, walls of the building. At the projecting corner of the yard, next the house on the north-west, was a gate; a path running from this gate along the east end of the building to the rear, or south wall, where was a smaller gate opening into a corral, in the rear of the house. Passing through this corral to the south-west corner of the building, we come to a door leading to a small hall and broad staircase, which was the only, then, means of access to the second story of the building. Facing the north, we ascend five or six steps, reach a square landing, turn to the right, facing the east, and ascend twelve or fourteen steps, reaching the hall which extends through the building from north to south. Turning to the right, we find two doors, one on each side of the hall.

The one to the right leads into a room in the south-west corner of the building, where were kept surplus arms. Turning to the left, from the head of the staircase we find two other doors, one on each side of the hall, and still another at the north end, which opens on a porch, facing the street on the north. The door on the left, or west side of the hall, led to a room appropriated to the confinement of prisoners, over whom I kept a guard. The door on the right, or east side of the hall, opened into a large room, occupied by me as an office, passing through which, another door opens into the north-east apartment, which I assigned to the guard, in which to confine The Kid. The necessity of this description will soon be understood by the reader, whether the description is lucid or not.

During the few days The Kid remained in confinement, I had several conversations with him. He appeared to have a plausible excuse for each and every crime charged against him, except, perhaps, the killing of Carlyle. I said to him one day: "Billy, I pass no judgment as to whether your sentence is just for the killing of Brady, but, had you been acquitted on that charge, you would, most surely, have been hung for the murder of Jimmy Carlyle, and I would have pronounced that sentence just. That was the most detestable crime ever charged against you." He seemed abashed and dejected, and only remarked: "There's more about that than people know of." In our conversations, he would sometimes seem on the point of opening his heart, either in confession or justification, but it always ended in an unspoken intimation that it would all be of no avail, as no one would give him credence, and he scorned to beg for sympathy. He expressed no enmity towards me for having been the instrument through which he was brought to justice, but evinced respect and confidence in me, acknowledging that I had only done my duty, without malice, and had treated him with marked leniency and kindness.

As to his guards, he placed confidence in Deputy Sheriff Bell, and appeared to have taken a liking to him. Bell was in no manner connected with the Lincoln County War, and had no animosity or grudge against The Kid. The natural abhorrence of an honest man towards a well-known violator of the law was intensified in Bell's case, by the murder of Carlyle, who was a friend of his; but never, by word or action, did he betray his prejudice, if it existed. As to Deputy Marshal Olinger, the case was altogether different. They had met, opposed in arms, frequently during the past years of anarchy. Bob Beckwith was a bosom friend of Olinger's—The Kid had killed him. The Kid charged that Olinger had killed friends of his. There existed a reciprocal hatred between these two, and neither attempted to disguise or conceal his antipathy for the other.

On the evening of April 28th, 1881, Olinger took all the other prisoners across the street to supper, leaving Bell in charge of The Kid in the guard room. We have but The Kid's tale, and the sparse information elicited from Mr. Geiss, a German employed about the building, to determine the facts in regard to events immediately following Olinger's departure. From circumstances, indications, information from Geiss, and The Kid's admissions, the popular conclusion is that:

At The Kid's request, Bell accompanied him down stairs and into the back corral. As they returned, Bell allowed The Kid to get considerably in advance. As The Kid turned on the landing of the stairs, he was hidden from Bell. He was light and active, and, with a few noiseless bounds, reached the head of the stairs, turned to the right, put his shoulder to the door of the room used as an armory (though locked, this door was well known to open by a firm push), entered, seized a six-shooter, returned to the head of the stairs just as Bell faced him on the landing of the stair-case, some twelve steps beneath, and fired. Bell turned, ran out into the corral and towards the little gate. He fell dead before reaching it. The Kid ran to the window at the south end of the hall, saw Bell fall, then slipped his handcuffs over his hands, threw them at the body, and said: "Here, d—n you, take these, too." He then ran to my office and got a double-barreled shotgun. This gun was a very fine one, a breech-loader, and belonged to Olinger. He had loaded it that morning, in presence of The Kid, putting eighteen buckshot in each barrel, and remarked, "The man that gets one of those loads will feel it." The Kid then entered the guard-room and stationed himself at the east window, opening on the yard.

Olinger heard the shot and started back across the street, accompanied by L. M. Clements. Olinger entered the gate leading into the yard as Geiss appeared at the little corral gate and said, "Bob, The Kid has killed Bell." At the same instant The Kid's voice was heard above: "Hello, old boy," said he.

"Yes, and he's killed me, too," exclaimed Olinger, and fell dead, with eighteen buckshot in his right shoulder and breast and side. The Kid went back through the guard room, through my office, into the hall, and out on the balcony. From here he could see the body of Olinger, as it lay on the projecting corner of the yard, near the gate. He took deliberate aim and fired the other barrel, the charge taking effect in nearly the same place as the first; then breaking the gun across the railing of the balcony, he threw the pieces at Olinger, saying, "Take it, d—n you, you won't follow me any more with that gun." He then returned to the back room, armed himself with a Winchester and two revolvers. He was still encumbered with his shackles, but hailing old man Geiss, he commanded him to bring a file. Geiss did so, and threw it up to him in the window. The Kid then ordered the old man to go and saddle a horse that was in the stable, the property of Billy Burt, deputy clerk of probate, then went to a front window, commanding a view of the street, seated himself, and filed the shackles from one leg. Bob Brookshire came out on the street from the hotel opposite, and started down towards the plaza. The Kid brought his Winchester down on him and said, "Go back, young fellow, go back. I don't want to hurt you, but I am fighting for my life. I don't want to see anybody leave that house."

In the meantime, Geiss was having trouble with the horse, which broke loose and ran around the corral and yard awhile, but was at last brought to the front of the house. The Kid was all over the building, on the porch, and watching from the windows. He danced about the balcony, laughed, and shouted as though he had not a care on earth. He remained at the house for nearly an hour after the killing before he made a motion to leave. As he approached to mount, the horse again broke loose and ran towards the Rio Bonito. The Kid called to Andrew Nimley, a prisoner, who was standing by, to go and catch him. Nimley hesitated, but a quick, imperative motion by The Kid started him. He brought the horse back and The Kid remarked, "Old fellow, if you hadn't gone for this horse, I would have killed you." And now he mounted and said to those in hearing, "Tell Billy Burt I will send his horse back to him," then galloped away, the shackles still hanging to one leg. He was armed with a Winchester and two revolvers. He took the road west, leading to Fort Stanton, but turned north about four miles from town and rode in the direction of Las Tablas.

This, to me, was a most distressing calamity, for which I do not hold myself guiltless. The Kid's escape, and the murder of his two guards, was the result of mismanagement and carelessness, to a great extent. I knew the desperate character of the man whom the authorities would look for at my hands on the 13th day of May—that he was daring and unscrupulous, and that he would sacrifice the lives of a hundred men who stood between him and liberty, when the gallows stared him in the face, with as little compunction as he would kill a coyote. And now realize how all inadequate my precautions were. Yet, in self-defense, and hazarding the charge of shirking the responsibility and laying it upon dead men's shoulders, I must say that my instructions as to caution and the routine of duty were not heeded and followed.

On the bloody 28th of April, I was at White Oaks. I left Lincoln on the day previous to meet engagements to receive taxes. Was at Las Tablas on the 27th, and went from there to White Oaks. On the 29th, I received a letter from John C. Delaney, Esq., of Fort Stanton, merely stating the fact of The Kid's escape and the killing of the guard. The same day Billy Nickey arrived from Lincoln and gave me the particulars. I returned to Lincoln on the 30th, and went out with some volunteer scouts to try and find The Kid's trail, but was unsuccessful. A few days after, Billy Burt's horse came in dragging a rope. The Kid had either turned him loose, or sent him in by some friend, who had brought him into the vicinity of the town and headed him for home.

The next heard of The Kid, after his escapade at Lincoln, was that he had been at Las Tablas and had there stolen a horse from Andy Richardson. He rode this horse to a point a few miles of Fort Sumner, where he got away from him, and The Kid walked into the town. If he made his presence known to any one there, I have not heard of it. At Sumner he stole a horse from Montgomery Bell, who lives some fifty miles above, but was there on business. He rode this horse out of town bareback, going in a southerly direction. Bell supposed the horse had been stolen by some Mexican, and got Barney Mason and Mr. Curington to go with him and hunt him up. Bell left his companions and went down the Rio Pecos. Mason and Curington took another direction. Mason had a rifle and a six- shooter, whilst Curington was unarmed. They came to a Mexican sheep-camp, rode up close to it, and The Kid stepped out and hailed them. The Kid had designated Mason as an object of his direct vengeance. On the sudden and unexpected appearance of The Kid, Mason's business "laid rolling." He had no sight on his gun, but wore a new pair of spurs. In short, Mason left. Curington stopped and talked to The Kid, who told him that he had Bell's horse, and to tell Bell he was afoot, and must have something to ride out of the country, that, if he could make any other arrangements, he would send the horse to him; if not, he would pay him for it.

The Kid led a fugitive life, hovering, spite of danger, around the scenes of his past two years of lawless adventure. He had many friends who were true to him, harbored him, kept him supplied with territorial newspapers, and with valuable information concerning his safety. The end was not yet, but fast approaching.

* * *

During the weeks following The Kid's escape, I was censured by some for my seeming unconcern and inactivity in the matter of his re-arrest. I was egotistical enough to think I knew my own business best, and preferred to accomplish this duty, if possible at all, in my own way. I was constantly, but quietly, at work, seeking sure information and maturing my plans of action. I did not lay about The Kid's old haunts, nor disclose my intentions and operations to anyone. I stayed at home, most of the time, and busied myself about the ranch. If my seeming unconcern deceived the people and gave The Kid confidence in his security, my end was accomplished. It was my belief that The Kid was still in the country and haunted the vicinity of Fort Sumner; yet there was some doubt mingled with my belief. He was never taken for a fool, but was credited with the possession of extraordinary forethought and cool judgment, for one of his age. It seemed incredible that, in his situation, with the extreme penalty of law, the reward of detection, and the way of successful flight and safety open to him—with no known tie to bind him to that dangerous locality—it seemed incredible that he should linger in the Territory. My first task was to solve my doubts.

Early in July, I received a reply from a letter I had written to Mr. Brazil. I was at Lincoln when this letter came to me. Mr. Brazil was dodging and hiding from The Kid. He feared his vengeance on account of the part which he, Brazil, had taken in his capture. There were many others who "trembled in their boots" at the knowledge of his escape; but most of them talked him out of his resentment, or conciliated him in some manner.

Brazil's letter gave me no positive information. He said he had not seen The Kid since his escape, but, from many indications, believed he was still in the country. He offered me any assistance in his power to recapture him. I again wrote to Brazil, requesting him to meet me at the mouth of Tayban Arroyo an hour after dark on the night of the 13th day of July.

A gentleman named John W. Poe, who had superseded Frank Stewart, in the employ of the stockmen of the Canadian, was at Lincoln on business, as was one of my deputies, Thomas K. McKinney. I first went to McKinney, and told him I wanted him to accompany me on a business trip to Arizona, that we would go down home and start from there. He consented. I then went to Poe and to him I disclosed my business and all its particulars, showing him my correspondence. He also complied with my request that he should accompany me.

We three went to Roswell and started up the Rio Pecos from there on the night of July 10th. We rode mostly in the night, followed no roads, but taking unfrequented routes, and arrived at the mouth of Tayban Arroyo, five miles south of Fort Sumner one hour after dark on the night of July 13th. Brazil was not there. We waited nearly two hours, but he did not come. We rode off a mile or two, staked our horses, and slept until daylight. Early in the morning we rode up into the hills and prospected awhile with our field glasses.

Poe was a stranger in the county and there was little danger that he would meet any one who knew him at Sumner. So, after an hour or two spent in the hills, he went into Sumner to take observations. I advised him, also, to go on to Sunnyside, seven miles above Sumner, and interview M. Rudolph, Esq., in whose judgment and discretion I had great confidence. I arranged with Poe to meet us that night at moonrise, at La Punta de la Glorietta, four miles north of Fort Sumner. Poe went on to the plaza, and McKinney and myself rode down into the Pecos Valley, where we remained during the day. At night we started out circling around the town and met Poe exactly on time at the trysting place.

Poe's appearance at Sumner had excited no particular observation, and he had gleaned no news there. Rudolph thought, from all indications, that The Kid was about; and yet, at times, he doubted. His cause for doubt seemed to be based on no evidence except the fact that The Kid was no fool, and no man in his senses, under the circumstances, would brave such danger.

I then concluded to go and have a talk with Peter Maxwell, Esq., in whom I felt sure I could rely. We had ridden to within a short distance of Maxwell's grounds when we found a man in camp and stopped. To Poe's great surprise, he recognized in the camper an old friend and former partner, in Texas, named Jacobs. We unsaddled here, got some coffee, and, on foot, entered an orchard which runs from this point down to a row of old buildings, some of them occupied by Mexicans, not more than sixty yards from Maxwell's house. We approached these houses cautiously, and when within ear shot, heard the sound of voices conversing in Spanish. We concealed ourselves quickly and listened;

but the distance was too great to hear words, or even distinguish voices. Soon a man arose from the ground, in full view, but too far away to recognize. He wore a broad-brimmed hat, a dark vest and pants, and was in his shirt-sleeves. With a few words, which fell like a murmur on our ears, he went to the fence, jumped it, and walked down towards Maxwell's house.

Little as we then suspected it, this man was The Kid. We learned, subsequently, that when he left his companions that night, he went to the house of a Mexican friend, pulled off his hat and boots, threw himself on a bed, and commenced reading a newspaper. He soon, however, hailed his friend, who was sleeping in the room, told him to get up and make some coffee, adding:— "Give me a butcher knife and I will go over to Pete's and get some beef; I'm hungry." The Mexican arose, handed him the knife, and The Kid, hatless and in his stocking-feet, started to Maxwell's, which was but a few steps distant.

When The Kid, by me unrecognized, left the orchard, I motioned to my companions, and we cautiously retreated a short distance, and, to avoid the persons whom we had heard at the houses, took another route, approaching Maxwell's house from the opposite direction. When we reached the porch in front of the building, I left Poe and McKinney at the end of the porch, about twenty feet from the door of Pete's room, and went in. It was near midnight and Pete was in bed. I walked to the head of the bed and sat down on it, beside him, near the pillow. I asked him as to the whereabouts of The Kid. He said that The Kid had certainly been about, but he did not know whether he had left or not. At that moment a man sprang quickly into the door, looking back, and called twice in Spanish, "Who comes there?" No one replied and he came on in. He was bareheaded. From his step I could perceive he was either barefooted or in his stocking-feet, and held a revolver in his right hand and a butcher knife in his left.

He came directly towards me. Before he reached the bed, I whispered: "Who is it, Pete?" but received no reply for a moment. It struck me that it might be Pete's brother-in-law, Manuel Abreu, who had seen Poe and McKinney, and wanted to know their business. The intruder came close to me, leaned both hands on the bed, his right hand almost touching my knee, and asked, in a low tone:

"Who are they Pete?"—at the same instant Maxwell whispered to me. "That's him!" Simultaneously The Kid must have seen, or felt, the presence of a third person at the head of the bed. He raised quickly his pistol, a self cocker, within a foot of my breast. Retreating rapidly across the room he cried: "*Quien es? Quien es?*" ("Who's that? Who's that?") All this occurred in a moment. Quickly as possible I drew my revolver and fired, threw my body aside, and fired again. The second shot was useless; The Kid fell dead. He never spoke. A struggle or two, a little strangling sound as he gasped for breath, and The Kid was with his many victims.

Maxwell had plunged over the foot of the bed on the floor, dragging the bed-clothes with him. I went to the door and met Poe and McKinney there. Maxwell rushed past me, out on the porch; they threw their guns down on him, when he cried: "Don't shoot, don't shoot." I told my companions I had got The Kid. They asked me if I had not shot the wrong man. I told them I had made no blunder, that I knew The Kid's voice too well to be mistaken. The Kid was entirely unknown to either of them. We now entered the room and examined the body. The ball struck him just above the heart, and must have cut through the ventricles. Poe asked me how many shots I fired; I told him two, but that I had no idea where the second one went. Both Poe and McKinney said The Kid must have fired then, as there were surely three shots fired. I told them that he had fired one shot, between my two. Maxwell said that The Kid fired; yet, when we came to look for bullet marks, none from his pistol could be found. We searched long and faithfully—found both my bullet marks and none other; so, against the impression and senses of four men, we had to conclude that The Kid did not fire at all. We examined his pistol—a self-cocker, calibre 41. It had five cartridges and one shell in the chambers, the hammer resting on the shell, but this proves nothing, as many carry their revolvers in this way for safety; besides, this shell looked as though it had been shot some time before.

It will never be known whether The Kid recognized me or not. If he did, it was the first time, during all his life of peril, that he ever lost his presence of mind, or failed to shoot first and hesitate afterwards. He knew that a meeting with me meant surrender or fight. He told several persons about Sumner that he bore no animosity against me, and had no desire to do me injury. He also said that he knew, should we meet, he would have to surrender, kill me, or get killed himself. So, he declared his intention, should we meet, to commence shooting on sight.

On the following morning, the Alcalde, Alejandro Segura, held an inquest on the body. Hon. M. Rudolph, of Sunnyside, was fore-man of the coroner's jury. They found a verdict that William H. Bonney came to his death from a gunshot wound, the weapon in the hands of Pat F. Garrett, that the fatal wound was inflicted by the said Garrett in the discharge of his official duty as sheriff, and that the homicide was justifiable.

The body was neatly and properly dressed and buried in the military cemetery at Fort Sumner, July 15, 1881. His exact age, on the day of his death, was 21 years, 7 months, and 21 days.

Again I say that The Kid's body lies undisturbed in the grave—and I speak of what I know.

CHAPTER VIII.

THE DALTONS

By Emerson Hough

What is true for Texas, in the record of desperadoism, is equally applicable to the country adjoining Texas upon the north, long known under the general title of the Indian Nations; although it is now rapidly being divided and allotted under the increasing demands of an ever-advancing civilization.

The great breeding ground of outlaws has ever been along the line of demarcation between the savage and the civilized. Here in the Indian country, as though in a hotbed especially contrived, the desperado has flourished for generations. The Indians themselves retained much of their old savage standards after they had been placed in this supposedly perpetual haven of refuge by the government. They have been followed, ever since the first movement

THE DALTONS

of the tribes into these reservations, by numbers of unscrupulous whites such as hang on the outskirts of the settlements and rebel at the requirements of civilization. Many white men of certain type married among the Indians, and the half-breed is reputed as a product inheriting the bad traits of both races and the good ones of neither—a sweeping statement not always wholly true. Among these also was a large infusion of negro blood, emanating from the slaves brought in by the Cherokees, and added to later by negroes moving in and marrying among the tribes. These mixed bloods seem to have been little disposed toward the ways of law and order. Moreover, the system of law was here, of course, altogether different from that of the States. The freedom from restraint, the exemption from law, which always marked the border, here found their last abiding place. The Indians were not adherents to the white man's creed, save as to the worst features, and they kept their own creed of blood. No man will ever know how many murders have been committed in these fair and pleasant savannahs, among these rough hills or upon these rolling grassy plains from the time William Clark, the "Red Head Chief," began the government work of settling the tribes in these lands, then supposed to be far beyond the possible demands of the white population of America.

Life could be lived here with small exertion. The easy gifts of the soil and the chase, coupled with the easy gifts of the government, unsettled the minds of all from those habits of steady industry and thrift which go with the observance of the law. If one coveted his neighbor's possessions, the ready arbitrament of firearms told whose were the spoils. Human life has been cheap here for more than half a hundred years; and this condition has endured directly up to and into the days of white civilization. The writer remembers very well that in his hunting expeditions of twenty years ago it was always held dangerous to go into the Nations; and this was true whether parties went in across the Neutral Strip, or farther east among the Osages or the Creeks. The country below Coffeyville was wild and remote as we saw it then, although now it is settling up, is traversed by railroads, and is slowly passing into the hands of white men in severalty, as fast as the negroes release their lands, or as fast as the government allows the Indians to give individual titles. In those days it was a matter of small concern if a traveler never returned from a journey among the timber clad mountains, or the black jack thickets along the rivers; and many was the murder committed thereabouts that never came to light.

159

In and around the Indian Nations there have also always been refugees from the upper frontier or from Texas or Arkansas. The country was long the natural haven of the lawless, as it has long been the designated home of a wild population. In this region the creed has been much the same even after the wild ethics of the cow men yielded to the scarcely more lawful methods of the land boomer.

Each man in the older days had his own notion of personal conduct, as each had his own opinions about the sacredness of property. It was natural that train robbing and bank looting should become recognized industries when the railroads and towns came into this fertile region, so long left sacred to the chase. The gangs of such men as the Cook boys, the Wickcliffe boys, or the Dalton boys, were natural and logical products of an environment. That this should be the more likely may be seen from the fact that for a decade or more preceding the great rushes of the land grabbers, the exploits of the James and Younger boys in train and bank robbing had filled all the country with the belief that the law could be defied successfully through a long term of years. The Cook boys acted upon this basis, until at length marshals shot them both, killed one and sent the remnants of the other to the penitentiary.

Since it would be impossible to go into any detailed mention of the scores and hundreds of desperadoes who have at different times been produced by the Nations, it may be sufficient to give a few of the salient features of the careers of the band which, as well as any, may be called typical of the Indian Nations brand of desperadoism—the once notorious Dalton boys.

The Dalton family lived in lower Kansas, near Coffeyville, which was situated almost directly upon the border of the Nations. They engaged in farming, and indeed two of the family were respectable farmers near Coffeyville within the last three or four years. The mother of the family still lives near Oklahoma City, where she secured a good claim at the time of the opening of the Oklahoma lands to white settlement. The father, Lewis Dalton, was a Kentucky man and served in the Mexican war. He later moved to Jackson county, Missouri, near the home of the notorious James and Younger boys, and in 1851 married Adelaide Younger, they removing some years later from Missouri to Kansas. Thirteen children were born to them, nine sons and four daughters. Charles, Henry, Littleton, and Coleman Dalton were respected and quiet citizens. All the boys had nerve, and many of them reached office as deputy marshals. Franklin Dalton was killed while serving as deputy United States marshal near Fort Smith, in 1887, his brother Bob being a member of the same posse at the time his fight was made with a band of horse thieves who resisted arrest. Grattan Dalton, after the death of his brother Franklin, was made a deputy United States marshal, after the curious but efficient Western fashion of setting dangerous men to work at catching dangerous men. He and his posse in 1888 went after a bad Indian, who, in the melée, shot Grattan in the arm and escaped. Grattan later served as United States deputy marshal in Muskogee district, where the courts certainly needed men of stern courage as executives, for they had to deal with the most desperate and fearless class of criminals the world ever knew. Robert R. Dalton, better known as Bob Dalton, served on the posses of his brothers, and soon learned what it was to stand up and shoot while being shot at. He turned out to be about the boldest of the family, and was accepted as the clan leader later on in their exploits. He also was a deputy United States marshal at the dangerous stations of Fort Smith and Wichita, having much to do with the desperadoes of the Nations. He was chief of the Osage police for some time, and saw abundance of violent scenes. Emmett Dalton was also possessed of cool nerve, and was soon known as a dangerous man to affront. All the boys were good shots, but they seemed to have cared more for the Winchester than the six-shooter in their exploits, in which they were perhaps wise, for the rifle is of course far the surer when it is possible of use; and men mostly rode in that country with rifle under leg.

Uncle Sam is obliged to take such material for his frontier peace officers as proves itself efficient in serving processes. A coward may be highly moral, but he will not do as a border deputy. The personal character of some of the most famous Western deputies would scarcely bear careful scrutiny, but the government at Washington is often obliged to wink at that sort of thing. There came a time when it remained difficult to wink any longer at the methods of the Daltons as deputies. In one case they ran off with a big bunch of horses and sold them in a Kansas town. On account of this episode, Grattan, William, and Emmett Dalton made a hurried trip to California. Here they became restless, and went back at their old trade, thinking that no one even on the Pacific Slope had any right to cause them fear. They held up a train in Tulare county and killed a fireman, but were repulsed. Later arrested and tried, William was cleared, but Grattan was sentenced to twenty years in the penitentiary. He escaped from jail before he got to the penitentiary, and rejoined Emmett at the old haunts in the Nations, Emmett having evaded arrest in California. The Southern Pacific railway had a standing offer of $6,000 for the robbers at the time they were killed.

The Daltons were now more or less obliged to hide out, and to make a living as best they could, which meant by robbery. On May 9, 1891, the Santa Fe train was held up at Wharton, Oklahoma Territory, and the express car was robbed, the bandits supposedly being the Daltons. In June of the following year another Santa Fé train was robbed at Red Rock, in the Cherokee strip. The 'Frisco train was robbed at Vinita, Indian Territory. An epidemic of the old methods of the James and Younger bands seemed to have broken out in the new railway region of the Southwest. The next month the Missouri, Kansas, and Texas train was held up at Adair, Indian Territory, and a general fight ensued between the robbers and the armed guard of the train, assisted by citizens of the town. A local physician was killed and several officers and citizens wounded, but none of the bandits was hurt, and they got away with a heavy loot of the express and baggage cars. At Wharton they had been less fortunate, for though they killed the station agent, they were rounded up and one of their men, Dan Bryant, was captured, later killing and being killed by United States deputy Ed. Short, as mentioned in an earlier chapter. Dick Broadwell joined the Dalton gang about now, and they nearly always had a few members besides those of their own family; their gang being made up and conducted on much the same lines of the James boys gang of Missouri, whose exploits they imitated and used as text for their bolder deeds. In fact it was the boast of the leader, Bob Dalton, in the Coffeyville raid, that he was going to beat anything the James boys ever did: to rob two banks in one town at the same time.

Bank robbing was a side line of activity with the Daltons, but they did fairly well at it. They held up the bank at El Reno, at a time when no one was in the bank except the president's wife, and took $10,000, obliging the bank to suspend business. By this time the whole country was aroused against them, as it had been against the James and Younger boys. Pinkerton detectives had blanket commissions offered, and railway and express companies offered rewards running into the thousands. Each train across the Indian Nations was accompanied for months by a heavily armed guard concealed in the baggage and express cars. Passengers dreaded the journey across that country, and the slightest halt of the train for any cause was sure to bring to the lips of all the word of fear, "the Daltons!" It seems almost incredible of belief that, in these modern days of fast railway service, of the telegraph and of rapidly increasing settlements, the work of these men could so long have been continued; but such, none the less, was the case. The law was powerless, and demonstrated its own unfitness to safeguard life and property, as so often it has in this country. And, as so often has been the case, outraged society at length took the law into its own hands and settled the matter.

The full tale of the Dalton robberies and murders will never be known, for the region in which they operated was reticent, having its own secrets to protect; but at last there came the climax in which the band was brought into the limelight of civilized publicity. They lived on the border of savagery and civilization. Now the press, the telegraph, the whole fabric of modern life, lay near at hand. Their last bold raid, therefore, in which they crossed from the country of reticence into that of garrulous news gathering, made them more famous than they had ever been before. The raid on Coffeyville, October 5, 1892, both established and ended their reputation as desperadoes of the border.

The rumor got out that the Daltons were down in the Nations, waiting for a chance to raid the town of Coffeyville, but the dreaded attack did not come off when it was expected. When it was delivered, therefore, it found the town quite unprepared. Bob Dalton was the leader in this enterprise. Emmett did not want to go. He declared that too many people knew them in Coffeyville, and that the job would prove too big for them to handle. He consented to join the party, however, when he found Bob determined to make the attempt in any case. There were in the band at that time Bob, Emmett, and Grattan Dalton, Bill Powers, and Dick Broadwell. These lay in rendezvous near Tulsa, in the Osage country, two days before the raid, and spent the night before in the timber on Onion creek, not far below town. They rode into Coffeyville at half-past nine the following morning. The street being somewhat torn up, they turned aside into an alley about a hundred yards from the main street, and, dismounting, tied their horses, which were thus left some distance from the banks, the First National and the bank of C. M. Condon & Co., which were the objects of their design.

Grattan Dalton, Dick Broadwell, and Bill Powers stepped over to the Condon bank, which was occupied at the time by C. T. Carpenter, C. M. Ball, the cashier, and T. C. Babb, a bookkeeper. Grattan Dalton threw down his rifle on Carpenter, with the customary command to put up his hands; the others being attended to by Powers and Broadwell. Producing a two-bushel sack, the leader ordered Carpenter to put all the cash into it, and the latter obeyed, placing three thousand dollars in silver and one thousand in currency in the sack. Grattan wanted the gold, and demanded that an inner safe inside the vault should be opened. The cashier, Ball, with a shifty falsehood, told him that they could not open that safe, for it was set on a time lock, and no one could open it before half-past nine o'clock. He told the outlaw that it was now twenty minutes after nine (although it was really twenty minutes of ten); and the latter said they could wait ten minutes. He was, however, uneasy, and was much of the mind to kill Ball on the spot, for he suspected treachery, and knew how dangerous any delay must be.

It was a daring thing to do—to sit down in the heart of a civilized city, in broad daylight and on the most public street, and wait for a time lock to open a burglar-proof safe. Daring as it was, it was foolish and futile. As the robbers stood uneasily guarding their prisoners, the alarm was spread. A moment later firing began, and the windows of the bank were splintered with bullets. The robbers were trapped, Broadwell being now shot through the arm, probably by P. L. Williams from across the street. Yet they coolly went on with their work as they best could, Grattan Dalton ordering Ball to cut the string of the bag and pour out the heavy silver, which would have encumbered them too much in their flight. He asked if there was not a back way out, by which they could escape. He was shown a rear door, and the robbers stepped out, to find themselves in the middle of the hottest street fight any of them had ever known. The city marshal, Charles T. Connolly, had given the alarm, and citizens were hurrying to the street with such weapons as they could find at the hardware stores and in their own homes.

Meantime Bob and Emmett Dalton had held up the First National Bank, ordering cashier Ayres to hand out the money, and terrorizing two or three customers of the bank who happened to be present at the time. Bob knew Thos. G. Ayres, and called him by his first name, "Tom," said he, "go into the safe and get out that money—get the gold, too." He followed Ayres into the vault, and discovered two packages of $5,000 each in currency, which he tossed into his meal sack. The robbers here also poured out the silver, and having cleaned up the bank as they supposed, drove the occupants out of the door in front of them. As they got into the street they were fired upon by George Cubine and C. S. Cox; but neither shot took effect. Emmett Dalton stood with his rifle under his arm, coolly tying up the neck of the sack which held the money. They then both stepped back into the bank, and went out through the back door, which was opened for them by W. H. Shepherd, the bank teller, who, with Tom Ayres and B. S. Ayres, the bookkeeper, made the bank force on hand. J. H. Brewster, C. H. Hollingsworth, and A. W. Knotts were in the bank on business, and were joined by E. S. Boothby; all these being left unhurt.

The firing became general as soon as the robbers emerged from the two bank buildings. The first man to be shot by the robbers was Charles T. Gump, who stood not far from the First National Bank armed with a shotgun. Before he could fire Bob Dalton shot him through the hand, the same bullet disabling his shotgun. A moment later, a young man named Lucius Baldwin started down the alley, armed with a revolver. He met Bob and Emmett, who ordered him to halt, but for some reason he kept on toward them. Bob Dalton said, "I'll have to kill you," and so shot him through the chest. He died three hours later.

Bob and Emmett Dalton now passed out of the alley back of the First National Bank, and came into Union Street. Here they saw George B. Cubine standing with his Winchester in his hands, and an instant later Cubine fell dead, with three balls through his body. Near him was Charles Brown, an old man, who was also armed. He was the next victim, his body falling near that of Cubine, though he lived for a few hours after being shot. All four of these victims of the Daltons were shot at distances of about forty or fifty yards, and with rifles, the revolver being more or less uncertain at such ranges even in practiced hands. All the gang had revolvers, but none used them.

Thos. G. Ayres, late prisoner in the First National Bank, ran into a store nearby as soon as he was released, caught up a Winchester and took a station near the street door, waiting for the bandits to come out at that entrance of the bank. Here he was seen by Bob Dalton, who had gone through the alley. Bob took aim and at seventy-five yards shot Ayres through the head. Friends tried to draw his body back into the store, but these now met the fire of Grattan Dalton and Powers, who, with the crippled Broadwell, were now coming out of their alleyway.

T. A. Reynolds, a clerk in the same store, who went to the door armed, received a shot through the foot, and thus made the third wounded man then in that building. H. H. Isham, one of the owners of the store, aided by M. A. Anderson and Charles K. Smith, joined in the firing. Grattan Dalton and Bill Powers were shot mortally before they had gone more than a few steps from the door of the Condon bank. Powers tried to get into a door when he was shot, and kept his feet when he found the door locked, managing to get to his horse in the alley before he was killed by a second shot. Grattan Dalton also kept his feet, and reached cover back of a barn about seventy yards from Walnut Street, the main thoroughfare. He stood at bay here, and kept on firing. City marshal Connolly, carrying a rifle, ran across to a spot near the corner of this barn. He had his eye on the horses of the bandits, which were still hitched in the alley. His back was turned toward Grattan Dalton. The latter must have been crippled somewhere in his right arm or shoulder, for he did not raise his rifle to his face, but fired from his hip, shooting Connolly down at a distance of about twenty feet or so.

There was a slight lull at this point of the street fight, and during this Dick Broadwell, who had been wounded again in the back, crawled into concealment in a lumber yard near by the alley where the horses were tied. He crept out to his horse and mounted, but just as he started away met the liveryman, John J. Kloehr, who did some of the best shooting recorded by the citizens. Kloehr was hurrying thither with Carey Seaman, the latter armed with a shotgun. Kloehr fired his rifle and Seaman his shotgun, and both struck Broadwell, who rode away, but fell dead from his horse a short distance outside the town.

Bob and Emmett Dalton, after killing Cubine and Brown and shooting Ayres, hurried on to join their companions and to get to their horses. At an alleyway junction they spied F. D. Benson climbing out of a window, and fired at him, but missed. An instant later, as Bob stepped into full view of those who were firing from the Isham store, he was struck by a ball and badly wounded. He walked slowly across the alley and sat down on a pile of stones, but like his brother Grattan, he kept his rifle going, though mortally shot. He fired once at Kloehr, but was unsteady and missed him. Rising to his feet he walked a few paces and leaned against the corner of a barn, firing two more shots. He was then killed by Kloehr, who shot him through the chest.

By this time Grattan Dalton was feebly trying to get to his horse. He passed the body of Connolly, whom he had killed, faced toward his pursuers and tried to fire. He, too, fell before Kloehr's Winchester, shot through the throat, dropping close to the body of Connolly.

Emmett Dalton was now the only one of the band left alive. He was as yet unwounded, and he got to his horse. As he attempted to mount a number of shots were fired at him, and these killed the two horses belonging to Bob Dalton and Bill Powers, who by this time had no further use for horses. Two horses hitched to an oil wagon in the street were also killed by wild shots. Emmett got into his saddle, but was shot through the right arm and through the left hip and groin. He still clung to the sack of money they had taken at the First National Bank, and he still kept his nerve and his wits even under such pressure of peril. He might have escaped, but instead he rode back to where Bob was lying, and reached down his hand to help him up behind himself on the horse. Bob was dying and told him it was no use to try to help him. As Emmett stooped down to reach Bob's arm, Carey Seaman fired both barrels of his shotgun into his back, Emmett dropping near Bob and falling upon the sack, containing over $20,000 in cash. Men hurried up and called to him to throw up his hands. He raised his one unhurt arm and begged for mercy. It was supposed he would die, and he was not lynched, but hurried away to a doctor's office nearby.

In the little alley where the last scene of this bloody fight took place there were found three dead men, one dying man, and one badly wounded. Three dead horses lay near the same spot. In the whole fight, which was of course all over in a few moments, there were killed four citizens and four outlaws, three citizens and one outlaw being wounded. Less than a dozen citizens did most of the shooting, of which there was considerable, eighty bullet marks being found on the front of the Condon bank alone.

The news of this bloody encounter was instantly flashed over the country, and within a few hours the town was crowded with sightseers who came in by train loads. The dead bandits were photographed, and the story of the fight was told over and over again, not always with uniformity of detail. Emmett Dalton, before he was sent to the penitentiary, confessed to different crimes, not all of them hitherto known, which the gang had at different times committed.

So ended in blood the career of as bloody a band as might well be discovered in the robber history of any land or time of the world. Indeed, it is doubtful if any country ever saw leagues of robbers so desperate as those which have existed in America, any with hands so red in blood. This fact is largely due to the peculiar history of this country, with its rapid development under swift modern methods of transportation. In America the advance to the westward of the fighting edge of civilization, where it meets and mingles with savagery, has been more rapid than has ever been known in the settlement of any country of the world. Moreover, this has taken place at precisely that time when weapons of the most deadly nature have been invented and made at a price permitting all to own them and many to become extremely skilled with them. The temptation and the means of murder have gone hand in hand. And in time the people,

not the organized law courts, have applied the remedy when the time has come for it. Today the Indian Nations are no more than a name. Civilization has taken them over. Statehood has followed territorial organization. Presently rich farms will make a continuous sea of grain across what was once a flood of crime, and the wheat will grow yellow, and the cotton white, where so long the grass was red.

Chapter IX.

EVOLUTION OF A TRAIN ROBBER

By Edgar Beecher Bronson

Life was never dull in Grant County, New Mexico, in the early eighties. There was always something doing—usually something the average law-abiding, peace-loving citizen would have been glad enough to dispense with. To say that life then and there was insecure is to describe altogether too feebly a state of society and an environment wherein Death, in one violent form or another, was ever abroad, seldom long idle, always alert for victims.

When the San Carlos Apaches, under Victoria, Ju, or Geronimo, were not out gunning for the whites, the whites were usually out gunning for one another over some trivial difference. Everybody carried a gun and was more or less handy with it. Indeed, it was a downright bad plan to carry one unless you were handy. For with gunning—the game most played, if not precisely the most popular—everyone was supposed to be familiar with the rules and to know how to play; and in a game where every hand is sure to be "called," no one ever suspected another of being out on a sheer "bluff." Thus the coroner invariably declared it a case of suicide where one man drew a gun on another and failed to use it.

This highly explosive state of society was not due to the fact that there were few peaceable men in the country for there were many of them, men of character and education, honest, and as law-abiding as their peculiar environment would permit. Moreover, the percentage of professional "bad men"—and this was a profession then—was comparatively small. It was due rather to the fact that every one, no matter how peaceable his inclinations, was compelled to carry arms habitually for self-defense, for the Apaches were constantly raiding outside the towns, and white outlaws inside. And with any class of men who constantly carry arms, it always falls out that a weapon is the arbiter of even those minor personal differences which in the older and more effete civilization of the East are settled with fists or in a petty court.

The prevailing local contempt for any man who was too timid to "put up a gun fight" when the etiquette of a situation demanded it, was expressed locally in the phrase that one "could take a corncob and a lightning bug and make him run himself to death trying to get away." It is clearly unnecessary to explain why the few men of this sort in the community did not occupy positions of any particular prominence. Their opinions did not seem to carry as much weight as those of other gentlemen who were known to be notably quick to draw and shoot.

I even recall many instances where the pistol entered into the pastimes of the community. One instance will stand telling:

A game of poker (rather a stiff one) had been going on for about a fortnight in the Red Light Saloon. The same group of men, five or six old friends, made up the game every day. All had varying success but one, who lost every day. And, come to think of it, his luck varied too, for some days he lost more than others. While he did not say much about his losings, it was observed that temper was not improving. This sort of thing went on for thirteen days. The thirteenth day the loser happened to come in a little late, after the game was started. It also happened that on this particular day one of the players had brought in a friend, a stranger in the town, to join the game, When the loser came in, therefore, he was introduced to the stranger and sat down. A hand was dealt him. He started to play it, stopped, rapped on the table for attention, and said:

"Boys, I want to make a personal explanation to this yere stranger. Stranger, this yere game is sure a tight wad for a smoothbore. I'm loser in it, an' a heavy one, for exactly thirteen days, and these boys all understand that the first son of a gun I find I can beat, I'm going to take a six-shooter an' make him play with me a week. Now, if you has no objections to my rules, you can draw cards."

Luckily for the stranger, perhaps, the thirteenth was as bad for the loser as its predecessors.

Outside the towns there were only three occupations in Grant County in those years, cattle ranching, mining and fighting Apaches, all of a sort to attract and hold none but the sturdiest types of real manhood, men inured to danger and reckless of it. In the early eighties no faint-heart came to Grant County unless he blundered in—and any such were soon burning the shortest trail out. These men were never better described in a line than when, years ago, at a banquet of California Forty-niners, Joaquin Miller, the poet of the Sierras, speaking of the splendid types the men of forty-nine represented, said:

"The cowards never started, and all the weak died on the road!"

Within the towns, also, there were only three occupations: first, supplying the cowmen and miners whatever they needed, merchandise wet and dry, law mundane and spiritual, for although neither court nor churches were working overtime, they were available for the few who had any use for them; second, gambling, at monte, poker, or faro; and, third, figuring how to slip through the next twenty-four hours without getting a heavier load of lead in one's system than could be conveniently carried, or how to stay happily half shot and yet avoid coming home on a shutter, unhappily shot, or, having an active enemy on hand, how best to "get" him.

Thus, while plainly the occupations of Grant County folk were somewhat limited in variety, in the matter of interest and excitement their games were wide open and the roof off.

Nor did all the perils to life in Grant County lurk within the burnished grooves of a gun barrel, according to certain local points of view, for always it is the most unusual that most alarms, as when one of my cowboys "allowed he'd go to town for a week," and was back on the ranch the evening of the second day. Asked why he was back so soon, he replied:

"Well, fellers, one o' them big depot water tanks burnt plumb up this maw-nin', an' reckonin' whar that'd happen a feller might ketch fire anywhere in them little old town trails, I jes' nachally pulled my freight for camp!"

171

But a cowboy is the subject of this story—Kit Joy. His genus, and striking types of the genus, have been cleverly described, especially by Lewis and by Adams (some day I hope to meet Andy) that I need say little of it here. Still, one of the cowboy's most notable and most admirable traits has not been emphasized so much as it deserves: I mean his downright reverence and respect for womanhood. No real cowboy ever wilfully insulted any woman, or lost a chance to resent any insult offered by another. Indeed, it was an article of the cowboy creed never broken, and all well knew it. So it happened that when one day a cowboy, in a crowded car of a train held up by bandits, was appealed to by an Eastern lady in the next seat:

"Heavens! I have four hundred dollars in my purse which I cannot afford to lose; please, sir, tell me how I can hide it."

Instantly came the answer:

"Shucks! Miss, stick it in yer sock; them fellers has nerve enough to hold up a train an' kill any feller that puts up a fight, but nary one o' them has nerve enough to go into a woman's sock after her bank roll!"

Kit Joy was a cowboy working on the X ranch on the Gila. He was a youngster little over twenty. It was said of him that he had left behind him in Texas more or less history not best written in black ink, but whether this was true or not I do not know. Certain it is that he was a reckless daredevil, always foremost in the little amenities cowboys loved to indulge in when they came to town such as shooting out the lights in saloons and generally "shelling up the settlement"—which meant taking a friendly shot at about everything that showed up on the streets. Nevertheless, Kit in the main was thoroughly good-natured and amiable.

Early in his career in Silver City it was observed that perhaps his most distinguishing trait was curiosity. Ultimately his curiosity got him into trouble, as it does most people who indulge it. His first display of curiosity in Silver was a very great surprise, even to those who knew him best. It was also a disappointment.

A tenderfoot, newly arrived, appeared on the streets one day in knickerbockers and stockings. Kit was in town and was observed watching the tenderfoot. To the average cowboy a silk top hat was like a red flag to a bull, so much like it in fact that the hat was usually lucky to escape with less than half a dozen holes through it. But here in these knee-breeches and stockings was something much more bizarre and exasperating than a top hat, from a

172

cowboy's point of view. The effect on Kit was therefore closely watched by the bystanders.

No one fancied for a moment that Kit would do less than undertake to teach the tenderfoot "the cowboy's hornpipe," not a particularly graceful but a very quick step, which is danced most artistically when a bystander is shooting at the dancer's toes. Indeed, the ball was expected to open early. To every one's surprise and disappointment, it did not. Instead, Kit dropped in behind the tenderfoot and began to follow him about town—followed him for at least an hour. Every one thought he was studying up some more unique penalty for the tenderfoot. But they were wrong, all wrong.

As a matter of fact, Kit was so far consumed with curiosity that he forgot everything else, forgot even to be angry. At last, when he could stand it no longer, he walked up to the tenderfoot, detained him gently by the sleeve and asked in a tone of real sympathy and concern: "Say, mistah! 'Fo' God, won't yo' mah let yo' wear long pants?"

Naturally the tenderfoot's indignation was aroused and expressed, but Kit's sympathies for a man condemned to such a juvenile costume were so far stirred that he took no notice of it.

Kit was a typical cowboy, industrious, faithful, uncomplaining, of the good old Southern Texas breed. In the saddle from daylight till dark, riding completely down to the last jump in them two or three horses a day, it never occurred to him even to growl when a stormy night, with thunder and lightning, prolonged his customary three-hour's turn at night guard round the herd to an all-night's vigil. He took it as a matter of course. And his rope and running iron were ever ready, and his weather eye alert for a chance to catch and decorate with the X brand any stray cattle that ventured within his range. This was a peculiar phase of cowboy character. While not himself profiting a penny by these inroads on neighboring herds, he was never quite so happy as when he had added another maverick to the herd bearing his employer's brand, an increase always obtained at the expense of some of the neighbors.

One night on the Spring round-up, the day's work finished, supper eaten, the night horses caught and saddled, the herd in hand driven into a close circle and bedded down for the night in a little glade in the hills, Kit was standing first relief. The day's drive had been a heavy one, the herd was well grazed and watered in the late afternoon, the night was fine; and so the twelve hundred or fifteen hundred cattle in the herd were lying down quietly, giving no trouble to the night herders. Kit, therefore, was jogging slowly round the herd, softly jingling his spurs and humming some rude love song of the sultry sort cowboys never tire of repeating. The stillness of the night superinduced reflection. With naught to interrupt it, Kit's curiosity ran farther afield than usual. Recently down at Lordsburg, with the outfit shipping a train load of beeves, he had seen the Overland Express empty its load of passengers for supper, a crowd of well-dressed men and women, the latter brilliant with the bright colors cowboys love and with glittering gems. Tonight he got to thinking about them.

Wherever did they all come from? However did they get so much money? Surely they must come from 'Frisco. No lesser place could possibly turn out such magnificence. Then Kit let his fancy wander off into crude cowboy visions of what 'Frisco might be like, for he had never seen a city.

"What a buster of a town 'Frisco must be!" Kit soliloquized. "Must have more'n a hundred saloons an' more slick gals than the X brand has heifers. What a lot o' fun a feller could have out thar! Only I reckon them gals wouldn't look at him more'n about onct unless he was well fixed for dough. Reckon they don't drink nothin' but wine out thar, nor eat nothin' but oysters. An' wine an' oysters costs money, oodles o' money! That's the worst of it! S'pose it'd take more'n a month's pay to git a feller out thar on the kiars, an' then about three months' pay to git to stay a week. Reckon that's jes' a little too rich for Kit's blood. But, jiminy! Wouldn't I like to have a good, big, fat bank roll an' go thar!"

Here was a crisis suddenly come in Kit's life, although he did not then realize it. It is entirely improbable he had ever before felt the want of money. His monthly pay of thirty-five dollars enabled him to sport a pearl-handled six-shooter and silver-mounted bridle bit and spurs, kept him well clothed, and gave him an occasional spree in town. What more could any reasonable cowboy ask?

But tonight the very elements and all nature were against him. Even a light dash of rain to rouse the sleeping herd, or a hungry cow straying out into the darkness, would have been sufficient to divert and probably save him; but nothing happened. The night continued fine. The herd slept on. And Kit was thus left an easy prey, since covetousness had come to aid curiosity in compassing his ruin.

"A bank roll! A big, fat, full-grown, long-horned, four-year-old roll! *That's* what a feller wants to do 'Frisco right. Nothin' less. But whar's it comin' from, an' when? S'pose I brands a few mavericks an' gits a start on my own? No use, Kit; that's too slow! Time you got a proper roll you'd be so old the skeeters wouldn't even bite you, to say nothin' of a gal a-kissin' of you. 'Pears like you ain't liable to git thar very quick, Kit, 'less you rustles mighty peart somewhar. Talkin' of rustlin', what's the matter with that anyway?"

A cold glitter came in Kit's light blue eyes. The muscles of his lean, square jaws worked nervously. His right hand dropped caressingly on the handle of his pistol.

"That's the proper caper, Kit. Why didn't you think of it before? Rustle, damn you, an', ef you're any good, mebbe so you can git to 'Frisco afore frost comes, or anywhere else you likes. Rustle! By jiminy, I've got it; I'll jes' stand up that thar Overland Express. Them fellers what rides on it's got more'n they've got any sort o' use for. What's the matter with makin' 'em whack up with a feller! 'Course they'll kick, an' thar'll be a whole passle o' marshals an' sheriffs out after you, but what o' that? Reckon Old Blue'll carry you out o' range. He's the longest-winded chunk o' horse meat in these parts. Then you'll have to stay out strictly on the scout fer a few weeks, till they gits tired o' huntin' of you, so you can slip out o' this yere neck o' woods 'thout leavin' a trail.

"An' Lord! but won't it be fun! 'Bout as much fun, I reckon, as doin' 'Frisco. Won't them tenderfeet beller when they hears the guns a-crackin' an' the boys a-yellin'! Le' see; wonder who I'd better take along?"

Scruples? Kit had none. Bred and raised a merry freebooter on the unbranded spoils of the cattle range, it was no long step from stealing a maverick to holding up a train.

With a man of perhaps any other class, a plan to engage in a new business enterprise of so much greater magnitude than any of those he had been accustomed to would have been made the subject of long consideration. Not so with Kit. Cowboy life compels a man to think quickly, and often to act quicker than he finds it convenient to think. The hand skilled to catch the one possible instant when the wide, circling loop of the lariat may be successfully thrown, and the eye and finger trained to accurate snap-shooting, do not well go with a mind likely to be long in reaching a resolution or slow to execute one.

So Kit at once began to cast about for two or three of the right sort of boys to join him. Three were quickly chosen out of his own and a neighboring outfit.

They were Mitch Lee and Taggart, two white cowboys of his own type and temper, and George Cleveland, a negro, known as a desperate fellow, game for anything. It needed no great argument to secure the cooperation of these men. A mere tip of the lark and the loot to be had was enough.

The boys saw their respective bosses. They "allowed they'd lay off for a few days and go to town." So they were paid off, slung their Winchesters on their saddles, mounted their favorite horses, and rode away. They met in Silver City, coming in singly. There they purchased a few provisions. Then they separated and rode singly out of town, to rendezvous at a certain point on the Miembres River.

The point of attack chosen was the little station of Gage (tended by a lone operator), on the Southern Pacific Railway west of Deming, a point then reached by the west-bound express at twilight. The evening of the second day after leaving the Gila, Kit and his three compadres rode into Gage. One or two significant passes with a six-shooter hypnotized the station agent into a docile tool. A dim red light glimmered away off in the east. As the minutes passed, it grew and brightened fast. Then a faint, confused murmur came singing over the rails to the ears of the waiting bandits. The light brightened and grew until it looked like a great dull red sun, and then the thunder of the train was heard.

Time for action had come!

The agent was made to signal the engineer to stop. With lever reversed and air brakes on, the train was nearly stopped when the engine reached the station. But seeing the agent surrounded by a group of armed men, the engineer shut off the air and sought to throw his throttle open. His purpose discovered, a quick snapshot from Mitch Lee laid him dead, and, springing into the cab, Mitch soon persuaded the fireman to stop the train.

Instantly a fusillade of pistol shots and a mad chorus of shrill cowboy yells broke out, that terrorized train crew and passengers into docility.

Within fifteen minutes the express car was sacked, the postal car gutted, the passengers were laid under unwilling contribution, and Kit and his pals were riding northward into the night, heavily loaded with loot. Riding at great speed due north, the party soon reached the main travelled road up the Miembres, in whose loose drifting sands they knew their trail could not be picked up. Still forcing the pace, they reached the rough hill-country east of Silver early in the night, cached their plunder safely, and a little after midnight were carelessly bucking a monte game in a Silver City saloon. The next afternoon they quietly rode out of town and joined their respective outfits, to wait until the excitement should blow over.

Of course the telegraph soon started the hue and cry. Officers from Silver, Deming, and Lordsburg were soon on the ground, led by Harvey Whitehill, the famous old sheriff of Grant County. But of clue there was none. Naturally the station agent had come safely out of his trance, but with that absence of memory of what had happened characteristic of the hypnotized. The trail disappeared in the sands of the Miembres road. Shrewd old Harvey Whitehill was at his wits' end.

Many days passed in fruitless search. At last, riding one day across the plain at some distance from the line of flight north from Gage, Whitehill found a fragment of a Kansas newspaper. As soon as he saw it he remembered that a certain merchant of Silver came from the Kansas town where this paper was published. Hurrying back to Silver, Whitehill saw the merchant, who identified the paper and said that he undoubtedly was its only subscriber in Silver. Asked if he had given a copy to any one, he finally recalled that some time before, about the period of the robbery, he had wrapped in a piece this newspaper some provisions he had sold to a negro named Cleveland and a white man he did not know.

Here was the clue, and Whitehill was quick to follow it. Meeting a negro on the street, he pretended to want to hire a cook. The negro had a job. Well, did he not know someone else? By the way, where was George Cleveland?

"Oh, boss, he done left de Gila dis week an' gone ober to Socorro," was the answer.

Two days later Whitehill found Cleveland in a Socorro restaurant, got the "drop" on him, told him his pals were arrested and had confessed that they were in the robbery, but that he, Cleveland, had killed Engineer Webster. This brought the whole story.

"'Foh God, boss, I nebber killed dat engineer. Mitch Lee done it, an' him an' Taggart an' Kit Joy, dey done lied to you outrageous."

Within a few days, caught singly, in ignorance of Cleveland's arrest, and taken completely by surprise, Joy, Taggart, and Lee were captured on the Gila and jailed, along with Cleveland, at Silver City, held to await the action of the next grand jury.

But strong walls did not a prison make adequate hold these men. Before many weeks passed, an escape was planned and executed. Two other prisoners, one a man wanted in Arizona, and the other a Mexican horse thief, were allo-wed to participate in the outbreak.

Taken unawares, their guard was seized and bound with little difficulty. Quickly arming themselves in the jail office, these six desperate men dashed out of the jail and into a neighboring livery stable, seized horses, mounted, and rode madly out of town, firing at everyone in sight. In Silver in those days no gentleman's trousers fitted comfortably without a pistol stuck in the waistband. Therefore, the flying desperadoes received as hot a fire as they sent. By this fire Cleveland's horse was killed before they got out of town, but one of his pals stopped and picked him up.

Instantly the town was in an uproar of excitement. Everyone knew that the capture of these men meant a fight to the death. As usual in such emergencies, there were more talkers than fighters. Nevertheless, six men were in pursuit as soon as they could saddle and mount. The first to start was the driver of an express wagon, a man named Jackson, who cut his horse loose from the traces, mounted bareback, and flew out of town only a few hundred yards behind the prisoners. Six others, led by Charlie Shannon and La Fer, were not far behind Jackson. The men of this party were greatly surprised to find that a Boston boy of twenty, a tenderfoot lately come to town, who had scarcely ever ridden a horse or fired a rifle, was among their number, well mounted and armed—a man with a line of ancestry worthwhile, and himself a worthy survival of the best of it.

The chase was hot. Jackson was well in advance, engaging the fugitives with his pistol, while the fugitives were returning the fire and throwing up puffs of dust all about Jackson. Behind spurred Shannon and his party.

At length the pursuit gained. Five miles out of Silver, in the Piñon Hills to the northwest, too close pressed to run farther, the fugitives sprang from their horses and ran into a low post oak thicket covering about two acres, where, crouching, they could not be seen. The six pursuers sent back a man to guide the sheriff's party and hasten reinforcements, and began shelling the thicket and surrounding it. A few minutes later Whitehill rode up with seven more men, and the thicket was effectually surrounded. To the surprise of every one, a hot fire poured into the thicket failed to bring a single answering shot. Whitehill was no man to waste ammunition on such chance firing, so he orde-red a charge. His little command rode into and through the thicket at full speed, only to find their quarry gone, gone all save one. The Mexican lay dead, shot through the head! Kit's party had dashed through the thicket without stopping, on to another, and their trail was shortly found leading up a rugged canyon of the Pinos Altos Range.

Whitehill divided his party. Three men followed up the bottom of the canyon on foot, five mounted flankers were thrown out on either side. At last, high up the canyon, Kit's party was found at bay, lying in some thick underbrush. It was a desperate position to attack, but the pursuers did not hesitate. Dismounting, they advanced on foot with rifles cocked, but with all the caution of a hunter trailing a wounded grizzly. The negro opened the ball at barely twenty yards' range with a shot that drove a hole through the Boston boy's hat. Dropping at first with surprise, for he had not seen the negro till the instant he rose to fire, the Boston boy returned a quick shot that happened to hit the negro just above the centre of the forehead and rolled him over dead.

Approaching from another direction, Shannon was first to draw Taggart's fire. Taggart was lying hidden in the brush; Shannon standing out in the open. Shot after shot they exchanged, until presently a ball struck the earth in front of Taggart's face and filled his eyes full of gravel and sand. Blinded for the time, he called for quarter, and came out of the brush with his hands up and another man with him. Asked for his pistol, Taggart replied:

"Damn you, that's empty, or I'd be shooting yet."

Meantime, Whitehill was engaging Mitch Lee. In a few minutes, shot through and helpless, Lee surrendered.

It was quick, hot work!

All but Kit were now killed or captured. He had been separated from his party, and La Fer was seen trailing him on a neighboring hillside.

At this juncture the sheriff detailed Shannon to return to town and get a wagon to bring in the dead and wounded, while he started to join La Fer in pursuit of Kit.

An hour later, as Shannon was leaving town with a wagon to return to the scene of the fight, a mob of men, led by a shyster lawyer, joined him and swore they proposed to lynch the prisoners. This was too much for Shannon's sense of frontier proprieties. So, rising in his wagon, he made a brief but effective speech.

"Boys, none of our men are hurt, although it is no fault of our prisoners. A dozen of us have gone out and risked our lives to capture these men. You men have not seen fit, for what motives we will not discuss, to help us. Now, I tell you right here that any who want can come, but the first man to raise a hand against a prisoner I'll kill."

Shannon's return escort was small.

But once more back in the hills of the Pinos Altos, Shannon found a storm raised he could not quell, even if his own sympathies had not drifted with it when he learned its cause. His friend La Fer lay dead, filled full of buckshot by Kit before Whitehill's reinforcements had reached him, while Kit had slipped away through the underbrush, over rocks that left no trail.

La Fer's death maddened his friends. There was little discussion. Only one opinion prevailed: Taggart and Lee must die.

Nothing was known of the prisoner wanted in Arizona, so he was spared.

Taggart and Lee were put in the wagon, the former tightly bound, the latter helpless from his wound. Short rope halters barely five feet long were stripped from the horses, knotted round the prisoners' necks, and fastened to the limb of a juniper tree. Taggart climbed to the high wagon seat, took a header and broke his neck. The wagon was then pulled away and Lee strangled.

With Cleveland, Lee, and Taggart dead, Engineer Webster and La Fer were fairly well avenged. But Kit was still out, known as the leader and the man who shot La Fer, and for days the hills were full of men hunting him. Hiding in the rugged, thickly timbered hills of the Gila, taking needed food at night, at the muzzle of his gun, from some isolated ranch, he was hard to capture.

Had Kit chosen to mount himself and ride out of the country, he might have escaped for good. But this he would not do. Dominated still by the fatal curiosity and covetousness that first possessed him, later mastered him, and then drove him into crime, bound to repossess himself of his hidden treasure and go out to see the world, Kit would not leave the Gila. He was alone, unaided, with no man left his friend, with all men on the alert to capture or to kill him, the unequal contest nevertheless lasted for many weeks.

There was only one man Kit at all trusted, a "nester" (small ranchman) named Racketty Smith. One day, looking out from a leafy thicket in which he lay hid, he saw Racketty going along the road. A lonely outcast, craving the sound of a human voice, believing Racketty at least neutral, Kit hailed him and approached. As he drew near, Racketty covered him with his rifle and ordered him to surrender. Surprised, taken entirely unawares, Kit started to jump for cover, when Racketty fired, shattered his right leg and brought him to earth. To spring upon and disarm Kit was the work of an instant.

Kit was sentenced to imprisonment at Santa Fe. A few years ago, having gained three years by good behavior, Kit was released, after having served fourteen years.

However Kit may still hanker for "a big, fat, four-year-old, long-horned bank roll," and whatever may be his curiosity to "do 'Frisco proper," it is not likely he will make any more history as a train robber, for at heart Kit was always a better "good man" than "bad man."

CHAPTER

BAT MASTERSON

By Wyatt Earp

Five men, riding to the summit of a knoll, caught sight of a deserted adobe house in the hollow at their feet. As the sun sank toward the edge of the prairie they found their refuge for the night.

The solitude of the building was more painful than the solitude of the plains; the yellowish walls glimmered like the walls of a vault in the gloom that had settled in the hollow as sediment settles in a glass. But these things did not matter, for there was water close by, and those grim walls were thick to stop bullets as well as arrows.

The five men watered their weary horses at the creek, and then drove picket-pins into the ground within a stone's throw of the house, where there was plenty of grass, and tethered the animals thereto with their lariats. Next they unlimbered their heavy saddles and carried them into the house. The plainsman's saddle is more precious to him than jewels. In this case, bacon, coffee, and army biscuits were involved. More important still, there was ammunition, and plenty of it.

It was a quarter century ago [Earp penned this tribute to his friend in 1896]. The five men were scouts, carrying dispatches from Dodge City to Camp Supply, through a country depopulated and laid waste by the Cheyennes. Their camping place was within forty miles of camp supply, in the heart of that no-man's-land known as the Panhandle of Texas.

When the first rays of the sun came slanting over the prairie one of the men went out to water the horses, while his comrades prepared breakfast. *Ping!* A rifle-shot startled the solitude. The four men rushed to the door. The fifth was lying face downward two hundred yards from the house. The horses were plunging and tugging at the ropes. In another second or two they had broken lariats or torn up picket-pins and galloped madly away. A horse can smell an Indian.

Another moment, and a hail of bullets and arrows splattered against the 'dobe walls. The five hundred yelling Indians galloped from behind a knoll and charged the building.

The four surviving scouts were ready for them. Everything was orderly and precise. It did not need that many words should be spoken. What few laconic orders that were given came from the youngest man in the party. He was a mere boy—a bright sturdy boy, whose wide, round eyes expressed the alert pugnacity of a blooded bull-terrier. To look at him one could not doubt that nature has molded him for a fighter.

The plan of defense was very simple. Like all buildings in that wild country, the old 'dobe house was provided with portholes on every side. It was a question of shooting fast and shooting straight through those portholes, and the scouts knew how to shoot both fast and straight. The fire was more than the Cheyennes could stand. With a baffled yell they wheeled and retreated, picking up their killed and wounded as they galloped to cover behind one of the many knolls that encompassed the house like the might billows of a frozen ocean.

That one charge was the history of the day. It was repeated again and again, first on one side of the house then on another. Each charge found the scouts prepared, and each time the Indians carried a dozen or more of their dead off the field.

Toward evening there was a brief breathing spell.

"I'm going to bring him," said the youngest scout—the boy with the bull-terrier eyes—pointing at the body lying on its face near the stampeded picket.

"Better not try, Bat, they'll get ye sure."

"We can't leave him lying there like that."

And taking his rifle in hand the boy went. He ran out under fire and he staggered back under fire with the body in his arms.

More charges, followed by a sleepless night, to guard against surprises. And at daybreak the fighting began again. Never before were the Indians known to make such a stubborn fight. Never before did such a handful hold such a horde at bay. The face of the plain was freckled with blood up to a radius of fifty yards of the house, but how many dead Indians had been carried off the beleaguered men had no means of knowing. One of them had his leg half shot away and all were sick from exhaustion, when at mid-afternoon a company of cavalry came riding over the plain and the Indians fled.

Thus was fought the "battle of 'dobe walls." The event which made young Bat Masterson a hero on the frontier.

It was not long afterward that Bat drifted to Sweetwater, where he became a lively citizen if as lively a town as ever subsisted on the patronage of a frontier army post. Bat was no more of a laggard in love than he was a dastard in war, and Annie Chambers was as proud of her handsome little hero as he was fond of his dashing, red-haired beauty. I had never met Bat at that time, but I had known Annie both in Leavenworth and Ellsworth. She was as fine a girl as ever set a frontier town by the ears, and she was better educated than most woman of her kind.

Sergeant King, one of the most notorious bullies and gun-fighters in the army, wanted to dance with Annie one night and because she refused he pulled his six-shooter and shot her in the breast. Even as she fell, dying, into Bat's arms the latter jerked his gun on the soldier and shot him dead, but not before King had pumped some lead into Bat's groin.

That was one of the killings for which Bat Masterson has been held up by some ignorant writers as a shocking example of ferocity and lawlessness. But of the many men he killed there was not one who was not in the wrong, and not one who did not start it with the best of the fight. Shocking as it may seem to civilized souls, we had our crude code of honor on the frontier. When I speak of a fair fighter I mean a man who will not fight for what he knows to be a bad cause, and who will not take his enemy at a disadvantage. Such a man was Bat Masterson.

Bat was acquitted, of course, and soon afterward came over to Dodge City, where I had just been installed as City Marshal.

His fame as hero of 'dobe walls and the slayer of Sergeant King had preceded Bat to Dodge, and he attracted no end of respectful attention as he limped from one gambling house to another, still pale and weak from the effect of King's bullet. Bat was somewhat of a dandy in those days, but before all else he was a man. Not that his physique entitled him to attention beyond other men, for in his case nature had packed a big consignment of dynamic energy into a small compass and corded it up tight. But there was something in the way his bullet-shaped head was mounted on his square shoulders, something in the grain of his crisp, wiry hair, something in the tilt of his short nose that bespoke animal courage such as not every man is endowed withal.

Mere animal courage has made many a man a brute and an assassin, but Bat Masterson had a wealth of saving graces which shone from the honest fullness of his face. I have spoken of his eyes. They were well-nigh unendurable in conflict—so bold, so bright, so unmitigable was their gaze; but in moments of peace they danced with mischief, with generosity, with affection. A small and carefully nurtured coal-black mustache, half hid a mouth which was readier to soften in mirth than to harden in anger, and the stubborn chin beneath was cleft with the dimple physiognomists interpret as the symbol of a kindly heart.

In moving from Wichita to take up the Marshalship of Dodge City at my own salary I had stipulated that I should have the appointment of my own police force. A fair judge of manhood as I esteemed myself, what wonder that I should have fastened hungry official eyes upon the hero of 'dobe walls?

"Bat," said I, "will you join the force?"

"I'd like it first-rate," he replied.

"Then throw away that cane and get to work,' I said.

And forthwith Bat was sworn in to protect the peace.

During the summer that he served with me—before he ran for Sheriff and was elected—stirring events came to pass in Dodge City. And like the Arizona feud of which I have already written, they all arose out of one incident. That incident was the killing of "The Nightingale."

One night a Texas desperado named Kennedy was diverting himself at a dancehall by flourishing his six-shooter. Mayor Kelly happened to be there, and as there was an officer present to restrain the Texan, he took it upon himself to interfere.

"You'd better give them guns to the bartender, my boy," he said kindly, "or some of my men will arrest ye."

Kennedy resented the suggestion and there was a dispute. But there was no word or thought of killing at that time. The mayor's remonstrance rankled in Kennedy's mind, however, and at two o'clock in the morning he started out to kill the Chief Executive.

Mounting his horse, so as to be in readiness for flight, the Texan rode down to the house where Kelly lived. The room where the Mayor and his wife slept opened on to the street, and Kennedy knew the direction in which the bed lay at the opposite end of the room. On the other side of a slender partition was another bed, occupied by Willet and his wife. Willet was a clerk for a neighboring grocer; his wife was a vaudeville woman of varied experiences on the frontier, and so sweet a singer that she was called "The Nightingale." Ask any man who knew Deadwood or Dodge in its prime to tell you how she sang "Killarney."

And so, making a careful estimation of the Mayor's bed, Kennedy began to empty his Winchester through the panels of the door. He calculated well, for two bullets went through the down comforter under which the Kellys slumbered. Nearly all the shots penetrated the partition behind their bed.

About that time Willet half awoke and turned over on his side, throwing his arm around his wife. At the touch her body fluttered like that of a wounded bird, and something bubbled up in her throat. Willet was wide awake in an instant—he did not know why. His hand touched something wet upon her breast and he asked her what it was; but there was no reply. A bullet had torn its way clear through her body. The Nightingale was dead.

Poor Willet ran over to me and I pulled on my clothes in a hurry. The only house where there was a light was the Long Branch saloon, so I went in there for information.

Kennedy was there, sitting on a monte table, swinging his legs.

"Was he here when the shots were fired?" I whispered to the bartender.

"For God's sake don't say anything here,' was the reply. "Come into the back room and I'll tell you about it."

"Kennedy's the man," he continued excitedly, when we had retired out of earshot. "He left here with another man just before the shooting and immediately afterward took a big drink of whiskey."

I ran back to the bar, but Kennedy had gone.

Bat joined me just then. He had been down to the house and the mayor had told him all about the trouble in the dance hall. In searching the town for Kennedy we ran across the man in whose company he had left the Saloon, and this fellow more than confirmed our suspicions of the Texan's guilt. Moreover, he led us to the alley where the murderer had tied his horse, and from there we picked up a clear trail leading out of the city.

At daylight, Bat, Bill Tillghman and I started out on the trail, taking this man along with us. For two days we followed it across the prairie toward the Texas Border, and then a heavy rainstorm came up and swept away all vestige of a hoofprint.

At a distance of nearly one hundred miles from Dodge we made a circuit of fifteen miles in order to get to a ranch for the night.

"Some of these here Texans are going home pretty early ain't they?" was the ranchman's greeting. "Kennedy was here yesterday afternoon, and he seemed in a hurry too."

Thus we picked up another trail, only to lose it again next day, when we were overtaken by more rain. In this predicament we made for a ranch twenty miles further on and reached the place at three o'clock in the afternoon. Our horses were fagged out, so we turned them out to grass and prepared to rest ourselves. After a while we caught sight of a horseman four or five miles away across the prairie, evidently making for the ranch. We watched him with idle curiosity, and when he came within a couple of miles of us Bat said, with conviction: "That's Kennedy. I know him by the way he rides; and besides, I know his horse." And when the stranger had arrived within a mile of the ranch we all knew that Bat, who had the eye of a hawk, was right.

Our horses were scattered over the pasture and it was too late to attempt to capture them. We agreed that it would be unwise to wait until Kennedy should get too close, lest he should recognize our horses and wheel in his tracks. So we ambushed ourselves behind a heap of earth that had thrown up from a new well, first agreeing that if he should scent danger and turn to make a run for it I should kill the horse and Bat attend to the man.

When he came within seventy-five yards of us we rose up and called him to halt.

He whipped out his gun, firing at us as he wheeled his horse. True to our agreement I shot the horse, which dropped just as Bat landed a bullet in Kennedy's shoulder.

Well, we took away his six-shooters and his Winchester, hired a team, and drove him back to Dodge. But the Brute was never convicted. He was the son of a multi-millionaire cattleman by a Mexican mother, and his father's money procured him endless delays, and finally an acquittal.

But the incidents connected with the wounding and capture of Kennedy for the murder of the Nightingale deepened the hatred bestowed upon Bat Masterson and myself by the Texan rustlers from whose violence we tried to protect the citizens of Dodge. Dodge had become the center of the cattle trade then, and the periodic incursions of cowboys, whose chief ambition was to be able to go back to Texas and boast of having "killed an orf'cer" were the curse of the community. The townspeople hated the Texans, and the Texans despised the townspeople. In the vernacular of the feud the Southerners were "long horns," the Northerners "short horns."

It was after Bat Masterson had been returned as Sheriff that I paid a visit to Mexico, during which I first met Doc Holliday and Big-nose Kate, as told in a previous story. During my absence Ed Masterson, Bat's elder brother, acted as my deputy. A crowd of cowboys started shooting in the Birdcage dance hall one night and Ed went over to see about it. He disarmed them all and made them pile their guns behind the bar. Then he returned across the deadline—the avenue formed by the railroad tracks, which divided the decent from the disreputable part of the town. Not long afterward, however, the cowboys recovered their six-shooters and began firing again. Ed went back to restore order and tried to disarm the first cowboy he encountered. The two men were scuffling for possession of the gun, when another cowboy fired at Ed Masterson and killed him.

Just at that moment Bat Masterson had appeared, attracted by the shooting. He saw his brother fall and with a quick drop killed the man who had fired the shot. The rest began to run away, shooting, and Bat winged the man with whom Ed had been scuffling. He died a few days later, while they were taking him back to Texas.

Thus perpetrated another of the so-called atrocities with which the hero of 'dobe walls was to be reproached in after years by writers whose knowledge of the frontier was derived from Bowery melodramas.

In view of the bloody complications closing in on my narrative it is high time that I introduced Bob Wright, the deus ex machina of much of the violent work that followed. Bob Wright was a tower of strength to the Texas faction. He had lived in their country and he depended on their patronage for the prosperity of his store, which was one of the largest in the city. He was a legislator, too—a duly elected representative from the county.

Bob Wright sought to interfere with me one night because I was taking one ill-behaved cattleman, who happened to be worth some millions of dollars, to the calaboose. My prisoner had tried to kill an inoffensive Dutch fiddler for not playing his favorite tune often enough to please him. The cattleman appealed to Wright, and threatened to have me put off the city force if I persisted in the arrest. The upshot of it was that I threw Wright into the calaboose to keep his friend company for the night. It was soon after that incident that the Texans began to hatch plots to kill me by foul means or fair—preferably the former.

The first attempt fell to the lot of a desperado named Hoyt, who was no 'prentice in the art of assassination. I was standing on the sidewalk outside a saloon on a bright moonlight night, talking to Eddie Foy, who was leaning against the doorway, when Hoyt came riding down the street on a white horse. I noticed that he had his right hand by his side, but did not suspect anything until he came to within ten steps of where I was standing. The he threw his gun over like lightening and took a shot at me. By the time he was on a level with me he had taken another shot, but both missed.

I ran out, intending to pull him off his horse, and, failing that, I tried to grab his horse's tail as it passed me. But the horse was too quick for me, and as Hoyt dug in his spurs he wheeled in his saddle and fired at me again. With that I crouched down in the middle of the road for a steady aim, and emptied my gun after him as he torn down the road. I saw him disappear over the bridge that spanned the Arkansas river, and made sure that I had missed him. But five minutes later, when I was telling the story to Bat Masterson and a crowd of citizens, the white horse came galloping back, mounted by a boy, who told us that its rider was lying, badly shot, just beyond the bridge. Half suspecting an ambush, Bat and I took shotguns and went back with the boy. There, sure enough, was Hoyt, full of lead and remorse, groaning most dolefully. Two or three days later he died.

This episode was not without its humorous side, for to this day Eddie Foy, the comedian, is fond of telling how, at the first shot, the threw himself under a monte table and stayed there until the shooting was over.

Undeterred by Hoyt's fate, the plotters sent Clay Allison, and the noted Colorado gunfighter hastened to Dodge City to kill the City Marshal. Let not the gentle reader, unused to frontier ways, jump to the conclusion that Allison was a hired bravo. He would probably have resented the imputation with deadly alacrity. It was reputation he was after, not money. To have killed me would mean for him to bask in the chaste effulgence of frontier fame for the rest of his days.

And so Clay Allison came to town, and for a whole day behaved like a veritable Chesterfield. But the next morning one of my policemen woke me up to tell me that the bad man from Colorado was loaded up with rum and searching for me everywhere with a pair of six-shooters and a mouthful of threats. Straightaway I put my guns on and went down the street with Bat Masterson. Now, Bat had a shotgun in the District Attorney's office, which was behind a drugstore just opposite Wright's store. He thought the weapon might come in handy in case of trouble, so he skipped across the street to get it. But not caring to be seen with such a weapon before there was occasion for it, he stayed over there, talking to some people outside the drug store, while I went into Webster's saloon looking for Allison. I saw at a glance that my man wasn't there, and had just reached the sidewalk to turn into the Long Branch, next door, when I met him face to face.

We greeted each other with caution thinly veiled by insouciance, and as we spoke backed carelessly against the wall, I on the right. There we stood, measuring each other with sideways glances. An onlooker across the street might have thought we were old friends.

"So," said Allison truculently, "you're the man that killed my friend Hoyt."

"Yes, I guess I'm the man you're looking for," I said.

His right hand was stealing round to his pistol pocket, but I made no move. Only I watched him narrowly. With my own right hand I had a firm grip on my six-shooter, and with my left I was ready to grab Allison's gun the moment he jerked it out. He studied the situation in all its bearings for the space of a second or two. I saw the change in his face.

"I guess I'll go round the corner," he said abruptly.

"I'd guess you'd better," I replied.

And he went.

In the meantime ten or a dozen of the worst Texans in town were laying low in Bob Wright's store, with their Winchesters, ready to cover Allison's retreat out of town, or help him in the killing, if necessary. From where he had stationed himself Bat Masterson could see them, but I did not know they were there. After the encounter with Allison I moved up the street and would have passed Bob Wright's door had not Bat, from across the street, signaled to me to keep out of range. A moment later Allison, who had mounted his horse, rode out in front of Webster's and called to me.

"Come over here, Wyatt," he said, "I want to talk to you."

"I can hear you all right here," I replied. "I think you came here to make a fight with me, and if you did you can have it right now."

Several friends of mine wanted me to take a shotgun, but I thought I could kill him all right with a six-shooter. At that moment, Bob Wright came running down the street to urge Allison to go out of town. He had experienced a sudden change of heart because Bat had crossed over to him with these portentous words: "If this fight comes up, Wright, you're the first man I'm going to kill." Allison listened to the legislator's entreaties with scowl.

"Well, I don't like you any too well," he said. "There were a lot of your friends to here this morning to help me out, but I don't see them around now.

"Earp," he continued, turning to me and raising his voice. "I believe you're a pretty good man from what I've seen of you. Do you know that these coyotes sent for me to make a fight with you and kill you? Well, I'm going to ride out of town, and I wish you good luck."

And so Clay Allison made his exit. Ten days later he reappeared within a mile of town and sent a messenger asking my permission to come to Dodge and attend to some business regarding his cattle. I sent him word that he was welcome to come so long as he behaved himself. He availed himself of the offer, and for two weeks he behaved like an exemplary citizen. It was a fourteen days wonder, for Allison had never in his life before conducted himself like a Christian. Indeed, it had been his practice to force every store, saloon, and bank other than those he patronized to close up during such time as he honored the frontier town with a visit.

A year or so later Allison came to an ignominious end by falling off a wagon and breaking his neck.

It was a day or two after my bloodless encounter with the famous Colorado fighter that Wright came to me with the olive branch, made a clean break of the Hoyt and Allison conspiracies, and offered me his friendship in return for my protection from his erstwhile friends, the Texans.

Even the Allison adventure was topped off with an epilogue of a grimly humorous kind, which I cannot forbear telling. Bat Masterson was speculating on the havoc his shotgun would have wreaked in the ranks of the cowboys if he had enjoyed a chance to use it that morning, and for the sake of a change of air and a little target practice he and I rode out of town, upended a broad plank, and began firing at it. First of all Bat fired both barrels of his shotgun, which was loaded just as he had picked it up at the District Attorney's office when I was looking for Allison. Walking up to the board he found to his dismay that the gun had been loaded, not with buckshot, as he had thought, but with the finest of birdshot. Somebody, he learned afterwards, had borrowed the gun for a day's sport, and left it loaded on returning it to its place.

"It would have been just the same," grumbled Bat, "if a good man's life had depended on that charge in that gun."

And now for the last, but not the least dramatic episode by which Bat's memory and mine are linked with Dodge City—not the Dodge City of cowboy revelry and bloodshed, but the Dodge City of what I can't help thinking a decadent if more decorous era.

As the town grew civilized, Bat Masterson and I drifted to Tombstone. Jim Masterson, another of Bat's brothers, remained in Dodge, a partner with Uptograph and Peacock in possession of a saloon and gambling house. Jim had a dispute with his partners about the distribution of the profits, and three or four of their creatures jumped on him. He escaped to his room with the intention of getting a gun and they surrounded the place, keeping him prisoner a whole day. Some of his friends telegraphed for Bat, and he traveled the 1,500 miles to make a fight with his brother's enemies.

He arrived in Dodge at nine o'clock one morning, and had hardly stepped from the train when the other faction, who knew of his coming, started across the deadline to meet him. When they got to within fifty yards of him they gave him a shot or two by way of welcome, and he returned the fire with such effect as to inflict a mortal wound on Uptograph.

Thereupon Mayor Webster appeared with a double barreled shotgun and arrested Bat, who was afterwards fined ten dollars and ordered to leave Dodge for the rest of his life. You see, Dodge had become so civilized that it had no further use for the men who had been its best protectors in the days of the Texas Terror.

It was not long after Bat's banishment that this very Webster, the Mayor, fell foul of another frontiersman—no less redoubtable a gambler and gun fighter than Luke Short. Luke and a man named Harris kept a gambling house next door to the one kept by the Mayor, and as Luke was well known in Texas and all over the frontier they enjoyed most of the patronage. In order to harass his rivals the Mayor had an ordinance passed denying women free access to the saloons—a prerogative which they had heretofore enjoyed in Dodge. Moreover, he secured a piano to add to the attractions of his own place and imported a professor to play it.

Short and Harris promptly furnished themselves with a handsomer piano and hired two girls to play and sing. Webster ordered a policeman to arrest these two girls, and they were taken to the calaboose. Luke went over to bail them out, but the policeman refused to accept his bonds. In the argument that ensued the policeman fired at Luke and Luke shot the policeman in the leg.

Thereupon Webster organized a shotgun brigade among his friends, and in the morning they marched Luke down to the depot, bundled him on board a train, and warned him never again to return to Dodge City. Apart from the ignominy of the thing and the natural desire to get square with his enemy, this was a serious matter for Luke, who had been dragged away from a profitable business in the city. So he telegraphed to Bat Masterson, and the pair of them, inspired by mutual friendship and a common grievance, tried to devise measures by which they could force the authorities of Dodge to receive them with the distinguished consideration which they conceived to be their due. Among other measures, they laid their grievance before the Governor of the State, who expressed his entire sympathy with them and advised them to fight their way into the city if necessary.

In this extremity they resorted to get my assistance, and Bat jumped on a train for Silverton, Col.,

where I was living at the time. (It should be understood that all this happened subsequent to the vendetta which resulted in my leaving Arizona.)

Our train got into Dodge at ten o'clock in the morning and we marched up the street to Luke's saloon, I with my Wells-Fargo shotgun and my men with their Winchesters. Body of Bacchus! No wonder Dodge City rubbed its eyes. There was Milsap, there was Shotgun Collins, there was Shoot-Your-Eye-Out Jack, who wore his hair down to his waist; and there was Crooked-Mouth Green, whose features had been so mutilated by a bullet that his mouth extended around to the back of his head. Faithful followers and quick fighters, every one of 'em.

We met the District Attorney going up the street and his face wore a care-worn, "come ye in peace now or come ye in war" look as he exclaimed:

"My God, Wyatt! Who are these people you've got with you?"

"Oh," said I carelessly, "they're just some bushwackers I've brought over from Colorado to straighten you people out."

"In whose interests?" he asked.

"Luke Short and Bat Masterson's," I replied.

A few paces further on I met Mayor Webster, who shook hands with me with an air of cordiality that the yellowish pallor of his cheeks belied. We all filed into Luke's saloon and there we were sworn in as deputies by Prairie Dog Dave, the Constable, who was with us blood and bones, as all good people in the town were. Indeed, the city was sick of the Webster reign of terror and glad to see a way out of it, and I soon had a following of a hundred or more fighters ready to do my bidding. It was no mean adventure to be deputized by Prairie Dog Dave, that enabled us to carry our arms without violating the law concerning which Dodge had become so sensitive.

The town council convened a hurried meeting and sent for me to ask my intentions. I told them I want Luke Short and Bat Masterson to return to Dodge at their pleasure. I added that if this were accomplished peacefully I would be so much better pleased, but that if necessary I was prepare to fight for my demands. In reply they offered to compromise. They would permit Luke Short to return for ten days to wind up his business. Bat Masterson they would not permit to enter the town. To this proposition I made no reply, but walked out of the council room. Soon afterward they sent for me again, and again I assured them that there would be no compromise—that Luke and Bat must be free to live in Dodge as long as they wanted to, provided they obey the laws.

Before the council had made any decision I wired to Luke Short to meet me at Kingsley, thirty miles away. I had an idea he might decide to return with me, so I gave orders to my followers to post themselves in front of Wright's and at other strategic points in case of disturbance. Luke and I dined together at Kingsley and, as I had anticipated, he resolved to come back with me. But we agreed that we would let the other fellows begin the fighting.

Luke and I jumped off the rear platform of the sleeper as the train slowed up, each with a double-barreled shotgun in readiness, and advanced up the street, fully expecting to make a stiff fight for it. But the enemy didn't appear. That night I telegraphed to Bat, telling him to come on the next train. He arrived in the morning and had no sooner alighted then a deputy sheriff demanded his shotgun, but I would not let him give it up.

I had hard work to persuade Bat to go into Webster's and shake hands with the Mayor, but he consented at last and the trouble was over in a few minutes. We had conquered Dodge City without firing a shot. It was a great moral victory, for Bat and Luke were unmolested from that time forth. Not that Bat stayed long to enjoy the fruits of his vindication, for he was then City Marshal of Trinidad.

Among other manifestations of exuberance at the successful issue of our invasion the citizens dubbed us "the Dodge City Peace Commission" and had us photographed in a group. Crooked-Mouth Green and my other picturesque henchmen did not figure in the group, as they felt sensitive about submitting their physiognomies to the fierce light of frontier history. Which is really a pity.

As everybody knows, Bat Masterson has now for many years been identified with Denver, where he is appreciated at his true worth. His association with the prize ring and other forms of sport all over the country has brought his name prominently before a younger and more effete generation. And he has fallen into flesh. But to me he will always be Bat Masterson, the quick fighter, the square gambler, the staunch friend and generous foe—the fastest of my frontier friends.

Chapter XI.

Wyatt Earp

By Bat Masterson

Thirty-five years ago that immense stretch of territory extending from the Missouri River west to the Pacific Ocean, and from the Brazos River in Texas north to the Red Cloud Agency in Dakota, knew no braver man nor more desperate man than Wyatt Earp, the subject of this narrative.

Wyatt Earp is one of the few men I personally knew in the West in the early days, whom I regarded as absolutely destitute of physical. I have often remarked, and I am not alone in my conclusion, that what goes for courage in a man is generally the fear of what other will think of him—in other words, personal bravery is largely made up of self-respect, egotism, and an apprehension of the opinion of others.

Wyatt Earp's daring and apparent recklessness in time of danger is wholly characteristic; personal fear doesn't enter into this equation, and when everything is said and done, I believe he values his own opinion of himself more than that of others, and it is his own good report that he seek to preserve. I may here cite an incident in his career that seems to me will go far toward establishing the correctness of the estimate I have made of him.

He was once engaged in running a faro game in Gunnison, Colorado, in the early days of that camp, and one day while away from the gambling house, another gambler by the name of Ike Morris, who had something of a local reputation as a bad man with a gun, and who was also running a faro game in another house in the camp, went into Wyatt's game and put down a roll of bills on one of the cards and told the dealer to turn.

The dealer did as he was told, and after making a turn or two, won the bet and reached out on the layout and picked up the roll of bills and deposited them in the money-drawer. Morris instantly made a kick and claimed that the cards were crooked, and demanded the return of his money. The dealer said he could not give back the money, as he was only working for wages, but advised him to wait until Mr. Earp returned, and then explain matters to him, and as he was the proprietor of the game he would perhaps straighten the matter up.

In a little while Wyatt returned, and Morris was on hand to tell him about the squabble with the dealer, and incidentally ask him for the return of the money he had bet and lost.

Wyatt told him to wait a minute and he would speak to the dealer about it; if things were as he represented he would see what could be done about it. Wyatt stepped over to the dealer and asked him about the trouble with Morris. The dealer explained the matter, and assured Wyatt that there was nothing wrong with the cards, and Morris had lost his money fairly and squarely.

By this time the house was pretty well filled up, as it noised about that Morris and Earp were likely to have trouble. A crowd had gathered in anticipation of seeing a little fun. Wyatt went over to where Morris was standing and stated that the dealer had admitted cheating him out of his money, and he felt very much like returning it on that account; but said Wyatt—"You are looked upon in this part of the country as a bad man and if I was to give you back your money you would say as soon as I left town, that you made me do it, and for that reason I will keep your money."

Morris said no more about the matter, and after inviting Wyatt to have a cigar, returned to his own house, and in a day or so left the camp.

There was really no reason why he should have gone away, for so far as Wyatt was concerned the incident was closed; but he had perhaps lost whatever prestige his reputation as a bad man had given him in camp, and concluded it would be best for him to move out before some other person of lesser note than Wyatt took a fall out of him. This he knew would be almost sure to happen if he remained in town after the Earp incident got noised about; every Tom, Dick, and Harry in camp would be anxious to take a kick at him, and that was perhaps the reason for his sudden departure for other fields where the fact of his punctured reputation was not so generally known. The course pursued by Earp on this occasion was undoubtedly the proper one—in fact, the only one, to preserve his reputation and self-respect. It would not have been necessary for him to have killed Morris in order to sustain his reputation, and very likely that was the very last thing he had in mind at the time, for he was not one of those human tigers who delight in shedding blood just for the fun of the thing. He never, at any time in his career, resorted to the pistol excepting in cases where such a course was absolutely necessary. Wyatt would scrape with his fists, and had often taken all the fight out of bad men, as they were called, with no other weapons than those provided by nature.

There were few men in the West who could whip Earp in a rough-and-tumble fight thirty years ago, and I suspect that he could give a tough youngster a hard tussle right now, even if he is sixty-one years of age. In all probability had Morris been known as a peaceable citizen, he would have had his money returned when he asked for it, as Wyatt never cared much for money; but being known as a bad man with a reputation as a gunfighter, his only chance to get his money back lay in his ability to "do" Earp, and that was a job he did not care to tackle.

I have known Wyatt Earp since early in the seventies, and I have seen him tried out under circumstances which made the test of manhood supreme. He landed in Wichita, Kansas in 1872, being then about twenty-six years old, and weighing in the neighborhood of one hundred and sixty pounds, all of it muscle. He stood six feet in height, with light blue eyes, and a complexion bordering on the blonde. He was born at Monmouth, Illinois, of a clean strain of American breeding, and served in an Iowa regiment the last three years of the Civil War, although he was only a boy at the time. He always arrayed himself on the side of law and order, and on a great many occasions, at the risk of his life, rendered valuable service in upholding the majesty of the law in those communities in which he lived. In the spring of 1876 he was appointed Assistant City marshal of Dodge City, Kansas, which was then the largest shipping point in the North for the immense herds of Texas cattle that were annually driven from Texas to the northern markets. Wyatt's reputation for courage and coolness was well known to many of the citizens of Dodge City—in fact it was his reputation that secured for him the appointment of Assistant City Marshal.

He was not very long on the force before one of the aldermen of the city, presuming somewhat on the authority of his position gave him over a police officer, ordered Wyatt one night to perform an official act that did not look exactly right to him, and Wyatt refused point blank to obey the order. The alderman, regarded as something of a scrapper himself, walked up to Wyatt and attempted to tear his official shield from his vest front where it was pinned. When that alderman woke up he was a greatly changed man. Wyatt knocked him down as soon as he laid his hands on him, and then reached down and picked him up with one hand and slammed a few cuts and upper-hooks into his face, dragged his limp form over to the city calaboose, and chucked him into one of the cells, just the same as he would any other disturber of the peace. The alderman's friends tried to get him out on bail during the night, but Wyatt gave it out that it was the calaboose for the alderman until the police

court opened up for business at nine o'clock the following morning, and it was. Wyatt was never bothered any more while he lived in Dodge City by aldermen.

While he invariably went armed, he seldom had occasion to do any shooting in Dodge City, and only once do I recall when he shot to kill, and that was a drunken cowboy who rode up to the Variety Theater where Eddie Foy, the now famous comedian, was playing an engagement. The cowboy rode straight by Wyatt, who was standing outside the main entrance to the show shop, but evidently he did not notice him, else he would not in all probability have acted as he did.

The building in which the show was being given was one of those pine-board affairs that were in general use in frontier towns. A bullet fired from a Colt's 45 calibre pistol would go through a half-dozen such buildings, and this the cowboy knew. Whether it was Foy's act that enraged him or whether he had been jilted by one of the chorus we never learned; at any rate he commenced bombarding the side of the building directly opposite the stage on which Eddie Foy was at that moment reciting that beautiful pathetic poem entitled "Kalamazoo in Michigan." The bullets tore through the side of the building, scattering pieces of the splintered pine-boards in all directions. Foy evidently thought the cowboy was after him, for he did not tarry long in the line of fire. The cowboy succeeded in firing three shots before Wyatt got his pistol in action. Wyatt missed the first shot which was probably due to the fact that the horse the cowboy was riding kept continually plunging around, which made it rather a hard matter to get a bead on him. His second shot however, did the work, and the cowboy rolled off his horse and was dead by the time the crowd reached him.

Wyatt's career in and around Tombstone, Arizona, in the early day of that bustling mining camp was perhaps the most thrilling and exciting of any he ever experienced in the thirty-five years he has lived on the lurid edge of civilization. He had four brothers besides himself who wagoned it into Tombstone as soon as it was announced that gold had been discovered in the camp.

Jim was the oldest of the brothers, Virgil came next, then Wyatt, then Morgan, and Warren, who was the kid of the family. Jim started in running a saloon as soon as one was built. Virgil was holding the position of Deputy U.S. Marshal. Wyatt operated a gambling house, and Morgan rode as a Wells Fargo shotgun messenger on the coach between Tombstone and Benson, which was the nearest railroad point. Morgan's duty was to protect the Wells

Fargo coach from the stage robbers with which the country at that time was infested.

The Earps and the stage robbers knew each other personally, and it was on this account that Morgan had been selected to guard the treasure the coach carried. The wells Fargo company believed that so long as it kept one of the Earp boys on their coach their property was safe; and it was, for no coach was ever held up in that country upon which one of the Earp boys rode as guard.

A certain band of these stage robbers who lived in the San Simone Valley, about fifty miles from Tombstone and very near the line of old Mexico, where they invariably took refuge when hard pressed by the authorities on the American side of the line, was made up of the Clanton Brothers, Ike and Billy, and the McLowry brothers, Tom and Frank. This was truly a quartet of desperate men, against whom the civil authorities of that section of the country at that time was powerless to act. Indeed, the United States troops from the surrounding posts who had been sent out to capture them dead or alive, had on more than one occasion returned to their posts after having met with both failure and disaster at the hands of the desperadoes.

Those were the men who had made up their minds to hold up and rob the Tombstone coach; but in order to do so with as little friction as possible, they must first get rid of Morgan Earp. They could as a matter of course, ambush him and shoot him dead from the coach; but that course would hardly do, as it would be sure to bring on a fight with the other members of the Earp family and their friends, of whom they had a great many. They finally concluded to try diplomacy. They sent word to Morgan to leave the employ of the Wells Fargo Express Company, as they intended to hold up the stage upon which he acted as guard, but didn't want to so long as the coach was in his charge. Morgan sent back word that he would not quit and that they had better not try to hold him up or there would be trouble. They sent word to Wyatt to have him induce Morgan, if such a thing was possible, to quit his job, as they had fully determined on holding up the coach and killing Morgan if it became necessary in order to carry out their purpose.

Wyatt sent back word that if Morgan was determined to continue riding as guard for Wells Fargo he would not interfere with him in any way, and that if they killed him he would hunt them down and kill the last one in the bunch. Just to show the desperate character of those men, they sent Virgil Earp, who was City Marshal of Tombstone at the time, word that on a certain day they would be in town prepared to give him and his brothers a battle to the death. Sure enough, on the day named, Ike and Billy Clanton, and Tom and Frank McLowry rode into Tombstone and put their horses up in one of the city corrals. They were in town some little time before the Earps knew it. They never suspected for a moment that the Clantons and McLowrys had any intention of carrying out their threat when they made it. When Virgil Earp finally realized that they were in town he got very busy. He knew it meant a fight and was not long in rustling up Wyatt and Morgan and "Doc" Holliday, the latter as desperate a man in a tight place as the West ever knew. This made the Marshal's party consist of the Marshal himself, his brothers Wyatt and Morgan, and "Doc" Holliday. Against them the two Clantons and the two McLowrys, an even thing so far as the numbers were concerned. As soon as Virgil Earp got his party together, he started for the corral, where he understood the enemy was entrenched, prepared to resist to the death the anticipated attack of the Earp forces.

Everybody in Tombstone seemed to realize that a bloody battle was about to be fought right in the very center of the town, and all those who could hastened to find points of vantage from which the impending battle could be viewed in safety. It took the City Marshal some time to get his men together, as both Wyatt and Holliday were still sound asleep in bed, and getting word to them and the time it took them to get up and dress themselves and get to the place Virge and Morgan were waiting, necessarily caused some delay. The invaders, who had been momentarily expecting an attack could not understand the delay, and finally concluded that the Earps were afraid and did not intend to attack them, at any rate while they were in the corral. This conclusion caused them to change their plan of battle. They instantly resolved that if "the mountain would not come to Mahomet—Mahomet would go to the mountain." If the Earps would not come to the corral, they would go and hunt up the Earps. Their horses were nearby, saddled, bitted and ready for instant use. Each man took his horse by the bridle-line and led him through the corral-gate to the street where they intended to mount.

But just as they reached the street, and before they had time to mount their horses, the Earp party came around the corner. Both sides were now within ten feet of each other. There were four men on a side, every one of whom had during his career been engage in other shooting scrapes and were regarded as being the most desperate of desperate men. The horses gave the rustlers quite an advantage in the position. The Earps were in the open street, while the invaders used their horses for breastworks. Virgil Earp as the City Marshal, ordered the Clantons and McLowrys to throw up their hands and surrender. This order they replied to with a volley from their pistols. The fight was on now. The Earps pressed in close, shooting as rapidly as they could. They fight was hardly started before it was over, and the result showed that nearly every shot fired by the Earp party went straight home to the mark.

As soon as the smoke from the battle cleared away sufficiently to permit of an accounting being made, it was seen that the two McLowrys and Billy Clanton were killed. They had been hit by no less than half a dozen bullets each, and died in their tracks. Morgan Earp was the only one of the Marshal's force that got hit. It was nothing more than a slight flesh wound in one of his arms. Ike Clanton made his escape, but in doing so he stamped himself as a coward of the first magnitude. No sooner had the shooting commenced than he threw down his pistol and with both hands above his head, he ran to Wyatt and begged him not to kill him. Here again Wyatt showed the kind of stuff that was in him, for instead of killing Clanton as most any other man would have done under the circumstances, he told him to run away, and he did.

The Earp party were all tried for this killing, and after a preliminary examination lasting several weeks, during which more than a hundred witnesses were examined, they were all exonerated. There were at this time two other outlaw bands in the country, who, when they heard of the killing of the McLowry brothers and Billy Clanton, swore to wipe out the Earp family and all their friends. They had no notion, however, of giving the Earps any more battles in the open. In future, killings would be done in ambush, and the first one to get potted by this guerilla system of warfare was Virge Earp, the City Marshal. As he was crossing one of the most prominent corners in Tombstone one night he was fired upon by someone not then known, but was afterwards learned to be "Curly Bill," who was concealed behind the walls of a building that was then in the course of construction on one of the corners. A shotgun loaded with buckshot was the weapon used. Most of the charge struck Virge in the left arm between the shoulder and the elbow, shattering the bone in a frightful manner. One or two of the other shot hit him but caused no serious injury. He was soon able to be about again, but never had use afterward of his left arm. As a matter of course the shock he sustained when the buckshot hit him caused him to fall, and the would-be assassin, thinking he had turned the trick successfully, made his escape in the dark to the foothills. The next to get murdered was Morgan Earp, who was shot through a window one night while playing a game of pinpool with a friend.

Wyatt the realized that it was only a question of time until he and all his friends would be killed in the same manner as his brother, if he remained in town. So he organized a party consisting of himself, "Doc" Holliday, Jack Vermillion, Sherman McMasters, and Bill Johnson, and after equipping it with horses, guns, and plenty of ammunition, started out on the warpath intending to hunt down and kill every one he could find who had any hand in the murder of his brother and the attempted assassination of Virge. Wyatt had in the meantime, learned that Pete Spence, Frank Stillwell, and a Mexican, by the name of Florentine, were the three who were interested in the killing of Morgan. Pete Spence had a ranch about twenty-five miles from Tombstone near the Dragoon Mountains, which was in reality nothing more than a rendezvous for cattle thieves and stage robbers.

Wyatt and his party headed straight for the Spence ranch as soon as he left Tombstone on his campaign of revenge. He found only the Mexican when he reached the ranch, and after making some inquiry as to the whereabouts of Spence, and learning that he had left early that morning for Tombstone by a different route from the ones the Earps had traveled, proceeded, with further ceremony to shoot the Mexican to pieces with buckshot. They left the greaser's body where it fell, and returned to Tombstone, where they expected to find Spence. He was there all right enough, but seemingly to anticipate what Wyatt intended doing, had gone to the sheriff, who was not on friendly terms with the Earp faction, and surrendered, having himself locked up in jail.

Of course, Wyatt had to let him go for the time being, and was getting ready to start out on another expedition when he received word from Tucson that Frank Stillwell and Ike Clanton were there. Wyatt and "Doc" Holliday immediately started for Benson where they took the train for Tucson, which was about sixty miles further south. Both were armed with shotguns, and just before the train came to a stop in Tucson station, Wyatt and "Doc" Holliday, from the platform of the rear coach saw Clanton and Stillwell standing on the depot platform. They immediately jumped off and started for the depot, intending to kill them both, but they were seen coming by the quarry who had evidently been made aware of Earp's movements and were on the lookout at the station. Clanton and Stillwell started to run as soon as they saw Wyatt and

Holliday approaching, Stillwell down the railroad track and Clanton towards town. Wyatt and Holliday immediately gave chase to Stillwell and succeeded after a short run in overtaking him. He threw up his hands and begged not to be killed, but it was too late. Besides Wyatt had given instructions that no prisoners should be taken, so they riddled his body with buckshot and left it where it fell, just as they had the Mexican. Wyatt and Holliday then returned to Tombstone, thinking there might still be a chance for a crack at Pete Spence, but the latter still clung to jail.

Meanwhile the sheriff of Tombstone had received telegraphic instructions from the sheriff of Tucson to arrest Wyatt and Holliday, as soon as they showed up, for the murder of Stillwell. When Wyatt got back to town, he hustled his men together for the purpose of going after Curly Bill, whom he believed to be the man who shot Virge from ambush. When the sheriff and his posse reached Wyatt, the latter and his crowd were about to mount their horses preparatory to going on the "Curly Bill" expedition.

"Wyatt, I want to see you," said the sheriff.

"You'll see me once to often," replied Wyatt, as he bounded up into the saddle. "And remember," continued Wyatt to the sheriff, "I'm going to get that hound you are protecting in jail when I come back, if I have to tear the jail down to do it."

The sheriff made no further attempt to arrest Wyatt and Holliday. The next night Wyatt killed Curly Bill at the Whetstone Spring about thirty miles from Tombstone and just to make his word good with the sheriff, he and his party returned to town. The sheriff, however, had during his absence released Spence and told him to get across the Mexican border with as little delay as possible if he valued his life, for the Earp gang would surely kill him if he didn't.

This ended the Earp campaign in Arizona for the time being. Much has been written about Wyatt Earp that is the veriest rot, and every once in a while a newspaper article will appear in which it is alleged that some person had taken a fall out of him, and that when he had been put to the test, had shown the white feather. Not long ago a story was published in different newspapers throughout the country that some Canadian police office somewhere in the Canadian Northwest has given Wyatt an awful call-down; had in fact, taken his pistol from him and in other ways humiliated him. The story went like wildfire, as all such stories do, and was printed and reprinted in all the big dailies in the country. There was not a word of truth in it, and the newspaper fakir who unloaded the story on the reading public very likely got no more than ten dollars for his work. Wyatt, to begin with, was never in the Canadian Northwest, and therefore was never in a position where a little Canadian police officer could have taken such liberties with him as those described by the author of the story. Take it from me, no one has ever humiliated this man Earp, nor made him show the white feather under any circumstances whatever. While he is now a man past sixty, there are still a great many so-called bad men in this country who would be found, if put to the test, to be much easier game to tackle than this same lean and lanky Earp.

Wyatt Earp, like many more of his character who lived in the West in its early days, has excited, by this display of great courage and nerve under trying conditions, the envy and hatred of those small minded creatures with which the world seem to be so abundantly peopled, and whose sole delight in life seems to be in fly-specking the reputations of real men. I have known him since the early seventies and have always found him a quiet, unassuming man, not given to brag or bluster, but at all times and under all circumstances a loyal friend and an equally dangerous enemy.

CHAPTER XII.

THE STATEMENT OF WYATT EARP

By Wyatt Earp

The following is Wyatt Earp's statement at the preliminary hearing looking into the facts surrounding what has become known as the Shootout at the O. K. Corral. Despite the myriad of speculation and various accounts in books, articles, movies, and television, this testimony remains the clearest, most accurate exposition of the circumstances surrounding the legendary gunfight.

Q. What is your name and age?

A. Wyatt S. Earp; age 32 last March.

Q. Where were you born?

A. Monmouth, Warren county, Illinois.

Q. Where do you reside and how long have you resided there?

A. Tombstone; since Dec. 1st, 1881 [misprint, should be: 1879]

Q. What is your business or profession?

A. Saloon keeper; have also been employed as a deputy sheriff, and also as a detective.

Q. Give any explanation you may think proper of the circumstances appearing in the testimony against you, and state any facts which you think will tend to your exculpation.

A. The difficulty between deceased and myself originated first when I followed Tom McLowry and Frank McLowry, with Virgil and Morgan Earp and Captain Hearst and four soldiers to look for six government mules which were stolen. A man named Estes told us at Charleston, that we would find the mules at McLowry's ranch, that the McLowrys were branding "D. S." over "US" We tracked the mules to McLowry's ranch, where we also found the brand. Afterwards some of those mules were found with the same brand. After we arrived at McLowry's ranch there was a man named Frank Patterson who made some kind of a compromise with Captain Hearst. Captain Hearst came to us boys and told us he had made this compromise and by so doing he would get the mules back. We insisted on following them up. Hearst prevailed upon us to go back to Tombstone, and so we came back. Hearst told us two or three weeks afterwards that they would not give up the mules to him after we left, saying they only wanted to get us away: that they could stand the soldiers off. Captain Hearst cautioned me and Virgil and Morgan to look out for those men; that they had made some hard threats against their lives. About one month after that, after those mules had been taken, I met Frank and Tom McLowry in Charleston. They tried to pick a fuss out of me, and told me that if I ever followed them up again as close as I did before that they would kill me.

Shortly after the time Budd Philpot was killed by those men who tried to rob the Benson stage, as a detective I helped trace the matter up, and I was satisfied that three men, named Billy Leonard, Harry Head and Jim Crane were in that robbery. I know that Leonard, Head and Crane were friends and associates of the Clantons and McLowrys and often stopped at their ranches. It was generally understood among officers, and those who have information about criminals, that Ike Clanton was a sort of chief among the cowboys; that the Clantons and McLowrys were cattle thieves, and generally in the secrets of the stage robbers; and that the Clanton and McLowrys ranches were the meeting place, and place of shelter for the gang.

I had an ambition to be sheriff of this county next election, and I thought it would be a great help to me with the people and the business men if I could capture the men who killed Philpot. There were rewards offered of about $1,200 each for the robbers. Altogether there was about $3,600 offered for their capture.

I thought that this amount might tempt Ike Clanton and Frank McLowry to give away Leonard, Head and Crane; so I went to Ike Clanton and Frank McLowry, when they came in town. I had an interview with them in the back yard of the Oriental saloon. I told them what I wanted. I told them I wanted the glory of capturing Leonard, Head and Crane; if I could do so, it would help me make the race for sheriff next election. I told them if they would put on the track of Leonard, Head and Crane—tell me where those men were hid—I would give them all the reward, and would never let anybody know where I got the information. Ike Clanton said that he would be glad to have Leonard captured, that Leonard claimed a ranch that he claimed, and if he could gel him out of the way he would have no opposition about the ranch.

Ike Clanton said that Leonard, Head and Crane would make a fight, that they would never be taken alive, and that I must first find out if the reward would be paid for the capture of the robbers dead or alive. I then went to Marshall Williams, the agent of Wells, Fargo & Co., in this town, and at my request he telegraphed to the agent of Wells, Fargo & Co., at San Francisco to find out if the reward would be paid for the robbers dead or alive. He received in June, 1881 a telegram which he gave me, promising that the reward should be paid dead or alive. I showed this telegram soon after I got it to Ike Clanton in front of the Alhambra and afterwards told Frank McLowry of its contents.

It was then agreed between us that they should have all the $3,600 reward outside of necessary expenses for horses in going after them and Joe Hill should go to where Leonard, Head, and Crane were hid, over near Eureka, in New Mexico, and lure them in near Frank and Tom McLowry's ranch near Soldier Holes, thirty miles from here, and I would be on hand with a posse and capture them. I asked Joe Hill, Ike Clanton and Frank McLowry what tale they would make to them to get them over here. They said they had agreed upon a plan to tell them that there would be a pay master going from Tombstone to Bisbee shortly to pay off the miners, and that they wanted them to come in and take them; Ike Clanton then sent Joe Hill to bring them in; before starting Joe Hill took on his watch and chain and between two and three hundred dollars in money, and gave it to Virgil Earp to keep for him until he got back. He was gone about ten days and returned with the word that he had got there a day too late; that Leonard and Harry Head had been killed the day before he got there by horse thieves. I learned afterward that the thieves had been killed subsequently by members of the Clanton and McLowry gang.

After that Ike Clanton and Frank McLowry said I had given them away to Marshal Williams and Doc Holliday, and when they came in town they shunned us, and Morgan and Virgil Earp and Doc Holliday and myself began to hear of their threats against us. I am a friend of Doc Holliday, because when I was city marshal of Dodge City, Kansas, he came to my rescue and saved my life, when I was surrounded by desperadoes. A month or so ago Morgan and I assisted to arrest Stillwell and Spence on the charge of robbing the Bisbee stage. The McLowrys and Clantons have always been friendly with Spence and Stillwell, and they laid the whole blame of their arrest on us, though the fact is, we only went as a sheriff's posse. After we got in town with Spence and Stillwell, Ike Clanton and Frank McLowry came in. Frank McLowry took Morgan into the middle of the street, where John Ringgold, Ike Clanton and the Hicks boys were standing, and commenced to abuse Morgan Earp for going after Spence and Stillwell. Frank McLowry said he would never speak to Spence again for being arrested by us. He said to Morgan, "If ever you come after me you will never take me." Morgan replied that if he ever had occasion to go after him he would arrest him. Frank McLowry then said to him, "I have threatened you boys' lives, and a few days ago I had taken it back, but since this arrest it now goes." Morgan made no reply, and walked off.

Before this and after this, Marshal Williams and Farmer Daly, and Ed Burns and three or four others, told us at different times of threats made to kill us, by Ike Clanton, Frank McLowry: Tom McLowry, Joe Hill and John Ringgold. I knew that all these men were desperate and dangerous, cattle thieves, robbers and murderers. I knew of the Clantons and McLowrys stealing six government mules. I heard of Ringgold shooting a man down in cold blood near Camp Thomas. I was satisfied that Frank and Tom McLowry killed and robbed Mexican in the Skeleton canyon two or three months ago, and I naturally keep my eyes open, and I did not intend that any of the gang should get the drop on me if I could help it.

Three or four weeks ago Ike Clanton met me at the Alhambra, and told me that I had told Holliday about this transaction, concerning the capture of Head and Leonard. I told him I never told Holliday anything. I told him when Holliday came up from Tucson I would prove it. Ike Clanton said that Holliday had told him so; when Holliday came I asked him and he said no; I told him that Ike Clanton had said so.

On the 25th of October Holliday met Ike Clanton in the Alhambra saloon and asked him about it. Clanton denied it, and they quarreled for three or four minutes. Holliday told Ike Clanton he was a d-d liar, if he said so. I was sitting eating lunch at the time. They got up and walked out on the street. I got through and walked out, and they were still talking about it. I then went to Holliday, who was pretty tight, and took him away. Then I came back alone and met Ike Clanton. He called me outside and said his gun was on the other side of the street at the hotel. I told him to leave it there. He said he would make a fight with Holliday any time he wanted to. I told him Holliday did not want to fight, but only to satisfy him this talk had not been made. I then went away and went to the Oriental, and in a few minutes Ike Clanton came over with his six shooter on. He said he was not fixed right; that in the morning he would have man for man that this fighting talk had been going on for a long time, and it was about time to fetch it to a close. I told him that I wouldn't fight no one if I could get away from it. He walked off and left me, saying, "I will be ready for all of you in the morning." He followed me into the Oriental, having his six shooter in plain sight. He said, "You mustn't think I won't be after you all in the morning." Myself and Holliday walked away and went to our rooms.

I got up next day, October 26, about noon. Before I got up, Ned Bolye came to me and told me that he met Ike Clanton on Allen street, near the telegraph office that morning; that Ike was armed; that he said, "As soon as those d—d Earps make their appearance on the street to day the battle will open," and, "We are here to make a fight, we are looking for the sons of b—s." Jones came to me after I got up and went to the saloon, and said, "What does all this mean?" I asked what he meant. He says, "Ike Clanton is hunting you Earp boys with a Winchester rifle and a six shooter." I said, "I will go down and find him and see what he wants." I went out, and on the corner of Fourth and Allen streets I met Virgil Earp, the marshal. He told me how he had heard that Ike Clanton was hunting us. I went up Allen street, and Virgil went down Fifth street and then Fremont street. Virgil found Ike Clanton on Fourth street in an alley. He walked up to him and said, "I hear you are hunting for some of us." Ike Clanton then threw his Winchester rifle around towards Virgil. Virgil grabbed it and hit Clanton with his six shooter and knocked him down. Clanton had his rifle, and his six shooter was exposed in his pants. By that time I came up, and Virgil and Morgan took his rifle and six shooter away and took them to the Grand Hotel after the examination, and took Ike Clanton before Justice

Wallace. Before the investigation Morgan Earp had Ike Clanton in charge, as Virgil Earp was out. A short time after I went into Wallace's court and sat down on a bench.

Ike Clanton looked over to me and says, "I will get even with all of you for this. If I had a six shooter I would make a fight with all of you." Morgan then said to him, "If you want to make a fight right bad I will give you this one." At the same time offering Ike Clanton his (Ike's) own six shooter. Ike Clanton started to get up to take it, when Campbell, the deputy sheriff, pushed him back on his seat, saying he wouldn't allow any fuse. I never had Ike Clanton's arms at any time as he has stated.

I would like to describe the position we occupied in the courtroom at that time. Ike Clanton sat down on a bench, with his face fronting to the north wall of the building. I myself sat down on a bench that was against the north wall right in front of Ike. Morgan Earp stood up against the north wall with his back against the north wall, two or three feet to my right. Morgan Earp had Ike Clanton's Winchester in his left hand and his six shooter in his right hand, one end of the rifle was on the floor. Virgil Earp was not in the court room any of the time, and Virgil Earp came there after I walked out.

I was tired of being threatened by Ike Clanton and his gang. I believed from what they had said to others and to me, and from their movements, that they intended to assassinate me the first chance they had, and I thought if I had to fight for my life against them, I had better make them face me in an open fight. So I said to Ike Clanton, who was then sitting about eight feet away from me, "you d—d dirty cur thief, you have been threatening our lives, and I know it. I think I should be justified shooting you down any place I should meet you, but if you are anxious to make a fight, I will go anywhere on earth to make a fight with you, even over to the San Simon among your own crowd." He replied, "All right, I will see you after I get through here. I only want four feet of ground to fight on." I walked out and just then outside the courtroom, near the justice's office, I met Tom McLowry. He came up to me and said to me, "If you want to make a fight I will make a fight with you anywhere." I supposed at the time he had heard what had first transpired between Ike Clanton and me. I knew of his having threatened me and I felt just as I did about Ike Clanton, that if the fight had to come, I had better have it come when I had an even show to defend myself, so I said to him all right "make a fight right here," and at the same time I slapped him in the face with my left hand, and drew my pistol with my right. He had a pistol in plain sight on his right hip, but made no move to draw it. I said to him, "Jerk, your gun. Use it." He made no reply and I hit him on the head with my six-shooter and walked away down to Hafford's corner. I went into Hafford's and got a cigar, and came out and stood by the door. Pretty soon after I saw Tom McLowry, Frank McLowry and William Clanton. They passed me and went down Fourth Street to the gunsmith shop. I followed down to see what they were going to do. When I got there Frank McLowry's horse was standing on the sidewalk with his head in the door of the gun shop. I took the horse by the bit, as I was deputy city marshal, and commenced to back him off the sidewalk. Frank and Tom McLowry and Billy Clanton came to the door, Billy Clanton had his hand on his six shooter. Frank McLowry took hold of the horse's bridle. I said "you will have to get this horse off the sidewalk." He backed him off on the street. Ike Clanton came up about that time and they all walked into the gunsmith's shop. I saw them in the shop changing cartridges into their belts. They came out of the shop and walked along Fourth street to the corner of Allen street. I followed them as far as the corner of Fourth and Allen streets, and then they went down Allen Street and over to Dunbar's corral. Virgil Earp was then city marshal; Morgan Earp was a special policeman for six weeks, wore a badge and drew pay. I had been sworn in Virgil's place to act for him while Virgil was gone to Tucson on Stillwell and Spence, on the charge of robbing the Bisbee stage trial. Virgil had been back several days, but I was still acting. I know it was Virgil's duty to disarm those men. He suspected he would have trouble in doing so; and I followed up to give assistance if necessary, especially as they had been threatening us, as I have already stated. About ten minutes afterwards, and while Virgil, Morgan, Doc Holliday and myself were standing in the center of Fourth and Allen streets several persons said, "there is going to be trouble with those fellows," and one man named Coleman said to Virgil Earp, "they mean trouble. They have just gone from Dunbar's corral into the O. K. Corral, all armed. I think you had better go and disarm them." Virgil turned around to Doc Holliday, Morgan Earp and myself and told us to come and assist him in disarming them. Morgan Earp said to me, "they have horses; had we not better get some horses ourselves, so that if they make a running fight we can catch them?" I said, "No, if they try to make a running fight we can kill their horses, and then capture them." We four then started through Fourth to Fremont street. When we turned the corner of Fourth and Fremont streets we could see them standing near or about the vacant space between Fly's photograph gallery and the next building west. I first saw Frank McLowry, Tom McLowry, Billy Clanton and Sheriff Behan standing there. We went down the left hand side of Fremont Street. When I got within about 150 feet of them I saw Ike Clanton, Billy Claiborne and another party. We had walked a few steps further when I saw Behan leave the party and come towards us, every few steps he would look back as if he apprehended danger. I heard Behan say to Virgil Earp, "For God's sake don't go down there or you will get murdered." Virgil replied, "I am going to disarm them"—he, Virgil Earp, being in the lead. When I and Morgan came up to Behan he said, "I have disarmed them." When he said this I took my pistol, which I had in my hand, under my coat, and put it in my overcoat pocket. Behan then passed up the street, and we walked on down. We came up on them close—Frank McLowry, Tom McLowry, and Billy Clanton standing all in a row against the east side of the building on the opposite side of the vacant space west of Fly's photography gallery. Ike Clanton and Billy Claiborne and a man I did not know were standing in the vacant space about halfway between the photograph gallery and the next building west. I saw that Billy Clanton and Frank McLowry and Tom McLowry had their hands by their sides and Frank McLowry's and Billy Clanton's six shooters were in plain sight. Virgil said, "Throw up your hands. I have come to disarm you." Billy Clanton and Frank McLowry had their hands on their six shooters. Virgil said, "Hold I don't mean that; I have come to disarm you." They—Billy Clanton and Frank McLowry—commenced to draw their pistols, at the same time Tom McLowry threw his hand to his right hip and jumped behind a horse. I had my pistol in my overcoat pocket where I had put it when Behan told us he had disarmed the other party. When I saw Billy and Frank draw their pistols I drew my pistol. Billy Clanton leveled his pistol at me but I did not aim at him. I knew that Frank McLowry had the reputation of being a good shot and a dangerous man, and I aimed at Frank McLowry. The two first shots which were fired were fired by Billy Clanton and myself; he shot at me, and I shot at Frank McLowry. I do not know which shot was first; we fired almost together. The fight then became general. After about four shots were fired Ike Clanton ran up and grabbed my arm. I could see no weapon in his hand and thought at the time he had none, and so I said to him, "The fight has now commenced go to fighting or get away." At the same time I pushed him off with my left hand. He started and ran down the side of the building and disappeared between the lodging house and the photograph gallery. My first shot struck Frank McLowry in the belly. He staggered off on the sidewalk but first fired one shot at me. When we told them to throw up their hands Claiborne held up his left hand, and then broke and ran. I never saw him afterwards until later in the afternoon, after the fight. I never drew my pistol or made a motion to shoot until after Billy Clanton and Frank McLowry drew their pistols. If Tom McLowry was unarmed I did not know it. I believe he was armed and that he fired two shots at our party before Holliday, who had the shotgun, fired at and killed him. If he was unarmed there was nothing to the circumstances or in what had been communicated to me, or in his acts or threats, that would have led me even to suspect his being unarmed. I never fired at Ike Clanton, even after the shooting commenced, because I thought he was unarmed and I believed then, and believe now, from the acts I have stated, and the threats I have related, and other threats communicated to me by different persons, as having been made by Tom McLowry, Frank McLowry and Isaac Clanton, that these men, last named, had formed a conspiracy to murder my brothers Morgan and Virgil, and Doc Holliday and myself. I believe I would have been legally and morally justified in shooting any of them on sight, but I did not do so or attempt to do so; I sought no advantage. When I went as deputy marshal to help disarm them and arrest them, I went as a part of my duty and under the direction of my brother the marshal. I did not intend to fight unless it became necessary in self defense, and in the performance of official duty. When Billy Clanton and Frank McLowry drew their pistols I knew it was a fight for life, and I drew and fired in defense of my own life and the lives of my brothers and Doc Holliday.

I have been in Tombstone since December 1, 1879. I came here from Dodge City, Kansas, where, against the protest of business men and officials, I resigned the office of City Marshal, which I held from 1876. I came to Dodge City from Wichita, Kansas. I was on the police force in Wichita, from 1874 until I went to Dodge City.

The testimony of Isaac Clanton that I had anything to do with any stage robbery, or any criminal enterprise, is a tissue of lies from beginning to end. Sheriff Behan made me an offer in his office on Allen Street, and in the back room of the cigar store, that if I would withdraw and not try to get appointed sheriff of Cochise county, that we would hire a clerk and divide the profits. I done so; and he never said another word to me afterward in regard to it. The reasons given by him here for not complying with his contract, are false.

I give here as a part of this statement, a document sent me from Dodge City, since my arrest, and marked Exhibit "A", and another document sent me from Wichita, since this arrest, which I wish attached to this statement, and marked Exhibit "B".

Myself and Doc Holliday happened to go to Charleston the night that Behan happened to go down to subpoena Ike Clanton. We went there for the purpose of getting a horse that had been stolen from us a few days after I came to Tombstone. I had heard several times that the Clantons had him. When I got there that night I was told by a friend of mine that the man that carried the dispatch from Charleston to Ike Clanton's ranch had my horse. At this time I did not know where Ike Clanton's ranch was. A short time afterward I was in the Huachucas, locating some water rights. I had started home to Tombstone, and had got within twelve or fifteen miles of Charleston, when I met a man named McMasters. He told me if I would hurry up I would find my horse in Charleston. I drove to Charleston, and saw my horse going through the streets toward the corral. I put up for the night at another corral. I went to Barnett's office, to get out papers to recover the horse. He was not at home, having gone to Sonora to see some coal fields that had been discovered. I telegraphed to Tombstone, to James Earp, and papers were made out and sent to Charleston, that night. While I was in town, waiting for the papers, Billy Clanton found out I was there. He went and tried to take the horse out of the corral. I told him that he could not take him out, that it was my horse. After the papers came he gave the horse up without the papers being served, and asked me "if I had any more horses to lose." I told him I would keep them in the stable after this, and not give him a chance to steal them.

In one of the conversations I had with Ike Clanton about giving away Leonard, Head and Crane, I told him one reason why I wanted to catch them was to prove to the citizens of Tombstone that Doc Holliday had nothing to do with it, as there were some false statements circulated to that effect. In following the trail of Leonard, Head and Crane, we struck it at the scene of the attempted robbery, and never lost the trail or hardly a footprint from the time that we started from Drew's ranch, on the San Pedro, until we got to Helm's ranch, in the Dragoons. After following about eight miles down the San Pedro river and capturing one of the men, named King that was supposed to be in with them, we then crossed the Catalina mountains within fifteen miles of Tucson, following their trail around the front of the mountain

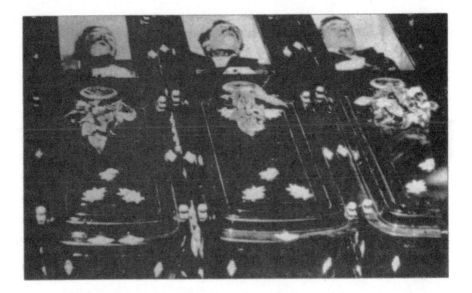

after they had crossed over to Tres Alamos, on the San Pedro river. We then started out from Helm's ranch and got on their trail. They had stolen fifteen or twenty head of stock so as to cover their trail. Wyatt Earp, Morgan Earp, R. H. Paul, Breckenridge, Johnny Behan and one or two others still follo-wed the trail up into New Mexico. Their trail never led south from Helm's ranch, as Ike Clanton has stated. We used every effort we could to capture these men. I was out ten days. Virgil Earp and Morgan Earp were out sixteen days, and we done all we could to capture these men, and I safely say if it had not been for myself and Morgan Earp, they would not have got King, as he started to run when we rode up to his hiding place, and was making for a big patch of brush on the river, and would have got in it if it had not been for us.

CHAPTER XIII.

THEODORE ROOSEVELT, LAWMAN

from *Theodore Roosevelt: An Autobiography*

By Theodore Roosevelt

When I went West, the last great Indian wars had just come to an end, but there were still sporadic outbreaks here and there, and occasionally bands of marauding young braves were a menace to outlying and lonely settlements. Many of the white men were themselves lawless and brutal, and prone to commit outrages on the Indians. Unfortunately, each race tended to hold all the members of the other race responsible for the misdeeds of a few, so that the crime of the miscreant, red or white, who committed the original outrage too often invited retaliation upon entirely innocent people, and this action would in its turn arouse bitter feeling which found vent in still more indiscriminate retaliation. The first year I was on the Little Missouri some Sioux bucks ran off all the horses of a buffalo-hunter's outfit. One of the buffalo-hunters tried to get even by stealing the horses of a Cheyenne hunting party, and when pursued made for a cow camp, with, as a result, a long-range skirmish between the cowboys and the Cheyennes. One of the latter was wounded; but this particular wounded man seemed to have more sense than the other participants in the chain of wrong-doing, and discriminated among the whites. He came into our camp and had his wound dressed.

A year later I was at a desolate little mud road ranch on the Deadwood trail. It was kept by a very capable and very forceful woman, with sound ideas of justice and abundantly well able to hold her own. Her husband was a worthless devil, who finally got drunk on some whisky he obtained from an outfit of Missouri bull-whackers—that is, freighters, driving ox wagons. Under the stimulus of the whisky he picked a quarrel with his wife and attempted to beat her. She knocked him down with a stove-lid lifter, and the admiring bull-whackers bore him off, leaving the lady in full possession of the ranch. When I visited her she had a man named Crow Joe working for her, a slab-sided, shifty-eyed person who later, as I heard my foreman explain, "skipped the country with a bunch of horses." The mistress of the ranch made first-class buckskin shirts of great durability. The one she made for me, and which I used for years, was used by one of my sons in Arizona a couple of winters ago. I had ridden down into the country after some lost horses, and visited the ranch to get her to make me the buckskin shirt in question. There were, at the moment, three Indians there, Sioux, well behaved and self-respecting, and she explained to me that they had been resting there waiting for dinner, and that a white man had come along and tried to run off their horses. The Indians were on the lookout, however, and, running out, they caught the man; but, after retaking their horses and depriving him of his gun, they let him go. "I don't see why they let him go," exclaimed my hostess. "I don't believe in stealing Indians' horses any more than white folks'; so I told 'em they could go along and hang him—I'd never cheep. Anyhow, I won't charge them anything for their dinner," concluded my hostess. She was in advance of the usual morality of the time and place, which drew a sharp line between stealing citizens' horses and stealing horses from the Government or the Indians.

A fairly decent citizen, Jap Hunt, who long ago met a violent death, exemplified this attitude towards Indians in some remarks I once heard him make. He had started a horse ranch, and had quite honestly purchased a number of broken-down horses of different brands, with the view of doctoring them and selling them again. About this time there had been much horse-stealing and cattle-killing in our Territory and in Montana, and under the direction of some of the big cattle-growers a committee of vigilantes had been organized to take action against the rustlers, as the horse thieves and cattle thieves were called. The vigilantes, or stranglers, as they were locally known, did their work thoroughly; but, as always happens with bodies of the kind, toward the end they grew reckless in their actions, paid off private grudges, and hung men on slight provocation. Riding into Jap Hunt's ranch, they nearly hung him because he had so many horses of different brands. He was finally let off. He was much upset by the incident, and explained again and again, "The idea of saying that I was a horse thief! Why, I never stole a horse in my life—leastways from a white man. I don't count Indians nor the Government, of course." Jap had been reared among men still in the stage of tribal morality, and while they recognized their obligations to one another, both the Government and the Indians seemed alien bodies, in regard to which the laws of morality did not apply.

On the other hand, parties of savage young bucks would treat lonely settlers just as badly, and in addition sometimes murder them. Such a party was generally composed of young fellows burning to distinguish themselves. Some one of their number would have obtained a pass from the Indian Agent allowing him to travel off the reservation, which pass would be flourished whenever their action was questioned by bodies of whites of equal strength. I once had a trifling encounter with such a band. I was making my way along the edge of the bad lands, northward from my lower ranch, and was just crossing a plateau when five Indians rode up over the further rim. The instant they saw me they whipped out their guns and raced full speed at me, yelling and flogging their horses. I was on a favorite horse, Manitou, who was a wise old fellow, with nerves not to be shaken by anything. I at once leaped off him and stood with my rifle ready.

It was possible that the Indians were merely making a bluff and intended no mischief. But I did not like their actions, and I thought it likely that if I allowed them to get hold of me they would at least take my horse and rifle, and possibly kill me. So I waited until they were a hundred yards off and then drew a bead on the first. Indians—and, for the matter of that, white men—do not like to ride in on a man who is cool and means shooting, and in a twinkling every man was lying over the side of his horse, and all five had turned and were galloping backwards, having altered their course as quickly as so many teal ducks.

After this one of them made the peace sign, with his blanket first, and then, as he rode toward me, with his open hand. I halted him at a fair distance and asked him what he wanted. He exclaimed, "How! Me good Injun, me good Injun," and tried to show me the dirty piece of paper on which his agency pass was written. I told him with sincerity that I was glad that he was a good Indian, but that he must not come any closer. He then asked for sugar and tobacco. I told him I had none. Another Indian began slowly drifting toward me in spite of my calling out to keep back, so I once more aimed with my rifle, whereupon both Indians slipped to the other side of their horses and galloped off, with oaths that did credit to at least one side of their acquaintance with English. I now mounted and pushed over the plateau on to the open prairie. In those days an Indian, although not as good a shot as a white man, was infinitely better at crawling under and taking advantage of cover; and the worst thing a white man could do was to get into cover, whereas out in the open if he kept his head he had a good chance of standing off even half a dozen assailants. The Indians accompanied me for a couple of miles. Then I reached the open prairie, and resumed my northward ride, not being further molested.

In the old days in the ranch country we depended upon game for fresh meat. Nobody liked to kill a beef, and although now and then a maverick yearling might be killed on the round-up, most of us looked askance at the deed, because if the practice of beef-killing was ever allowed to start, the rustlers—the horse thieves and cattle thieves—would be sure to seize on it as an excuse for general slaughter. Getting meat for the ranch usually devolved upon me. I almost always carried a rifle when I rode, either in a scabbard under my thigh, or across the pommel. Often I would pick up a deer or antelope while about my regular work, when visiting a line camp or riding after the cattle. At other times I would make a day's trip after them. In the fall we sometimes took a wagon and made a week's hunt, returning with eight or ten deer carcasses, and perhaps an elk or a mountain sheep as well. I never became more than a fair hunter, and at times I had most exasperating experiences, either failing to see game which I ought to have seen, or committing some blunder in the stalk, or failing to kill when I fired. Looking back, I am inclined to say that if I had any good quality as a hunter it was that of perseverance. "It is dogged that does it" in hunting as in many other things. Unless in wholly exceptional cases, when we were very hungry, I never killed anything but bucks.

Occasionally I made long trips away from the ranch and among the Rocky Mountains with my ranch foreman Merrifield; or in later years with Tazewell Woody, John Willis, or John Goff. We hunted bears, both the black and the grizzly, cougars and wolves, and moose, wapiti, and white goat. On one of these trips I killed a bison bull, and I also killed a bison bull on the Little Missouri some fifty miles south of my ranch on a trip which Joe Ferris and I took together. It was rather a rough trip. Each of us carried only his slicker behind him on the saddle, with some flour and bacon done up in it. We met with all kinds of misadventures. Finally one night, when we were sleeping by a slimy little prairie pool where there was not a stick of wood, we had to tie the horses to the horns of our saddles; and then we went to sleep with our heads on the saddles. In the middle of the night something stampeded the horses, and away they went, with the saddles after them. As we jumped to our feet Joe eyed me with an evident suspicion that I was the Jonah of the party, and said: "O Lord! I've never done anything to deserve this. Did you ever do anything to deserve this?"

In addition to my private duties, I sometimes served as deputy sheriff for the northern end of our county. The sheriff and I crisscrossed in our public and private relations. He often worked for me as a hired hand at the same time that I was his deputy. His name, or at least the name he went by, was Bill Jones, and as there were in the neighborhood several Bill Joneses—Three Seven Bill Jones, Texas Bill Jones, and the like—the sheriff was known as Hell Roaring Bill Jones. He was a thorough frontiersman, excellent in all kinds of emergencies, and a very game man. I became much attached to him. He was a thoroughly good citizen when sober, but he was a little wild when drunk. Unfortunately, toward the end of his life he got to drinking very heavily. When, in 1905, John Burroughs and I visited the Yellowstone Park, poor Bill Jones, very much down in the world, was driving a team in Gardiner outside the park. I had looked forward to seeing him, and he was equally anxious to see me. He kept telling his cronies of our intimacy and of what we were going to do together, and then got drinking; and the result was that by the time I reached Gardiner he had to be carried out and left in the sage-brush. When I came out of the park, I sent on in advance to tell them to be sure to keep him sober, and they did so. But it was a rather sad interview. The old fellow had gone to pieces, and soon after I left he got lost in a blizzard and was dead when they found him.

Bill Jones was a gun-fighter and also a good man with his fists. On one occasion there was an election in town. There had been many threats that the party of disorder would import section hands from the neighboring railway stations to down our side. I did not reach Medora, the forlorn little cattle town which was our county seat, until the election was well under way. I then asked one of my friends if there had been any disorder. Bill Jones was standing by. "Disorder hell!" said my friend. "Bill Jones just stood there with one hand on his gun and the other pointing over toward the new jail whenever any man who didn't have a right to vote came near the polls. There was only one of them tried to vote, and Bill knocked him down. Lord!" added my friend, meditatively, "the way that man fell!" "Well," struck in Bill Jones, "if he hadn't fell I'd have walked round behind him to see what was propping him up!"

In the days when I lived on the ranch I usually spent most of the winter in the East, and when I returned in the early spring I was always interested in finding out what had happened since my departure. On one occasion I was met by Bill Jones and Sylvane Ferris, and in the course of our conversation they mentioned "the lunatic." This led to a question on my part, and Sylvane Ferris began the story: "Well, you see, he was on a train and he shot the newsboy. At first they weren't going to do anything to him, for they thought he just had it in for the newsboy. But then somebody said, 'Why, he's plumb crazy, and he's liable to shoot any of us!' and then they threw him off the train. It was here at Medora, and they asked if anybody would take care of him, and Bill Jones said he would, because he was the sheriff and the jail had two rooms, and he was living in one and would put the lunatic in the other." Here Bill Jones interrupted: "Yes, and more fool me! I wouldn't take charge of another lunatic if the whole county asked me. Why," (with the air of a man announcing an astounding discovery), "that lunatic didn't have his right senses! He wouldn't eat, till me and Snyder got him down on the shavings and made him eat." Snyder was a huge, happy-go-lucky, kind-hearted Pennsylvania Dutchman, and was Bill Jones's chief deputy. Bill continued: "You know, Snyder's soft-hearted, he is. Well, he'd think that lunatic looked peaked, and he'd take him out for an airing. Then the boys would get joshing him as to how much start he could give him over the prairie and catch him again." Apparently the amount of the start given the lunatic depended upon the amount of the bet to which the joshing led up. I asked Bill what he would have done if Snyder hadn't caught the lunatic. This was evidently a new idea, and he responded that Snyder always did catch him. "Well, but suppose he hadn't caught him?" "Well," said Bill Jones, "if Snyder hadn't caught the lunatic, I'd have whaled hell out of Snyder!"

Under these circumstances Snyder ran his best and always did catch the patient. It must not be gathered from this that the lunatic was badly treated. He was well treated. He became greatly attached to both Bill Jones and Snyder, and he objected strongly when, after the frontier theory of treatment of the insane had received a full trial, he was finally sent off to the territorial capital. It was merely that all the relations of life in that place and day were so managed as to give ample opportunity for the expression of individuality, whether in sheriff or ranchman. The local practical joker once attempted to have some fun at the expense of the lunatic, and Bill Jones described the result. "You know Bixby, don't you? Well," with deep disapproval, "Bixby thinks he is funny, he does. He'd come and he'd wake that lunatic up at night, and I'd have to get up and soothe him. I fixed Bixby all right, though. I fastened a rope on the latch, and next time Bixby came I let the lunatic out on him. He 'most bit Bixby's nose off. I learned Bixby!"

Bill Jones had been unconventional in other relations besides that of sheriff. He once casually mentioned to me that he had served on the police force of Bismarck, but he had left because he "beat the Mayor over the head with his gun one day." He added: "The Mayor, he didn't mind it, but the Superintendent of Police said he guessed I'd better resign." His feeling, obviously, was that the Superintendent of Police was a martinet, unfit to take large views of life.

It was while with Bill Jones that I first made acquaintance with Seth Bullock. Seth was at that time sheriff in the Black Hills district, and a man he had wanted—a horse thief—I finally got, I being at the time deputy sheriff two or three hundred miles to the north. The man went by a nickname which I will call "Crazy Steve"; a year or two afterwards I received a letter asking about him from his uncle, a thoroughly respectable man in a Western State; and later this uncle and I met at Washington when I was President and he a United States Senator. It was some time after "Steve's" capture that I went down to Deadwood on business, Sylvane Ferris and I on horseback, while Bill Jones drove the wagon. At a little town, Spearfish, I think, after crossing the last eighty or ninety miles of gumbo prairies, we met Seth Bullock. We

had had rather a rough trip, and had lain out for a fortnight, so I suppose we looked somewhat unkempt. Seth received us with rather distant courtesy at first, but unbent when he found out who we were, remarking, "You see, by your looks I thought you were some kind of a tin-horn gambling outfit, and that I might have to keep an eye on you!" He then inquired after the capture of "Steve"—with a little of the air of one sportsman when another has shot a quail that either might have claimed—"My bird, I believe?" Later Seth Bullock became, and has ever since remained, one of my staunchest and most valued friends. He served as Marshal for South Dakota under me as President. When, after the close of my term, I went to Africa, on getting back to Europe I cabled Seth Bullock to bring over Mrs. Bullock and meet me in London, which he did; by that time I felt that I just had to meet my own people, who spoke my neighborhood dialect.

When serving as deputy sheriff I was impressed with the advantage the officer of the law has over ordinary wrong-doers, provided he thoroughly knows his own mind. There are exceptional outlaws, men with a price on their heads and of remarkable prowess, who are utterly indifferent to taking life, and whose warfare against society is as open as that of a savage on the war-path. The law officer has no advantage whatever over these men save what his own prowess may—or may not—give him. Such a man was Billy the Kid, the notorious man-killer and desperado of New Mexico, who was himself finally slain by a friend of mine, Pat Garrett, whom, when I was President, I made collector of customs at El Paso. But the ordinary criminal, even when murderously inclined, feels just a moment's hesitation as to whether he cares to kill an officer of the law engaged in his duty. I took in more than one man who was probably a better man than I was with both rifle and revolver; but in each case I knew just what I wanted to do, and, like David Harum, I "did it first," whereas the fraction of a second that the other man hesitated put him in a position where it was useless for him to resist.

I owe more than I can ever express to the West, which of course means to the men and women I met in the West. There were a few people of bad type in my neighborhood—that would be true of every group of men, even in a theological seminary—but I could not speak with too great affection and respect of the great majority of my friends, the hard-working men and women who dwelt for a space of perhaps a hundred and fifty miles along the Little Missouri. I was always as welcome at their houses as they were at mine. Everybody worked, everybody was willing to help everybody else, and yet nobody asked any favors. The same thing was true of the people whom I got to know fifty miles east and fifty miles west of my own range, and of the men I met on the round-ups. They soon accepted me as a friend and fellow-worker who stood on an equal footing with them, and I believe the most of them have kept their feeling for me ever since. No guests were ever more welcome at the White House than these old friends of the cattle ranches and the cow camps—the men with whom I had ridden the long circle and eaten at the tail-board of a chuck-wagon—whenever they turned up at Washington during my Presidency. I remember one of them who appeared at Washington one day just before lunch, a huge, powerful man who, when I knew him, had been distinctly a fighting character. It happened that on that day another old friend, the British Ambassador, Mr. Bryce, was among those coming to lunch. Just before we went in I turned to my cow-puncher friend and said to him with great solemnity, "Remember, Jim, that if you shot at the feet of the British Ambassador to make him dance, it would be likely to cause international complications"; to which Jim responded with unaffected horror, "Why, Colonel, I shouldn't think of it, I shouldn't think of it!"

Not only did the men and women whom I met in the cow country quite unconsciously help me, by the insight which working and living with them enabled me to get into the mind and soul of the average American of the right type, but they helped me in another way. I made up my mind that the men were of just the kind whom it would be well to have with me if ever it became necessary to go to war. When the Spanish War came, I gave this thought practical realization.

Fortunately, Wister and Remington, with pen and pencil, have made these men live as long as our literature lives. I have sometimes been asked if Wister's "Virginian" is not overdrawn; why, one of the men I have mentioned in this chapter was in all essentials the Virginian in real life, not only in his force but in his charm. Half of the men I worked with or played with and half of the men who soldiered with me afterwards in my regiment might have walked out of Wister's stories or Remington's pictures.

There were bad characters in the Western country at that time, of course, and under the conditions of life they were probably more dangerous than they would have been elsewhere. I hardly ever had any difficulty, however. I never went into a saloon, and in the little hotels I kept out of the barroom unless, as sometimes happened, the barroom was the only room on the lower floor except the dining room. I always endeavored to keep out of a quarrel until self-respect forbade my making any further effort to avoid it, and I very rarely had even the semblance of trouble.

Of course amusing incidents occurred now and then. Usually these took place when I was hunting lost horses, for in hunting lost horses I was ordinarily alone, and occasionally had to travel a hundred or a hundred and fifty miles away from my own country. On one such occasion I reached a little cow town long after dark, stabled my horse in an empty outbuilding, and when I reached the hotel was informed in response to my request for a bed that I could have the last one left, as there was only one other man in it. The room to which I was shown contained two double beds; one contained two men fast asleep, and the other only one man, also asleep. This man proved to be a friend, one of the Bill Joneses whom I have previously mentioned. I undressed according to the fashion of the day and place, that is, I put my trousers, boots, chaps, and gun down beside the bed, and turned in. A couple of hours later I was awakened by the door being thrown open and a lantern flashed in my face, the light gleaming on the muzzle of a cocked .45. Another man said to the lantern-bearer, "It ain't him"; the next moment my bedfellow was covered with two guns, and addressed, "Now, Bill, don't make a fuss, but come along quiet." "I'm not thinking of making a fuss," said Bill. "That's right," was the answer, "we're your friends; we don't want to hurt you; we just want you to come along, you know why." And Bill pulled on his trousers and boots and walked out with them. Up to this time there had not been a sound from the other bed. Now a match was scratched, a candle lit, and one of the men in the other bed looked round the room. At this point I committed the breach of etiquette of asking questions. "I wonder why they took Bill," I said. There was no answer, and I repeated, "I wonder why they took Bill." "Well," said the man with the candle, dryly, "I reckon they wanted him," and with that he blew out the candle and conversation ceased. Later I discovered that Bill in a fit of playfulness had held up the Northern Pacific train at a nearby station by shooting at the feet of the conductor to make him dance. This was purely a joke on Bill's part, but the Northern Pacific people possessed a less robust sense of humor, and on their complaint the United States Marshal was sent after Bill, on the ground that by delaying the train he had interfered with the mails.

The only time I ever had serious trouble was at an even more primitive little hotel than the one in question. It was also on an occasion when I was out after lost horses. Below the hotel had merely a barroom, a dining room, and a lean-to kitchen; above was a loft with fifteen or twenty beds in it. It was late in the evening when I reached the place. I heard one or two shots in the barroom as I came up, and I disliked going in. But there was nowhere else to go, and it was a cold night. Inside the room were several men, who, including the bartender, were wearing the kind of smile worn by men who are making believe to like what they don't like. A shabby individual in a broad hat with a cocked gun in each hand was walking up and down the floor talking with strident profanity. He had evidently been shooting at the clock, which had two or three holes in its face.

He was not a "bad man" of the really dangerous type, the true man-killer type, but he was an objectionable creature, a would-be bad man, a bully who for the moment was having things all his own way. As soon as he saw me he hailed me as "Four eyes," in reference to my spectacles, and said, "Four eyes is going to treat." I joined in the laugh and got behind the stove and sat down, thinking to escape notice. He followed me, however, and though I tried to pass it off as a jest this merely made him more offensive, and he stood leaning over me, a gun in each hand, using very foul language. He was foolish to stand so near, and, moreover, his heels were close together, so that his position was unstable. Accordingly, in response to his reiterated command that I should set up the drinks, I said, "Well, if I've got to, I've got to," and rose, looking past him.

As I rose, I struck quick and hard with my right just to one side of the point of his jaw, hitting with my left as I straightened out, and then again with my right. He fired the guns, but I do not know whether this was merely a convulsive action of his hands or whether he was trying to shoot at me. When he went down he struck the corner of the bar with his head. It was not a case in which one could afford to take chances, and if he had moved I was about to drop on his ribs with my knees; but he was senseless. I took away his guns, and the other people in the room, who were now loud in their denunciation of him, hustled him out and put him in a shed. I got dinner as soon as possible, sitting in a corner of the dining-room away from the windows, and then went upstairs to bed where it was dark so that there would be no chance of any one shooting at me from the outside. However, nothing happened. When my assailant came to, he went down to the station and left on a freight.

There was one bit of frontier philosophy which I should like to see imitated in more advanced communities. Certain crimes of revolting baseness and cruelty were never forgiven. But in the case of ordinary offenses, the man who had served his term and who then tried to make good was given a fair chance; and of course this was equally true of the women. Everyone who has studied the subject at all is only too well aware that the world offsets the readiness with which it condones a crime for which a man escapes punishment, by its unforgiving relentlessness to the often far less guilty man who *is* punished, and who therefore has made his atonement. On the frontier, if the man honestly tried to behave himself there was generally a disposition to give him fair play and a decent show. Several of the men I knew and whom I particularly liked came in this class. There was one such man in my regiment, a man who had served a term for robbery under arms, and who had atoned for it by many years of fine performance of duty. I put him in a high official position, and no man under me rendered better service to the State, nor was there any man whom, as soldier, as civil officer, as citizen, and as friend, I valued and respected—and now value and respect—more.

Now I suppose some good people will gather from this that I favor men who commit crimes. I certainly do not favor them. I have not a particle of sympathy with the sentimentality—as I deem it, the mawkishness—which overflows with foolish pity for the criminal and cares not at all for the victim of the criminal. I am glad to see wrong-doers punished. The punishment is an absolute necessity from the standpoint of society; and I put the reformation of the criminal second to the welfare of society. But I do desire to see the man or woman who has paid the penalty and who wishes to reform given a helping hand—surely every one of us who knows his own heart must know that he too may stumble, and should be anxious to help his brother or sister who has stumbled. When the criminal has been punished, if he then shows a sincere desire to lead a decent and upright life, he should be given the chance, he should be helped and not hindered; and if he makes good, he should receive that respect from others which so often aids in creating self-respect—the most invaluable of all possessions.

Chapter XIV.

TOM HORN, CATTLE DETECTIVE

By Tom Horn

It's said Tom Horn set down his life's story—from which this sample is excerpted—to hurry the lagging time. That may be so, as the manuscript was written from a Laramie County jail cell in Cheyenne, Wyoming. The year was 1903, and Horn stood convicted of the murder of a fourteen-year-old boy (a thing he denied in court but, allegedly, he'd bragged about around town), had been sentenced to hang, and was awaiting the results of an appeal.

At the time of the killing Horn worked as a stock detective for the Swan Land & Cattle Company. His job was to hunt down rustlers, and to act generally as an enforcer for the company. More and more this had come to be a matter of ambush and assassination. Horn was known previously to have killed at least four men, and at the time of the trial, public opinion ran strongly against him. A great many people had had enough of big monied operations and their hired guns. There was also the age

233

of the victim. The case received much attention in the press, almost all of it against Horn. Lurid articles were written purporting to paint a true picture of this cowboy monster. Horn's brisk, truculent autobiography was his response. It's interesting that he doesn't even mention his arrest and trial. What does this mean?

Perhaps he thought the whole business was beneath contempt, or that his wealthy bosses would see him cleared. He might have defended himself, if only to restate the case he'd made at trial. Why not? Certainly he was stung by his portrayal in the press. But stung to silence? I believe Horn probably killed the boy. When Horn set down his story he had no idea that it would ever be published. He was writing for himself— and perhaps a few friends, who would know the truth. Why bother to lie to yourself?

It may or may not be a good idea to hurry along the lagging time—depending on how things turn out in the end. Eventually Horn's appeal was denied, and he was hanged, just a short time after he completed his story. This excerpt is the end of his account.

Early in April of 1887, some of the boys came down from the Pleasant Valley, where there was a big rustler war going on and the rustlers were getting the best of the game. I was tired of the mine and willing to go, and so away we went. Things were in a pretty bad condition. It was war to the knife between cow boys and rustlers, and there was a battle every time the two outfits ran together. A great many men were killed in the war. Old man Blevins and his three sons, three of the Grahams, a Bill Jacobs, Jim Payne, Al Rose, John Tewkesbury, Stolt, Scott, and a man named "Big Jeff" were hung on the Apache and Gila County line. Others were killed, but I do not remember their names now. I was the mediator, and was deputy sheriff under Bucky O'Neil, of Yavapai County, under Commodore Owens, of Apache County, and Glenn Reynolds, of Gila County. I was still a deputy for Reynolds a year later when he was killed by the Apache Kid, in 1888.

After this war in the Pleasant Valley I again went back to my mine and went to work, but it was too slow, and I could not stay at it. I was just getting ready to go to Mexico and was going down to clean out the spring at the mine one evening. I turned my saddle horse loose and let him graze up the canyon. After I got the spring cleaned out I went up the canyon to find my horse and saw a moccasin track covering the trail made by the rope my horse was dragging. That meant to go back, but I did not go back. I cut up the side of the mountain and found the trail where my horse had gone out. It ran into the trail of several more horses and they were all headed south. I went down to the ranch, got another horse and rode over to the Agency, about twenty miles, to get an Indian or two to go with me to see what I could learn about this bunch of Indians.

I got to the Agency about two o'clock in the morning and found that there had been an outbreak and mutiny among Sieber's police. It was like this: Sieber had raised a young Indian he always called "the Kid, "and now known as the "Apache Kid." This kid was the son of old Chief Toga-de-chuz, a San Carlos Apache. At a big dance on the Gila at old Toga-de-chuz's camp everybody got drunk and when morning came old Toga was found dead from a knife thrust. An old hunter belonging to another tribe of Indians and called "Rip," was accused of doing the job, but from what Sieber could learn, as he afterwards told me, everybody was too drunk to know how the thing did happen. The wound was given in a very skilful manner and as it split open old Toga's heart it was supposed to be given by one who knew where the heart lay.

Toga and old Rip had had a row over a girl about forty years before (they were both about sixty at this time), and Toga had gotten the best of the row and the girl to boot. Some say that an Indian will forget and forgive the same as a white man. I say no. There had elapsed forty years between the row and the time old Toga was killed.

Rip had not turned his horse loose in the evening before the killing, so it was supposed he had come there with the express intention of killing old Toga.

Anyway, the Kid was the oldest son of Toga-de-chuz and he must revenge the death of his father. He must, according to all Indian laws and customs, kill old Rip.

Sieber knew this and cautioned the Kid about doing anything to old Rip. The Kid never said a word to Sieber as to what he would do. The Kid was First Sergeant of the agency scouts. The Interior Department had given the agency over to the military and there were no more police, but scouts instead.

Shortly after this killing, Sieber and Captain Pierce, the agent, went up to Camp Apache to see about the distribution of some annuities to the Indians there, and the Kid, as First Sergeant of the scouts, was left in charge of the peace of the agency.

No sooner did Sieber and Captain Pierce get started than the Kid took five of his men and went over on the Aravaipo, where old Rip lived, and shot him. That evened up their account and the Kid went back to where his band was living; up above the agency. Sieber heard of this and he and Pierce immediately started to San Carlos.

When they got there, they found no one in command of the scouts; Sieber sent word up to the camp where the Kid's people lived to tell the Kid to come down. This he did escorted by the whole band of bucks.

Sieber, when they drew up in front of his tent, went out and spoke to the Kid and told him to get off his horse, and this the Kid did. Sieber then told him to take the arms of the other four or five men who had Government rifles. This also the Kid did. He took their guns and belts and then Sieber told him to take off his own belt and put down his gun and take the other deserters and go to the guard house.

Some of the bucks with the Kid (those who were not soldiers), said to the Kid to fight, and in a second they were at it—eleven bucks against Sieber alone. It did not make any particular difference to Sieber about being outnumbered. His rifle was in his tent. He jumped back and got it, and at the first shot he killed one Indian. All the other Indians fired at him as he came to the door of his tent, but only one bullet struck him; that hit him on the shin and shattered his leg all to pieces. He fell and the Indian ran away.

This was what Sieber told me when I got to the Agency. And then I knew it was the Kid who had my horse and outfit. Soldiers were already on his trail.

From where he had stolen my horse, he and his band crossed over the mountain to the Table Mountain district, and there stole a lot of Bill Atchley's saddle horses. A few miles further on they killed Bill Dihl, then headed on up through the San Pedro country, turned down the Sonoita River, and there they killed Mike Grace; then they were turned back north again by some of the cavalry that was after them.

They struck back north, and Lieutenant Johnson got after them about Pontaw, overtook them in the Rincon Mountains, and bad a fight, killing a couple of them, and put all the rest of them afoot. My horse was captured unwounded, and as the soldiers knew him, he was taken to the San Pedro and left there; they sent word to me, and eventually I got him, though he was pretty badly used up.

That was the way the Kid came to break out. He went back to the Reservation and later on he surrendered. He was tried for desertion, and given a long time by the Federal Courts, but was pardoned by President Cleveland, after having served a short term.

During the time the Kid and his associates were hiding around on the Reservation, previous to his first arrest, he and his men had killed a freighter, or he may have been only a whiskey peddler. Anyway, he was killed twelve miles above San Carlos, on the San Carlos River, by the Kid's outfit, and when the Kid returned to the Agency after he had done his short term, and had been pardoned by the President, he was re-arrested by the civil authorities of Oila County. Arizona, to be tried for the killing of this man at the Twelve Mile Point.

This was in the fall of 1888. I was deputy sheriff of Oila County at that time, and as it was a new county, Reynolds was the first sheriff. I was to be the interpreter at the Kid's trial, but on July 4th, of 1888, I had won the prize at Globe for tying down a steer, and there was a county rivalry among the cow boys all over the Territory as to who was the quickest man at that business. One Charley Meadows was making a big talk that he could beat me tying at the Territorial Fair, at Phoenix. Our boys concluded I must go to the fair and make a trial for the Territorial prize, and take it out of Meadows. I had known Meadows for years, and I thought I could beat him, and so did my friends.

The fair came off at the same time as did court in our new county, and since I could not very well be at both places, and, as they said, could not miss the fair, I was not at the trial.

While I was at Phoenix the trial came off and several of the Indians told him about the killing. (There were six on trial) and they were all sentenced to the penitentiary at Yuma, Arizona, for life. Reynolds and "Hunky Dory" Holmes started to take them to Yuma. There were the six Indians and a Mexican sent up for one year, for horse stealing. The Indians had their hands coupled together, so that there were three in each of the two bunches.

Where the stage road from Globe to Casa Grande (the railroad station on the Southern Pacific railroad) crosses the Gila River there is a very steep sand wash, up which the stage road winds. Going up this Reynolds took his prisoners out and they were all walking behind the stage. The Mexican was handcuffed and inside the stage. Holmes got ahead of Reynolds some little distance. Holmes had three Indians and Reynolds had three.

Just as Holmes turned a short bend in the road and got behind a point of rocks and out of sight of Reynolds, at a given signal, each bunch of prisoners turned on their guard and grappled with them. Holmes was soon down and they killed him. The three that had tackled Reynolds were not doing so well, but the ones that had killed Holmes got his ride and pistol and went to the aid of the ones grappling Reynolds. These three were holding his arms so he could not get his gun. The ones that came up killed him, took his keys, unlocked the cuffs and they were free.

Gene Livingston was driving the stage, and he looked around the side of the stage to see what the shooting was about. One of the desperadoes took a shot at him, striking him over the eye, and down he came. The Kid and his men then took the stage horses and tried to ride them, but there was only one of the four that they could ride.

The Kid remained an outlaw after that, till he died a couple of years ago of consumption. The Mexican, after the Kid and his men left the stage (they had taken off his handcuffs), struck out for Florence and notified the authorities. The driver was only stunned by the shot over the eye and is today a resident and business man of Globe.

Had I not been urged to go to the fair at Phoenix, this would never have happened, as the Kid and his comrades just walked along and put up the job in their own language, which no one there could understand but themselves. Had I not gone to the fair I would have been with Reynolds, and could have understood what they said and it would never have happened. I won the prize roping at the fair, but it was at a very heavy cost.

In the winter I again went home and in the following spring I went to work on my mine. Worked along pretty steady on it for a year, and in 1890 we sold it to a party of New Yorkers. We got $8,000 for it.

We were negotiating for this sale, and at the same time the Pinkerton National Detective Agency at Denver, Colorado, was writing to me to get me to come to Denver and go to work for them. I thought it would be a good thing to do, and as soon as all the arrangements for the sale of the mine were made I came to Denver and was initiated into the mysteries of the Pinkerton institution.

My work for them was not the kind that exactly suited my disposition; too tame for me. There were a good many Instructions and a good deal of talk given to the operative regarding the things to do and the things that had been done.

James McFarland, the superintendent, asked me what I would do if I was put on a train robbery ease. I told him if I had a good man with me I could catch up to them.

Well, on the last night of August, that year, at about midnight, a train was robbed on the Denver & Rio Grande Railway between Cotopaxi and Texas Creek. I was sent out there, and was told that C. W. Shores would be along in a day or so. He came on time and asked me how I was getting on. I told him

I had struck the trail, but there were so many men scouring the country that I, myself, was being held up all the time; that I had been arrested twice in two days and taken in to Salida to be identified!

Eventually all the sheriff's posses quit and then Mr. W. A. Pinkerton and Mr. McFarland told Shores and me to go at 'em. We took up the trail where I had left it several days before and we never left it till we got the robbers.

They had crossed the Sangre de Cristo range, come down by the Villa Grove iron mines, and crossed back to the east side of the Sangre de Oristos at Mosca pass, then on down through the Huerfano Canon, out by Cucharas, thence down east of Trinidad. They had dropped into Clayton, N. M., and got into a shooting scrape there in a gin mill. They then turned east again toward the "Neutral Strip" and close to Beaver City, then across into the "Pan Handle" by a place in Texas called Ochiltree, the county seat of Ochiltree county. They then headed toward the Indian Territory, and crossed into it below Canadian City. They then swung in on the head of the Washita River in the Territory, and kept down this river for a long distance.

We finally saw that we were getting close to them, as we got in the neighborhood of Paul's Valley. At Washita station we located one of them in the house of a man by the name of Wolfe. The robber's name was Burt Curtis. Shores took this one and came on back to Denver, leaving me to get the other one if ever he came back to Wolfe's.

After several days of waiting on my part, he did come back, and as he came riding up to the house I stepped out and told him someone had come. He was "Peg Leg" Watson, and considered by everyone in Colorado as a very desperate character. I had no trouble with him.

We had an idea that Joe McCoy, also, was in the robbery, but "Peg" said he was not, and gave me information enough so that I located him. He was wanted very badly by the sheriff of Fremont County, Colorado, for a murder scrape. He and his father had been tried previous to this for murder, had been found guilty and were remanded to jail to wait sentence, but before Joe was sentenced he had escaped. The old man McCoy got a new trial, and at the new trial was sentenced to eighteen years in the Canon City, Colorado, penitentiary.

When I captured my man, got to a telegraph station and wired Mr. McFarland that I had the notorious "Peg," the superintendent wired back: "Good! Old man McCoy got eighteen years today!" This train had been robbed in order to get money to carry McCoy's case up to the Supreme Court, or rather to pay the attorneys (Macons & Son), who had carried the case up.

Later on I told Mr. McFarland that T could locate Joe McCoy and he communicated with Stewart, the sheriff, who came to Denver and made arrangements for me to go with him and try to get McCoy.

We left Denver on Christmas Eve and went direct to Rifle, from there to Meeker and on down White River. When we got to where McCoy had been we learned that he had gone to Ashley, in Utah, for the Christmas festivities. We pushed on over there, reaching the town late at night, and could not locate our man. Next morning I learned where he got his meals and as he went in to get his breakfast I followed him in and arrested him. He had a big Colt's pistol, but did not shoot me. We took him out by Fort Duchesne, Utah, and caught the D. & R. G. train at Price station.

The judge under whom he had been tried had left the bench when McCoy finally was landed back in jail, and it would have required a new trial before he could be sentenced by another judge; he consented to plead guilty to involuntary manslaughter, and took six years in the Canon City pen. He was pardoned out in three years, I believe.

Peg Leg Watson and Hurt Curtis were tried in the United States court for robbing the United States mails on the highway, and were sentenced for life in the Detroit federal prison. In robbing the train they had first made the fireman break into the mail compartment of the compartment car. They then saw their mistake, and did not even take the amount of a one-cent postage stamp, but went and made the fireman break into the rear compartment, where they found the express matter and took it. But the authorities proved that it was mail robbery and their sentence was life.

While Pinkerton's is one of the greatest institutions of the kind in existence, I never did like the work, so I left them in 1894.

I then came to Wyoming and went to work for the Swan Land and Cattle Company, since which time everybody else has been more familiar with my life and business than I have been myself.

And I think that since my coming here the yellow journal reporters are better equipped to write my history than am I, myself!

Respectfully,
TOM HORN

CHAPTER XV.

EXPLOITS OF THE JAMES GANG

By J. A. Dacus

They used to say that the James Boys and the Younger Brothers might kill men who attempted to impose upon them, but they would not rob or steal. Those who rob men of life must be the greatest criminals, and the lesser crimes are included in the greater. The career they had chosen required the service which money alone can render. These men had need for money which their legitimate resources were inadequate to supply. Those who have taken many lives will not hesitate long to take a few dollars when their necessities require it. Such are the laws which govern human actions.

Long before many of the very respectable citizens of Clay, Clinton, and Jackson counties believed it, the sons of the excellent minister whom they had known were the most unscrupulous and daring highwaymen who had ever followed the roads on this continent. They were bold, but cautious; skilled in the school of cunning; trained in the art of killing; shrewd in planning; and swift in the execution of their designs.

They seldom attempted a robbery except in out-of-the-way places where the presence of robbers was not expected. Nor did they ever attempt robberies a second time at the same place. Their plan was to strike unexpected blows. This week they would rob a train at Gad's Hill, next week at Muncie, Kansas; again, they would arrest a stage on the Malvern and Hot Springs road, and then again they would flag a train at Big Springs, Wyoming Territory, a thousand miles from the scene of their last exploit.

It was a gray, raw day in January, 1874, when the regular stage running from Malvern, on the St. Louis, Iron Mountain & Southern Railway, to Hot Springs, pulled out from the little town. This is a narrow dell, shut in by abrupt hills, clad with a dense forest of pine and tangled underbrush and evergreen vines. At this particular place the valley widens, and there is a beautiful farm and lovely grounds bordering the roadside on the east and north side of the stream. West and south the deep, tangled forest crowns the hills, which rise to a great height. Here is a favorite halting place for travelers along that way. The clear waters of the Golpha afford refreshing draughts to the wearied teams.

It was a gray, raw morning in January. The long drive from Malvern over the stony roads inclined the passengers, as well as the horses, to rest. That particular Thursday morning the drivers had stopped, as usual, directly opposite the Gains residence, which is about two hundred yards from the road, toward the northeast. The spot is about five miles southeast from Hot Springs. A little beyond the stopping place the road crosses the stream at a ford. Beyond the creek the country is very rugged, and covered with forest trees. And in those trees a band of robbers were crouched, waiting the approach of the stage. The unsuspecting pilgrims were soon moving on, inwardly congratulating themselves on the near termination of their fatiguing journey.

The stage had proceeded well into the wood on the Hot Springs side of the Golpha, perhaps half a mile from "the watering place," when a strong, emphatic voice called out from the borders of the brush: "Stop! d—n you, or I'll blow your head off!" Thus commanded, of course the driver of the stage brought his team to a standstill. The passengers naturally threw aside the flaps of the vehicles and thrust out their heads to ascertain what the strange proceedings meant. They saw at once. Cocked revolvers yawned before them, and stern,

harsh voices exclaimed in chorus, "D—n you, tumble out!" "Certainly, under the circumstances, we will do so with alacrity," replied one of the passengers, a Mr. Charles Moore.

"Raise your hands, you d—d———." Of course every passenger promptly obeyed the order. One passenger, a rheumatic invalid, alone, was left undisturbed. Then the leader cried out:

"Come! Be quick, form a circle here!"

The order was obeyed. Then two of the robbers, one of whom was armed with a double-barrel shotgun and the other with a navy repeater, mounted guard over the prisoners, and made many sinister remarks, doubtless intended to be jocose, but which kept the prisoners in a tremor of apprehension all the while.

Then two of the brigands proceeded to examine the effects and pockets of the passengers.

It was a very good morning's work, and the bandits were so well pleased that they were inclined to indulge in a sort of grim facetiousness. One of them unharnessed the best stage horse, saddled him and mounted him, and after trying his gait by riding up and down the road a few times, called out:

"Boys, I reckon he'll do!"

Another one of the band went to each passenger as he stood in the circle. John Dietrich was the first to pass through the ordeal of cross-examination.

"Where are you from?"

"Little Rock," replied Dietrich.

"Ah, ha!"

"Yes, have a boot and shoe store there," remarked Dietrich.

"You'd better be there attending to it," was the observation of the chief of the bandits.

"Are there any Southern men here?"

"I am," replied Mr. Crump and three others.

"Any who served in the army?"

"I did," said Crump.

The leader then asked him what regiment he belonged to, and what part of the country he had served in. The answers were satisfactory, and then the robber handed Crump his watch and money, remarking as he did so:

"Well, you look like an honest fellow. I guess you're all right. We don't want to rob Confederate soldiers. But the d—d Yankees have driven us all into outlawry, and we will make them pay for it yet."

Mr. Taylor, of Lowell, Mass., was examined.

"Where are you from?"

"St. Louis."

"Yes, and d—n your soul, you are a reporter for the St. Louis *Democrat*, the vilest sheet in the land. Go to Hot Springs and send the dirty concern a telegram about this affair, and give them my compliments, will you?"

Then Governor Burbank felt encouraged to ask a favor of them.

"Will you please return me my papers?" asked the Governor. "They are valuable to me, but I am sure you can make no use of them."

"We'll see," said the leader, sententiously, and took the packet and kneeled down to examine them.

In a few moments he took up a paper with an official seal, that excited his ire, and before he paused to examine it sufficiently to enable him to determine its character, he reached the conclusion that the bearer was a detective, a class which he held in the utmost hatred.

"Boys, I believe he's a detective—shoot him, at once!" was the sententious command. In an instant Governor Burbank was covered by three ready cocked dragoon pistols. The ex-Governor was on the border of time.

"Stop!" cried the robber, "I reckon it's all right. Here, take your papers."

And the ex-Governor felt that a mighty load had suddenly been lifted from him, and that a dark cloud, which but a moment before had enshrouded the world in the deepest gloom, had drifted away, allowing the bright sun to shine out on the scenes of time.

The passenger from Syracuse asked for the return of $5, to enable him to telegraph home for assistance.

The chief looked at him rather sternly for a few moments, and said:

"So, you have no friends nor money. You had better go and die. Your death would be no loss to yourself or the country. You'll get nothing back, at any rate."

All this while one of the robbers, said to have been James Younger, held a double-barrel shotgun cocked in his hand, which he pointed ever and anon at Mr. Taylor, the supposed *Democrat* reporter, making such cheerful remarks as these:

"Boys, I'll bet a hundred dollar bill I can shoot his hat off his head and not touch a hair on it." And the others would respond with a banter of a very uncomfortable character, while the facetious bandit went on: "Now, wouldn't that button on his coat make a good mark. I'll bet a dollar I can clip it off and not cut the coat!" With such grim jests did he amuse himself and torment the captive.

Having thoroughly accomplished their work, the bandits made the drivers hitch up their teams and drive away. The whole transaction was completed in less than ten minutes. The robbers did not linger. In a few minutes they scattered through the brush. Some "struck out," as they expressed it, for the Nation, another for Texas, and one for Louisiana.

Of course, denials of complicity on the part of the Jameses in this affair were at once entered by their friends. But it has since been ascertained that the party who did the deed consisted of Frank and Jesse James, Coleman and James Younger, and Clell Miller, one of the associates of the daring outlaws.

* * *

During the morning of January 31, at the hour of 9:30, the St. Louis and Texas express train, with a goodly number of passengers, and the mails and valuable express freight, departed from the Plum street depot in St. Louis, bound for Texas, via the St. Louis, Iron Mountain, and Southern railroad. Mr. C. A. Alford was the conductor in charge of the train when it departed, and when the event which we are about to describe occurred.

The 31st of January, 1874, was a dreary, winter day. The cold gray clouds veiled the sky, and no ray of sunlight filtered through the wintry pall.

The day wore away, wearily enough, with the passengers on Mr. Alford's train. They had not yet been together a sufficient length of time to assimilate, and each one was left to his, or her, own device for amusement or entertainment. Slowly the hours passed away. The landscape was cold, dreary and forbidding; the winds came blowing from the north with a chill in their breath that made the passengers think longingly of "sweet home." Iron Mountain, and Pilot Knob, and Shepherd's Mountain, and the beautiful valley of Arcadia, in their winter dress, wore anything but a pleasing aspect. But in fact, it was a comfortless sort of day, which made the passengers feel anything but merry.

Nightfall was approaching. Already the thick atmosphere was becoming somber in hue, and it was evident the curtains of darkness were falling over the earth.

By this time it was about 5:30 in the afternoon. The train was approaching the little station dignified by the name of Gadshill. As the train drew near, the engineer saw the red flag displayed, and whistled "down brakes."

Before proceeding to relate what happened to the train and the passengers on it, we shall state what had happened at Gadshill before the train came.

About half-past three o'clock that afternoon, a party of seven men, splendidly mounted and armed to the teeth, rode to the station, secured the agent, then took in a blacksmith, and afterwards all the citizens and two or three countrymen, and one lad, who were waiting for the arrival of the train. Among the persons so detained was the son of Dr. Rock, at that time Representative in the Legislature from Wayne county. The captives were taken to the little station-house and confined there, under the surveillance of one of the armed robbers. Then the bandits set about completing their arrangements for executing the work which they had come to perform. The signal flag was displayed on the track and the lower end of the switch was opened, so that the train would be ditched if it attempted to pass. Then the bandits waited for their prey.

In due time the train came dashing down the road. The engineer saw the flag and gave the signal for stopping. Mr. Alford, the conductor, was ready to step upon the little platform as soon as the train came alongside. The robbers did not show themselves until the cars were at the station. No sooner had the train come to a full halt than Mr. Alford stepped off to the platform. He was instantly confronted by the muzzle of a pistol and greeted with the salutation:

"Give me your money and your watch, d—n your soul! Quick!"

Mr. Alford had no alternative. He gave up his pocketbook containing fifty dollars in money, and an elegant gold watch.

"Get in there!" they commanded, and Mr. Alford obeyed.

While this was going on, one of the brigands had covered the engineer with a revolver, and compelled him to leave his cab. Meanwhile, part of the band occupied the platforms at the ends of the passenger coaches, while two of them went through the train with a revolver in one hand and commanded the passengers to give up their money. Of course the defenseless travelers yielded their change to the uttermost farthing into the hands of the robbers.

The robbers made a clean sweep, taking money, watches, and jewelry from all. After having effectually stripped the passengers of worldly wealth, the robbers proceeded to the express car, broke open the safe, and secured the contents. The mail bags were next cut open and their contents rifled of everything of value. The whole amount of money secured by the robbers was somewhere between eight and ten thousand dollars. After completing their work the bandits went to Mr. Alford and remarked that as he was conductor he needed a watch, and they gave him back his timekeeper.

When they had satisfied themselves that there was no more plunder to be gained, they released the conductor and engineer, and told them to draw out at once.

As the robbers, whose part of the business it was to relieve the passengers of their spare cash, passed through the cars, they asked each one of the gentlemen passengers his name. One of the victims, a Mr. Newell, asked the brigands,

"What do you want to know that for?"

"D—n you, out with your name, and ask questions afterward!" was the profane reply.

"Well, my name is Newell, and here's my money, and now I want to know why you ask me for my name?" said Mr. Newell, with an attempt at pleasantry, fortified by a sort of grim smile.

"You seem to be a sort of jolly coon, anyhow," said the robber, "and I'll gratify you. That old scoundrel, Pinkerton, is on this train, or was to have been on it, and we want to get him, so that we can cut out his heart and roast it."

During the time they were in the cars among the passengers, they mentioned the name of Pinkerton many times, and exhibited the most intense hatred of the distinguished detective. It was very fortunate for Mr. Allan Pinkerton that he was not a passenger on the train.

This circumstance is confirmatory of the evidence that Jesse and Frank James were leaders in the Gadshill affair. They, for years, have cherished the most bitter animosity toward the detective, and the very mention of his name was sufficient to render them almost frantic with rage.

The citizens were released, and the robbers mounted their horses and rode away in the gathering darkness, over the forest-crowned hills to the west. Some of the features of this bold robbery were ludicrous in the extreme. The trepidation of the passengers made the job a quick one, because they were ready on demand to give up everything to the freebooters. One passenger complained at the hardship, and the following dialogue ensued:

"Give me your money, watch, and jewelry, you blamed cur! Quick!"

"Now, please, I—"

"Dry up, d—n you, and shell out!" And the robber thrust a pistol against his temple.

"Oh, yes! Excuse m-m-me, p-p-p-please, d-don't shoot. Here's a-all I've g-got in t-t-the world." And the poor fellow, all tremblingly, handed up his wealth.

"I'm a good mind to shoot you, anyhow," remarked the robber, "for being so white livered."

At this the alarmed traveler crouched down behind a seat.

It was nightfall when the robbers rode away. Gadshill is in the midst of a wilderness country. There are but few settlements among the hills, and it was impossible to organize an effective posse at once for pursuit. At Piedmont, on the arrival of the train, the news was telegraphed to St. Louis and Little Rock. The citizens of that vicinity were aroused, and before midnight a well armed posse of a dozen men were riding over the hills westward in pursuit.

But the robbers, who were all mounted on blooded horses, rode swiftly away. Before the dawn of day they were sixty miles from the scene of the crime. They called at the residence of a widow lady named Cook, one mile above Carpentersville, on the Current river, to obtain a breakfast. There were but five of them in the party, and these were each armed with a pair of pistols and a repeating rifle. They continued on, and passed Mr. Payne's on the Big Piney, in Texas county, and went to the house of the Hon. Mr. Mason, then a member of the State Legislature, and who was at that time absent attending its session, and demanded food and lodging from Mrs. Mason. They remained there all night, and proceeded westward in the morning. The same day that the five men took breakfast with Mrs. Cook, a dozen pursuers from Gadshill and Piedmont arrived at the same place, having tracked them sixty miles.

* * *

The bold act of brigandage at Gadshill aroused the whole country. The outlaws had become formidable. Missouri and Arkansas were alike interested, and the citizens of both states were ready to make personal sacrifices to aid in the capture of such daring brigands. But who were the robbers? Some said at once that it was the Jameses and the Youngers and their associates. Geo. W. Shepherd, one of Quantrell's most daring Guerrillas in Missouri, and one of those who separated from him when he went to Kentucky, was an intimate friend of the Jameses in the old Guerrilla times. After the war Shepherd emigrated to Kentucky and married at Chaplin, Nelson county, where he settled down. After Russellville, circumstances pointed to him as one of the persons implicated in the robbery. He was arrested, carried to Logan county and tried. The proof was of such a character that he was found guilty of aiding and abetting the robbers, and was sentenced to the penitentiary for a term of three years. At the expiration of his sentence he returned to Chaplin and learned that during his incarceration his wife had obtained a divorce and married another man. Shepherd had paid $600 on the house and lot which he found his ex-wife and husband occupying. But he left them there and took his departure from Kentucky. At the time of the Gadshill affair he was somewhere in Missouri. But there is not a particle of evidence to connect him with the robbery.

Bradley Collins was a noted desperado in those days, who figured in Texas and the Indian Territory as one of the worst outlaws in the business. He also rode at times with the Jameses and the Youngers. John Chunk was another daring outlaw who infested Texas and the Indian Territory, and often came into Missouri and co-operated with the brigands of that state.

Sid Wallace, afterwards hanged at Clarksville, Arkansas, was another noted outlaw between the years 1866 and 1874. He, too, was a "friend" of the Jameses. Cal Carter, Jim Reed, John Wes. Hardin, Sam Bass, Bill Longley, Tom Taylor and Jim Clark, all notorious in Texas and the Nation, often joined the Missouri outlaws and hunted with them. Indeed, it appears that there was a regularly organized band of brigands ramifying through the states of Missouri, Kansas, Colorado, Arkansas, the Indian Territory and Texas. This banditti was composed of the most desperate and daring men who had ever placed themselves beyond the pale of the law in this country.

Whatever doubts might once have existed concerning the personality of the bandits of Gadshill, they have all vanished in the light of subsequent events. Jesse and Frank James, some of the Youngers and their associates, were undoubtedly the men who rode to Gadshill.

Governor Woodson, of Missouri, offered a reward to the full extent of the law's provisions. Governor Baxter, of Arkansas, communicated to Governor Woodson his desire to aid in the capture of the outlaws, and also offered a reward. The express company offered a heavy reward for the capture of the bandits, and the United States authorities took an active interest in the movement set on foot to break up the formidable banditti. Stimulated by the prospect of gain, the detectives all over the country became active in the pursuit. The citizens, too, were on the move, and it seemed that the auguries all pointed to a speedy annihilation of this formidable gang.

Meanwhile another outrage was committed almost on the line of retreat from Gadshill, which still further agitated the public mind.

During the afternoon of the 11th of February, 1874, five men, splendidly mounted and well armed, rode into the town of Bentonville, Benton county, Arkansas. Their entrance was quiet. They rode to the store of Craig & Son; dismounted and entered the store; made prisoners of the proprietors and clerks at the muzzle of pistols, and proceeded to rifle the cash box. Fortunately for the firm of Craig & Son, they had made a deposit that day and the robbers only obtained about one hundred and fifty dollars in money. They helped themselves to about one hundred dollars' worth of goods; warned the proprietors and clerks not to give the alarm until they had passed out of town; went out; mounted their horses and rode away in the most nonchalant manner. In a saloon adjacent, there were more than twenty men who were uninformed as to what was taking place in the store of Messrs. Craig & Son, until after the robbers had departed. Pursuit was made, but the bandits escaped.

The weeks following the Gadshill outrage were busy ones with the detectives. A carefully planned campaign against the marauders was at once instituted and prosecuted with great vigor. Allan Pinkerton was employed by the express company to hunt the robbers down. The United States Government ordered the Secret Service force into the field, and the police and constabulary forces of Missouri and Arkansas, under orders from the Governors of the respective states, were acting in concert with the forces of detectives called into service by the General Government and the express company.

The brigands were successfully tracked through the wilds of southern Missouri, and their trail led into the hill country of St. Clair county, and across Jackson county on beyond the Missouri river. No doubt was left upon the minds of the man-hunters as to the personality of the Gadshill robbers. The James Boys and some of the Youngers were certainly engaged in it. The Youngers, at least John and Jim, had returned to Roscoe, St. Clair county, "flush with cash." The detectives were on their tracks. To the force was added Ed. B. Daniels, a courageous young man of Osceola, who was thoroughly acquainted with the country. The detective force in St. Clair county was under the direction of one of Allan Pinkerton's picked men, Captain W. J. Allen, whose real name was Lull. With him was a St. Louis "fly cop," well known, and distinguished for his shrewdness and daring, who for the time had assumed the name of Wright. Daniels was extremely serviceable as a guide.

One morning, when near the residence of Theodoric Snuffer, a short distance from Roscoe, these three men were suddenly surprised by John and James

Younger, who rode up behind them in the road. They were at Snuffer's house, and saw the detectives pass, and started out with the avowed purpose of capturing them. Approaching the three men in the rear, they raised their double-barrel shot-guns, and with an oath commanded them to hold up their hands and drop their pistols. Taken thus, at a disadvantage, the detectives complied, and dropped their belts of pistols in the road. James Younger dismounted to secure them, while John remained on horseback with a double-barrel gun covering them. For a moment he lowered his gun. That moment was fatal. Captain Lull drew a concealed Smith & Wesson revolver from his bosom, and fired. The ball took effect in John Younger's neck, severing the left jugular vein. In the very agonies of death, as he fell from his horse to die, John Younger raised a pistol and fired, the ball taking effect in the left arm and side of Captain Lull. Two more shots were fired, probably by James Younger, before Allen, or rather Lull, fell. James Younger then commenced firing at Ed. B. Daniels. That gentleman also had a concealed pistol, returned the fire, and inflicted a slight flesh wound on the person of James Younger. But his fate was sealed. A fatal bullet crashed through the left side of the neck, and Daniels fell, and soon afterward expired. This tragedy excited and alarmed the whole country. It was no longer possible for James Younger to remain in the country. He took the pistols which his dead brother, John, had worn, and departed for the house of a friend in Boone county, Arkansas, where he was soon joined by Cole and Bob.

Wright, who was riding a short distance in advance of Captain Lull and Ed. Daniels, hearing the summons of the Younger Brothers, turned, and at a glance saw the situation, and, putting spurs to his horse, dashed away. Although he was fired upon and pursued a short distance by James Younger, he managed to escape unharmed, aided as he was by a very fleet horse.

The hunters for the Jameses met with no better luck. One of the darkest tragedies which ever disgraced the state of Missouri followed the efforts of the detectives to capture the shrewdest and most daring outlaws who have yet appeared in this country. There is an air of mystery about this terrible episode which makes it all the more thrilling.

* * *

The James Boys were believed to have been the projectors and leaders of the Gadshill enterprise. Soon after that event they returned to Clay county.

Traces of their trail through Southern Missouri were soon discovered. The description given of two of the five travelers who took breakfast at Mrs. Cook's on Current river, and lodged at Mr. Mason's house in Texas county, answered well for Frank and Jesse James. The detectives caught at every clue. The James Boys were at Gadshill beyond a doubt. And so the brigand hunters passed into Clay county.

Meanwhile the James Boys and other members of the gang were resting in the vicinity of Kearney, in Clay county, at the residence of Dr. Samuels. Among those known to have been there were Jim Cummings and Clell Miller, Jim Anderson, a brother of Bill Anderson, of Centralia notoriety, and Bradley Collins, a Texas desperado. The sheriff of Clay county thought Arthur McCoy was probably at that time with the Jameses. On the 9th day of March, Jesse James spent a portion of the day in Kearney. The gang had several horses shod a few days before at a country blacksmith shop in that vicinity.

Wednesday, March 10, 1874, arrived at Liberty, the county seat of Clay county, Missouri, J. W. Whicher, from what place it mattered not to the citizens of Liberty. This man was in the very vigor of a matured manhood. He was just twenty-six years of age, lately married to an estimable and accomplished young lady, a resident of Iowa City.

Whicher was intelligent, shrewd, and daring. He was selected by his chief, Allan Pinkerton, who is acknowledged as a consummate judge of human nature, as the fittest instrument to execute the most dangerous enterprise which he had ever yet undertaken.

Immediately on arriving at Liberty, Whicher called at the Commercial Savings Bank to see Mr. Adkins, its president. To him he made known his errand into that section. At the same time he deposited in the bank some money and papers. Mr. Adkins was not able to give Whicher all the information which he desired, and sent him to Col. O. P. Moss, ex-sheriff of Clay county, for further information.

When he opened his plans to Moss, that gentleman advised him not to go. He gave him a terrible account of the prowess of the desperadoes; told him of their shrewdness and of their merciless nature when excited by the presence of an enemy, and warned him that he need not hope to secure such wary men by stratagem. Col. Moss was earnest in his efforts to dissuade Whicher from making the attempt.

But it was of no avail. Whicher had received what he regarded as positive evidence that the Jameses were the leaders of the Gadshill bandits, and, further, that they were now at home, near Kearney. Stimulated by the hope of "catching his game" and securing the large rewards, Whicher, who seems to have been destitute of any sense of fear, made his arrangements to go that very evening to the Jameses' place of retreat. Disguised in the garb of a farm laborer, with an old carpet bag swung on a stick, Whicher took the evening train for Kearney, and there made inquiries for work on a farm. He did not tarry long at the station, but soon started out toward the Samuels place.

There was a friend of the Jameses in Liberty that day—a fellow named Jim Latche, who had been expelled from Texas on account of his worthless qualities as a citizen and dangerous attributes as a criminal. Latche had met the James Boys, and had made a raid with them, on one occasion, down in Texas. He had been resting at their retreat for a few days, and was probably on a scout for them that day. At any rate, he was in Liberty when Whicher arrived. He observed his movements, because Whicher was a stranger; saw him go to the bank and make a deposit; waited while he conferred with Mr. Adkins, and then, tracked him to Col. Moss' office. He came to the conclusion that Whicher was a detective; and when afterward he saw that the detective had changed his clothes, he was convinced that he was right. Latche hastened away to give a report of what he had heard and observed.

When Whicher arrived at Kearney the Jameses knew of it, and suspected the truth concerning his mission. It was in the evening. Jim Anderson, Jesse James and Bradley Collins were in waiting on the roadside, about half a mile from the Samuels residence. Soon after Whicher came along. He was carrying a carpet-sack. Jesse James came out of their concealment alone, and met Whicher in the road.

"Good evening, sir," said Whicher.

"Where in h—ll are *you* going?" responded the other.

"Well, it's a rude response, but I will not answer as rudely again. I am seeking work. Can you tell me where I can get some work on a farm?"

"No, not much, you don't want any, either, you d—d thief. Old Pinkerton has already given you a job that will last you as long as you live, I reckon."

And Jesse laughed a cold, hard laugh that meant death. Of course Whicher was helpless, for the other had him under cover of a pistol from the moment he

came in sight. But Whicher was dauntless and wary, and, without exhibiting the least trepidation, he said:

"Who do you take me to be? What have I to do with Pinkerton or his business? I am a stranger in the country and want something to do. I don't see why you should keep that pistol pointed at me. I don't know you, and have never done you any wrong."

"Oh, d—n it, you are the kind of a dog that sneaks up and bites, are you? You will carry in the James Boys, will you? You are a nice sneaking cur, ain't you? Want work, do you? What say you, my sneak? Eh?"

The tantalizing manner of Jesse James did not disconcert the detective. He answered these taunts with perfect coolness:

"I don't understand you, sir. I am no cur, and know nothing of the James Boys. I addressed you politely, and you did not return the same. I said I wanted some employment, and you taunt me for it. I must bid you good evening."

With this, Whicher made a step forward. His progress was arrested by the harsh voice of Jesse James.

"You shall die if you move out of your tracks! Keep up your hands!"

Whicher realized by this time that his chance of escape was small, for he knew that Jesse James stood before him, and he had quickly made up his mind that he would sell his life dearly. He was cool, active, and expert with the pistol; his right hand was almost involuntarily seeking to grasp his weapon. But Jesse James evidently had him at a great disadvantage.

Instantly realizing this, he changed his purpose.

"Well, this is a singular adventure, I declare. Now, why you should make such a mistake concerning me is more than I can imagine. You are surely making sport of me. I tell you I know nothing of the persons of whom you speak, and why should you interrupt me? Let me go on, for I must find a place to stop tonight, anyhow."

Jesse James laughed outright. "What," said he, "were you doing at Liberty today? Why did you deposit money in the bank? What business did you have with Adkins and Moss? Where are the clothes you wore? Plotting to capture the James Boys, eh?" and Jesse laughed aloud, and Jim Anderson and Fox, another confederate of the Boys, came from their concealment, with pistols in hand. Poor Whicher saw this, and for the first time he fully realized the helplessness of his position.

Jesse James said, in a cold, dry tone:

"Young man, we want to hear no more from you. We know you. Move but a finger and you die now. Boys," he said, addressing Anderson and Fox, "I don't think it best to do the job here. It wouldn't take long, but for certain reasons I don't think this is the place. Shall we cross the river tonight?" The others answered they would.

All this time Whicher had stood still; not a muscle moved, and not a single wave of pallor had covered his features. He knew what they meant by "the job," and made up his mind to improve any incident, however slight, to have revenge on his murderers.

But there were no favorable incidents for him. He had been tried and condemned in a court from which he could not appeal. At what time the sentence would be executed he could not tell.

"Boys, relieve him of his burden and weapons," said Jesse James.

Quick as thought, Whicher's hand was thrust into the bosom of his coat. It was too late. Fox and Anderson sprang upon him, while Jesse James placed the muzzle of his pistol against his temple. To struggle was useless. He was compelled to yield, for just then Brad Collins and Jim Latche joined the others. The case of the detective was hopeless. In an instant they had disarmed him; he had brought only one Smith & Wesson pistol. Then the desperadoes felt his hands, and laughed at his pretensions as a farm-laborer.

* * *

Confident in the belief that he had been betrayed by one of the two gentlemen to whom he had applied at Liberty, Whicher made up his mind that he would make no whining petition to the murderers. If he had known the exact state of the case he would not have gone to Kearney, and if he had gone he would have been better prepared to encounter the Boys. But fate had ordained it otherwise, and another victim in the long, long catalogue of names which Jesse James had written in blood was the outcome of it all.

Darkness had fallen upon the fair scenes of nature while these things were Whicher was bound securely, and a gag was placed in his mouth that he might call for no aid or deliverance. The desperadoes placed him upon a horse, in the still hours of the night, and rode away. His legs were tied securely under the horse's belly, and his arms were pinioned with strong ropes. Jesse James, Bradley Collins and Jim Anderson were the executioners. In silence himself, Whicher, during that long, lonely ride heard the three discussing their bloody deeds with a thrill of horror, for they had told him what his fate was to be.

About three o'clock on the morning of the 11th of March, the drowsy ferryman at Blue Mills, on the Missouri river, was roused to wakefulness by the shouts of men on the north side, who signified their desire to cross over.

"Be in a hurry," cried the belated travelers. "We are after horse thieves and must cross quick if we catch them."

Thus appealed to the ferryman crossed the river to the northeastern shore, where the horse thief hunters awaited him.

When they came down to the boat, they said to the ferryman:

"We have caught the thief, and if you want to keep your head on your shoulders you had better put us across the river very quick."

So persuaded, the ferryman obeyed. They were soon on the south side of the river. The ferryman observed that one of the men was bound and gagged. It was poor Whicher on his way to his execution.

They rode away in the darkness. Just how they executed their purpose only the red-handed outlaws and the merciful God knows.

The next morning an early traveler on the road from Independence to Blue Mills, about half way between the places, in a lonely spot, saw a ghastly corpse with a bullet-hole through the forehead and another through the heart. It was all that remained of Whicher.

* * *

After Whicher's melancholy fate, Allan Pinkerton had motives aside from those of gain for pursuing to the death the celebrated border bandits, Frank and Jesse James. In one year, three of the most courageous and trusted men in the employ of the distinguished detective had been sent out after the Missouri outlaws, and were carried back cold in death, after conflicts with the desperadoes. And yet Frank and Jesse James, and their followers and allies, were free as the winds that blow, to come and go as interest or caprice might dictate to them. While this condition of affairs continued, Pinkerton must have felt that his reputation as a skillful entrapper of criminals suffered.

About the first of the year 1875, the great detective commenced a campaign against the renowned brigands which was meant to be finally effective. The most elaborate and careful preparations were made. Nothing was left undone which could in any way contribute to the success of the undertaking. The utmost secrecy was observed in every movement.

Several circumstances seemed to favor the detectives. Many of the most respectable citizens of Clay county had grown weary of the presence in their midst of persons of the evil reputation of the Jameses, and entered with alacrity and zeal into the scheme inaugurated for the capture of the Boys. Among those of the citizens most prominent in the movement which had for its design the annihilation of the band of which Jesse James was supposed to be the chief leader, were several of the old neighbors and acquaintances of the James and Samuels families.

With these citizens, Mr. William Pinkerton, who had gone from Chicago to Kansas City, to direct the movements of the detective forces, opened communication. A system of cipher signals was adopted, and communications constantly passed between the different persons engaged in the undertaking. The citizens in the neighborhood of Kearney were watchful, and keenly observed every movement in the vicinity of the residence of Dr. Samuels, and daily transmitted the results to their chief.

It was known to some of the immediate neighbors of Dr. Samuels that Frank and Jesse James were at home. They had been seen occasionally at the little railway station of Kearney, which is three miles distant from the residence which had been, and was still claimed, as the home of the outlaws. Near neighbors, in casually passing, had seen them about the barnyards. All these things had been faithfully reported to the chief detective at Kansas City.

At length the opportune time for striking a decisive blow was deemed to have arrived. Dispatches in cipher were sent to Chicago for reinforcements, and specific orders touching their movements after their arrival near the objective point, were given. The Kansas City division of the forces was held in readiness to cooperate with the force from the East. The citizens of Clay county, who had so zealously aided the detectives, received final instructions as to the part they were to take in the grand *coup*, by which their county was to be forever relieved of the presence of the dangerous outlaws.

Extraordinary precautions had been taken to maintain a profound secrecy as to the movements and purposes of the detectives. No strange men had been seen loitering about Kearney. Everything which could possibly be done to allay suspicion on the part of the outlaws had been done. But the Jameses had friends everywhere in Western Missouri—keen, shrewd, vigilant men, who noted everything, and whose suspicions were aroused by the slightest circumstance. The very quiet which prevailed was ominous of approaching danger. Somehow, too, they had learned of the sending and receiving of cipher messages by a Clay county man, at Liberty. This made them doubly watchful.

It was not until the night of the 25th of January, that the detectives made the final attack.

Jesse and Frank had been seen near the Samuels place that very evening, and no doubt was entertained that they were at home.

The detective forces destined for the attack on what was facetiously termed "Castle James," were divided into small squads, and began to arrive in Clay county on the afternoon of the 24th, from the East. Coming after night, they were met by citizens of Clay county and conducted to places of shelter in the most quiet and secret manner. After nightfall on the evening of the 25th, a special train came up by Kearney, and on it came another detachment from Kansas City. These were met by citizens well acquainted, and conducted to the place of rendezvous.

Secretly as these movements had been conducted, the ever-vigilant Jesse had his suspicions aroused by some trivial circumstance, which would have escaped the attention of almost any other man. Convinced that some formidable movement was going on, designed to consummate his destruction, Jesse James, his brother, and another member of the band rode away from the Samuels house after nightfall that very evening, and at the hour when the detectives arrived in the vicinity of the place where they expected to capture them, the Jameses were riding in the cold, well on their way to the house of a friend, miles away.

The detectives had no intimation that their intended victims had taken the alarm and departed from the place. They were assured that the outlaws had been seen in the vicinity of their home at a late hour in the afternoon, and it was believed that they were there still.

The night was cold and dark. It was late—perhaps near midnight, when the detective force arrived at the farmhouse. There were nine men selected from Pinkerton's force because of their shrewdness and courage, and several citizens of the vicinity who, like the detectives, were fully armed. The assailing forces took up their stations completely surrounding the house. Some balls of tow thoroughly saturated with kerosene oil and turpentine had been prepared, and the detectives carried with them some formidable hand grenades to be used in the assault. Two of the assailants approached a window at the rear of the house. The slight noise made in opening the shutters and raising the sash aroused a negro woman, an old family servant, who was sleeping in the apartment. She at once set up a shout of alarm which speedily brought to the room Mrs. Samuels, her husband, and several members of the family, some of them young children.

Just then a lighted ball of tow and oil was thrown into the room. The place was instantly brilliantly illuminated. The inmates of course, having just been aroused from slumber, were greatly agitated at this unexpected assault. The situation was truly appalling. Another lighted ball was hurled into the room.

The younger members of the family cried out piteously as they fled aghast from the lurid flames that shot toward the ceiling. Mrs. Samuels quickly recovered her presence of mind, and began to give directions and personally to exert herself in the work of subduing the flames. She was permitted only a moment to engage in this employment. There was a sudden crash as a great iron ball struck the floor, followed in an instant by a terrific explosion. Instantly the room was filled by a dense cloud of smoke, through which the white flames of the fireballs gleamed with a lurid red hue as if tinged with blood. There was a wail of agony from within that pandemonium of midnight horrors which might well have called emotion to a heart of stone. The piteous moans of childhood in dying throes, were mingled with the deeper groans of suffering age, and the shriller cries of terrified youth.

The work of the assailants in that particular line of attack was complete. And yet the noted outlaws did not appear. It was at once concluded that they

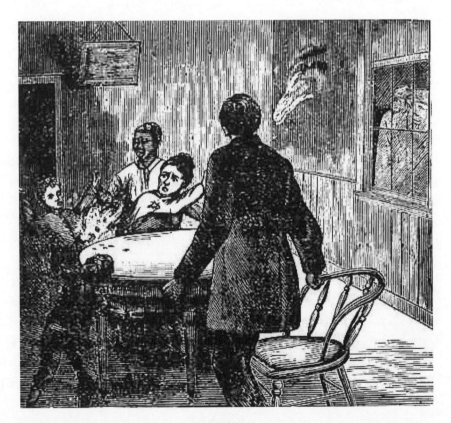

were not present or they would have shown themselves under such circumstances. The attacking force did not wait to ascertain the result of the explosion of their terrible missile. They realized only that the game they sought had escaped them, and they retired from the place without caring to learn anything more about the consequences of their effort. They had failed, and that was all they felt interested in ascertaining.

When the smoke had cleared away and the fires which had been kindled about the house were extinguished, the extent of the execution done by the explosion was fully revealed. The spectacle presented was awful. There, lying on the floor, in a pool of blood, poured out from his own young veins, was the mangled form of an eight-year old son of Mrs. Samuels, in the very throes of death; Mrs. Samuels' right arm hung helpless by her side, having been almost completely torn off above the elbow. Dr. Samuels was cut and bruised; the aged colored woman was wounded in several places; in fact, every member of the household was more or less injured. Blood was everywhere. Death was in the room; and pain and grief combined smote upon every soul in that stricken home.

Whatever the crimes of the boys of ill-favored reputation, they afforded no justification for this terrible assault in which innocent childhood was made the victim for the deeds of others. And the people of the state, without any exceptions, condemned the deed as wholly unjustifiable. The detectives made haste to leave the country, and the citizens who had assisted them returned to their homes and kept counsel with themselves.

The dead boy was taken away, and in his little grave under the snow they left him lying, the sinless victim of sin, over whose untimely fate many hearts have swelled with emotions too big for utterance.

The attack on the Samuels' home by the Pinkertons so outraged the country that a bill was tabled in the Missouri State Legislature offering amnesty to the gang. It was narrowly defeated.

By 1882, the James gang had largely dispersed. The Younger brothers were in prison, and Frank James had moved east and was living under an alias. Jesse had moved his family to Saint Joseph, Missouri, but he was still at loose ends, and so decided to put together another gang. Among the candidates for this new outfit were two brothers, Charlie and Bob Ford.

On the morning of April 3rd, 1882, Bob Ford shot Jesse James through the back of his head as he stood on a parlor chair to dust a picture frame.

The Ford brothers were immediately arrested and convicted of murder. Just as quickly the Governor of the state pardoned them. It later transpired that the Fords had been commissioned by the Governor to assassinate the famous outlaw.

Chapter XVI.

COLE YOUNGER

By Cole Younger

Bob and I had a close call with the St. Louis police in the fall of that year. The bank at Huntington, West Virginia, was robbed the first of September that year, and in the chase of the robbers Thompson McDaniels, who had fought with us in the war, was shot and fatally hurt. In his delirium he called for "Bud," and many, among whom was Detective Ely of Louisville, thought that he meant me, I having been known familiarly throughout the war as "Bud" Younger. This fact has made careless writers connect Brother Bob with some of my exploits, and in his case it served to throw suspicion on me when in fact it was probably "Bud" or Bill McDaniels, Thompson's brother, about whom he was raving. Bill was killed shortly before, escaping from arrest for complicity in the Muncie train robbery.

Shortly after this Huntington affair Bob and I were coming north from Florida. We had ridden as far as Nashville, and sold our horses there, carrying the saddle pockets with us. Shortly before we reached St. Louis we met the morning papers, full of the Huntington robbery, and the statement that the robbers were headed for Missouri. Knowing that we would be watched for in St. Louis, I told Bob we would have to go through anyway. There were some farmers' families on the train from White county, Tennessee, who were moving to the big bend of the Arkansas river, the men and goods having gone on ahead by freight. We determined to get in with these people and bluff it through. As they always do at St. Louis when on the lookout, a lot of detectives boarded the train at East St. Louis and came through, but I was busy showing one of the small boys the river, and Bob had a little girl who was equally interested in the strange city before her. Gathering up a lot of the baggage of the women folks, we went through the union depot. Chief of Detectives McDonough was standing by the gate and I saw him as I passed within a few feet of him, but he made no sign. We took the women downtown to the office where they got their rebates on their tickets, and then we took them back to the depot and left them, very grateful for our considerate attention, although, perhaps, we were under as deep obligations to them as they were to us, if they had known all the facts.

But I was determined to take no further chances, and told Bob to get in a hack that stood outside, and if we were stopped I would get on top and drive.

As we told the driver to go to a certain hotel we allayed the suspicion of a policeman who stood near and he made no effort to molest us. When we got around a corner and out of sight we paid the hackman and skipped out to Union, where we spent the night, and came up to Little Blue, on the Missouri Pacific, the next day.

* * *

There was no change in the situation in Missouri so far as the Younger brothers were concerned. Every daylight robbery in any part of the country, from the Alleghenies to the Rockies, was laid at our doors; we could not go out without a pair of pistols to protect ourselves from the attack of we knew not whom; and finally, after one of the young ruffians who had helped in the robbery of the Missouri Pacific express car at Otterville "confessed" that we were with the robbers we decided to make one haul, and with our share of the proceeds start life anew in Cuba, South America, or Australia.

Gen. Benjamin F. Butler, whom we preferred to call "Silver Spoons" Butler from his New Orleans experiences during the war, had a lot of money invested, we were told, in the First National bank at Northfield, Minnesota, as also had J. T. Ames, Butler's son-in-law, who had been the "carpet-bag" governor of Mississippi after the war.

Butler's treatment of the Southerners during the war was not such as to commend him to our regard, and we felt little compunction, under the circumstances, about raiding him or his.

Accordingly, about the middle of August we made up a party to visit Northfield, going north by rail. There were Jim, Bob and myself, Clell Miller, who had been accused of the Gad's Hill, Muncie, Corydon, Hot Springs and perhaps other bank and train robberies, but who had not been convicted of any of them; Bill Chadwell, a young fellow from Illinois, and three men whose names on the expedition were Pitts, Woods, and Howard.

We spent a week in Minneapolis, seeing the sights, playing poker and looking around for information, after which we spent a similar period in St. Paul.

I was accounted a fairly good poker player in those days, and had won about $3,000 the winter I was in Florida, while Chadwell was one of the best that ever played the game.

We both played our last game of poker in St. Paul that week, for he was soon to die at Northfield, and in the quarter of a century that has passed since such a change has come over me that I not only have no desire to play cards, but it disgusts me even to see boys gamble with dice for cigars.

This last game was at a gambling house on East Third street, between Jackson and Robert streets, about half a block from the Merchants' hotel, where we were stopping. Guy Salisbury, who has since become a minister, was the proprietor of the gambling house, and Charles Hickson was the bartender. It was upstairs over a restaurant run by Archie McLeod, who is still in St. Paul.

Chadwell and I were nearly $300 ahead of the game when Bob came along and insisted on sitting in, and we left the table. I never would play in a game where Bob was.

Early in the last week in August we started on the preliminary work for the Northfield expedition.

* * *

While Pitts and I were waiting for Bob and Chadwell we scouted about, going to Madelia and as far as the eastern part of Cotton-wood county, to familiarize ourselves with the country. Finally, a few days later, the boys joined us, having bought their horses at Mankato.

We then divided into two parties and started for Northfield by somewhat different routes. Monday night, Sept. 4, our party were at Le Sueur Center, and court being in session, we had to sleep on the floor. The hotel was full of lawyers, and they, with the judge and other court attendants, had a high old time that night. Tuesday night we were at Cordova, a little village in Le Sueur County, and Wednesday night in Millersburg, eleven miles west of Northfield. Bob and his party were then at Cannon City, to the south of Northfield. We reunited Thursday morning, Sept. 7, a little outside Northfield, west of the Cannon River.

We took a trip into town that forenoon, and I looked over the bank. We had dinner at various places and then returned to the camp. While we were planning the raid it was intended that I should be one of the party to go into the bank. I urged on the boys that whatever happened we should not shoot anyone.

"What if they begin shooting at us?" someone suggested.

"Well," said Bob, "if Cap is so particular about the shooting, suppose we let him stay outside and take his chances."

So at the last minute our plans were changed, and when we started for town Bob, Pitts and Howard went in front, the plan being for them to await us in the square and enter the bank when the second detachment came up with them. Miller and I went second to stand guard at the bank, while the rest of the party were to wait at the bridge for the signal—a pistol shot—in the event they were needed. There were no saddle horses in evidence, and we calculated that we would have a considerable advantage. Wrecking the telegraph office as we left, we would get a good start, and by night would be safe beyond Shieldsville, and the next day could ride south across the Iowa line and be in comparative safety.

But between the time we broke camp and the time they reached the bridge the three who went ahead drank a quart of whisky, and there was the initial blunder at Northfield. I never knew Bob to drink before, and I did not know he was drinking that day till after it was all over.

When Miller and I crossed the bridge the three were on some dry goods boxes at the corner near the bank, and as soon as they saw us went right into the bank, instead of waiting for us to get there.

When we came up I told Miller to shut the bank door, which they had left open in their hurry. I dismounted in the street, pretending to tighten my saddle girth. J. S. Allen, whose hardware store was near, tried to go into the bank, but Miller ordered him away, and he ran around the corner, shouting:

"Get your guns, boys; they're robbing the bank."

Dr. H. M. Wheeler, who had been standing on the east side of Division Street, near the Dampier house, shouted "Robbery! Robbery!" and I called to him to get inside, at the same time firing a pistol shot in the air as a signal to the three boys at the bridge that we had been discovered. Almost at this instant I heard a pistol shot in the bank. Chadwell, Woods and Jim rode up and joined us, shouting to people in the street to get inside, and firing their pistols to emphasize their commands. I do not believe they killed anyone, however. I have always believed that the man Nicholas Gustavson, who was shot in the street, and who, it was said, did not go inside because he did not understand English, was hit by a glancing shot from Manning's or Wheeler's rifle. If any of our party shot him it must have been Woods.

A man named Elias Stacy, armed with a shot-gun, fired at Miller just as he was mounting his horse, filling Clell's face full of bird shot. Manning took a shot at Pitts' horse, killing it, which crippled us badly. Meantime the street was getting uncomfortably hot. Every time I saw any one with a bead on me I would drop off my horse and try to drive the shooter inside, but I could not see in every direction. I called to the boys in the bank to come out, for I could not imagine what was keeping them so long. With his second shot Manning wounded me in the thigh, and with his third he shot Chadwell through the heart. Bill fell from the saddle dead. Dr. Wheeler, who had gone upstairs in the hotel, shot Miller, and he lay dying in the street.

At last the boys who had been in the bank came out. Bob ran down the street toward Manning, who hurried into Lee & Hitchcock's store, hoping in that way to get a shot at Bob from behind. Bob, however, did not see Wheeler, who was upstairs in the hotel behind him, and Wheeler's third shot shattered Bob's right elbow as he stood beneath the stairs. Changing his pistol to his left hand, Bob ran out and mounted Miller's mare. Howard and Pitts had at last come out of the bank. Miller was lying in the street, but we thought him still alive. I told Pitts to put him up with me, and I would pack him out, but when we lifted him I saw he was dead, and I told Pitts to lay him down again. Pitts's horse had been killed, and I told him I would hold the crowd back while he got out on foot. I stayed there pointing my pistol at any one who showed his head until Pitts had gone perhaps thirty or forty yards, and then, putting spurs to my horse, I galloped to where he was and took him up behind me.

"What kept you so long?" I asked Pitts.

Then he told me they had been drinking and had made a botch of it inside the bank. Instead of carrying out the plan originally formed, seizing the cashier at his window and getting to the safe without interruption, they leaped right over the counter and scared Heywood at the very start. As to the rest of the affair inside the bank I take the account of a Northfield narrator:

"With a flourish of his revolver one of the robbers pointed to Joseph L. Heywood, head bookkeeper, who was acting as cashier in the absence of that official, and asked:

"'Are you the cashier?'

"'No,' replied Heywood, and the same question was put to A. E. Bunker, teller, and Frank J. Wilcox, assistant bookkeeper, each of whom made the same reply.

"'You are the cashier,' said the robber, turning upon Heywood, who was sitting at the cashier's desk. 'Open that safe—quick or I'll blow your head off.'

"Pitts then ran to the vault and stepped inside, whereupon Heywood followed him and tried to shut him in.

"One of the robbers seized him and said:

"'Open that safe now or you haven't but a minute to live.'

"'There's a time lock on,' Heywood answered, 'and it can't be opened now.'"

Howard drew a knife from his pocket and made a feint to cut Heywood's throat, as he lay on the floor where he had been thrown in the scuffle, and Pitts told me afterward that Howard fired a pistol near Heywood's head to scare him.

Bunker tried to get a pistol that lay near him, but Pitts saw his movement and beat him to it. It was found on Charley when he was killed, so much more evidence to identify us as the men who were in Northfield.

"Where's the money outside the safe?" Bob asked.

Bunker showed him a box of small change on the counter, and while Bob was putting the money in a grain sack Bunker took advantage of the opportunity to dash out of the rear window. The shutters were closed, and this caused

Bunker an instant's delay that was almost fatal. Pitts chased him with a bullet. The first one missed him, but the second went through his right shoulder.

As the men left the bank Heywood clambered to his feet and Pitts, in his liquor, shot him through the head, inflicting the wound that killed him.

We had no time to wreck the telegraph office, and the alarm was soon sent throughout the country.

Gov. John S. Pillsbury first offered $1,000 reward for the arrest of the six who had escaped, and this he changed afterward to $1,000 for each of them, dead or alive. The Northfield bank offered $700 and the Winona & St. Peter railroad $500.

A little way out of Northfield we met a farmer and borrowed one of his horses for Pitts to ride. We passed Dundas on the run, before the news of the robbery had reached there, and at Millersburg, too, we were in advance of the news, but at Shieldsville we were behind it. Here a squad of men, who, we afterwards learned, were from Faribault, had left their guns outside a house. We did not permit them to get their weapons until we had watered our horses and got a fresh start. They overtook us about four miles west of Shieldsville, and shots were exchanged without effect on either side. A spent bullet did hit me on the "crazy bone," and as I was leading Bob's horse it caused a little excitement for a minute, but that was all.

We were in a strange country. On the prairie our maps were all right, but when we got into the big woods and among the lakes we were practically lost.

There were a thousand men on our trail, and watching for us at fords and bridges where it was thought we would be apt to go.

That night it started to rain, and we wore out our horses. Friday we moved toward Waterville, and Friday night we camped between Elysian and German lake. Saturday morning we left our horses and started through on foot, hiding that day on an island in a swamp. That night we tramped all night and we spent Sunday about four miles south of Marysburg. Meantime our pursuers were watching for horsemen, not finding our abandoned horses, it seems, until Monday or Tuesday.

Bob's shattered elbow was requiring frequent attention, and that night we made only nine miles, and Monday, Monday night, and Tuesday we spent in a deserted farmhouse close to Mankato. That day a man named Dunning discovered us and we took him prisoner. Some of the boys wanted to kill him, on the theory that "dead men tell no tales," while others urged binding him and leaving him in the woods. Finally we administered to him an oath not to betray our whereabouts until we had time to make our escape, and he agreed not to. No sooner, however, was he released than he made posthaste into Mankato to announce our presence, and in a few minutes another posse was looking for us.

Suspecting, however, that he would do so, we were soon on the move, and that night we evaded the guard at the Blue Earth river bridge, and about midnight made our way through Mankato. The whistle on the oil mill blew, and we feared that it was a signal that had been agreed upon to alarm the town in case we were observed, but we were not molested.

Howard and Woods, who had favored killing Dunning, and who felt we were losing valuable time because of Bob's wound, left us that night and went west. As we afterward learned, this was an advantage to us as well as to them, for they stole two horses soon after leaving us, and the posse followed the trail of these horses, not knowing that our party had been divided.

Accordingly, we were not pursued, having kept on a course toward Madelia to a farm where I knew there were some good horses, once in possession of which we could get along faster.

We had been living on scant rations, corn, watermelon and other vegetables principally, but in spite of this Bob's arm was mending somewhat. He had to sleep with it pillowed on my breast, Jim being also crippled with a wound in his shoulder, and we could not get much sleep. The wound in my thigh was troubling me and I had to walk with a cane I cut in the brush. One place we got a chicken and cooked it, only to be interrupted before we could have our feast, having to make a quick dash for cover.

At every stopping place we left marks of blood from our wounds, and could have been easily trailed had not the pursuers been led in the track of our recent companions.

It seems from what I have read since, however, that I had myself left with my landlord at Madelia, Col. Vought, of the Flanders house, a damaging suggestion which proved the ultimate undoing of our party. I had talked with him about a bridge between two lakes near there, and accordingly when it became known that the robbers had passed Mankato Vought thought of this bridge, and it was guarded by him and others for two nights. When they abandoned the guard, however, he admonished a Norwegian boy named Oscar Suborn to keep close watch there for us, and Thursday morning, Sept. 21, just two weeks after the robbery, Oscar saw us, and fled into town with the alarm. A party of forty was soon out in search for us, headed by Capt. W. W. Murphy, Col. Vought and Sheriff Glispin. They came up with us as we were fording a small slough, and unable to ford it with their horses, they were delayed somewhat by having to go around it. But they soon after got close enough so that one of them broke my walking stick with a shot. We were in sight of our long-sought horses when they cut us off from the animals, and our last hope was gone. We were at bay on the open prairie, surrounded by a picket line of forty men, some of whom would fight. Not prepared to stand for our last fight against such odds on the open field, we fell back into the Watonwan river bottoms and took refuge in some bushes.

We were prepared to wait as long as they would, but they were not of the waiting kind. At least some of them were not, and soon we heard the captain, who, we afterward learned, was W. W. Murphy, calling for volunteers to go in with him and rout us out. Six stepped to the front, Sheriff Glispin, Col. T. L. Vought, B. M. Rice, G. A. Bradford, C. A. Pomeroy, and S. J. Severson.

Forming in line four paces apart, he ordered them to advance rapidly and concentrate the fire of the whole line the instant the robbers were discovered.

Meanwhile we were planning, too.

"Pitts," I said, "if you want to go out and surrender, go on."

"I'll not go," he replied, game to the last. "I can die as well as you can."

"Make for the horses," I said. "Every man for himself. There is no use stopping to pick up a comrade here, for we can't get him through the line. Just charge them and make it if we can."

I got up as the signal for the charge and we fired one volley.

I tried to get my man, and started through, but the next I knew I was lying on the ground, bleeding from my nose and mouth, and Bob was standing up, shouting:

"Coward!"

One of the fellows in the outer line, not brave enough himself to join the volunteers who had come in to beat us out, was not disposed to believe in the surrender, and had his gun levelled on Bob in spite of the handkerchief which was waving as a flag of truce.

Sheriff Glispin, of Watonwan county, who was taking Bob's pistol from him, was also shouting to the fellow:

"Don't shoot him or I'll shoot you."

All of us but Bob had gone down at the first fire. Pitts, shot through the heart, lay dead. Jim, including the wound in the shoulder he received at Northfield, had been shot five times, the most serious being the shot which shattered his upper jaw and lay imbedded beneath the brain, and a shot that buried itself underneath his spine, and which gave him trouble to the day of his death. Including those received in and on the way from Northfield I had eleven wounds.

A bullet had pierced Bob's right lung, but he was the only one left on his feet. His right arm useless, and his pistol empty, he had no choice.

"I surrender," he had shouted. "They're all down but me. Come on. I'll not shoot."

And Sheriff Glispin's order not to shoot was the beginning of the protectorate that Minnesota people established over us.

We were taken into Madelia that day and our wounds dressed, and I greeted my old landlord, Col. Vought, who had been one of the seven to go in to get us. We were taken to his hotel and a guard posted.

Then came the talk of mob vengeance we had heard so often in Missouri. It was said a mob would be out that night to lynch us. Sheriff Glispin swore we would never be mobbed as long as we were his prisoners.

"I don't want any man to risk his life for us," I said to him, "but if they do come for us give us our pistols so we can make a fight for it."

"If they do come, and I weaken," he said, "you can have your pistols."

But the only mob that came was the mob of sightseers, reporters, and detectives.

* * *

Saturday we were taken to Faribault, the county seat of Rice County, in which Northfield is, and here there was more talk of lynching, but Sheriff Ara Barton was not of that kind either, and we were guarded by militia until the excitement had subsided. A Faribault policeman, who thought the militia guard was a bluff, bet five dollars he could go right up to the jail without being interfered with. He did not halt when challenged, and was fired upon and killed, the coroner's jury acquitting the militiaman who shot him. Some people blamed us for his death, too.

Chief of Detectives McDonough, of St. Louis, whom I had passed a few months before in the union depot at St. Louis, was among our visitors at Faribault.

Another was Detective Bligh, of Louisville, who believed then, and probably did ever afterward, that I had been in the Huntington, West Virginia, robbery, and tried to pump me about it.

Four indictments were found against us. One charged us with being accessory to the murder of Cashier Heywood, another with assaulting Bunker with intent to do great bodily harm, and the third with robbing the First National bank of Northfield. The fourth charged me as principal and my brothers as accessories with the murder of Gustavson.

Two witnesses had testified before the grand jury identifying me as the man who fired the shot that hit him, although I know I did not, because I fired no shot in that part of town.

Although not one of us had fired the shot that killed either Heywood or Gustavson, our attorneys, Thomas Rutledge of Madelia and Bachelder and Buckham of Faribault, asked, when we were arraigned, Nov. 9, that we be given two days in which to plead.

They advised us that as accessories were equally guilty with the principals, under the law, and as by pleading guilty we could escape capital punishment, we should plead guilty. There was little doubt, under the circumstances, of our conviction, and under the law as it stood then, an accused murderer who pleaded guilty was not subject to the death penalty. The state was new, and the law had been made to offer an inducement to murderers not to put the county to the expense of a trial.

The excitement that followed our sentence to state prison, which was popularly called "cheating the gallows," resulted in the change of the law in that respect.

The following Saturday we pleaded guilty, and Judge Lord sentenced us to imprisonment for the remainder of our lives in the state prison at Stillwater, and a few days later we were taken there by Sheriff Barton.

With Bob it was a life sentence, for he died there of consumption Sept. 16, 1889. He was never strong physically after the shot pierced his lung in the last fight near Madelia.

* * *

When the iron doors shut behind us at the Stillwater prison I submitted to the prison discipline with the same unquestioning obedience that I had exacted during my military service, and Jim and Bob, I think, did the same.

For ten years and a half after our arrival, Warden Reed remained. The first three years there was a popular idea that such desperate men as the Youngers would not stay long behind prison walls, and that especial watchfulness must be exercised in our case. Accordingly the three of us were put at work making buckets and tubs, with Ben Cayou over us as a special guard, when in our dreams we had been traveling to South America on Ben Butler's money.

Then we were put in the thresher factory. I made the sieves, while Jim sewed the belts, and Bob made the straw-carriers and elevators.

The latter part of the Reed regime I was in the storeroom.

Jan. 25, 1884, when we had been in the prison something over seven years, the main prison building was destroyed by fire at night. George P. Dodd, who was then connected with the prison, while his wife was matron, and who still lives in Buffalo, Minn., said of our behavior that night:

"I was obliged to take the female convicts from their cells and place them in a small room that could not be locked. The Youngers were passing and Cole asked if they could be of any service. I said: 'Yes, Cole. Will you three boys take care of Mrs. Dodd and the women?' Cole answered: 'Yes, we will, and if you ever had any confidence in us place it in us now.' I told him I had the utmost confidence and I slipped a pistol to Cole as I had two. Jim, I think, had an ax handle and Bob a little pinch bar. The boys stood before the door of the little room for hours and even took the blankets they had brought with them from their cells and gave them to the women to try and keep them comfortable as it was very cold. When I could take charge of the women and the boys were relieved, Cole returned my revolver."

Next morning Warden Reed was flooded with telegrams and newspaper sensations: "Keep close watch of the Youngers;" "Did the Youngers escape?" "Plot to free the Youngers," and that sort of thing.

The warden came to his chief deputy, Abe Hall, and suggested that we be put in irons, not that he had any fear on our account, but for the effect on the public.

"I'll not put irons on 'em," replied Hall.

And that day Hall and Judge Butts took us in a sleigh down town to the county jail where we remained three or four weeks. That was the only time we were outside the prison enclosure from 1876 till 1901.

* * *

In spite of the popular indignation our crime had justly caused, from the day the iron gates closed behind us in 1876, there were always friends who hoped and planned for our ultimate release. Some of these were misguided, and did us more harm than good.

Among these were two former guerrillas, who committed small crimes that they might be sent to prison and there plot with us for our escape. One of them was only sent to the county jail, and the other served a year in Stillwater prison without ever seeing us.

Well meaning, too, but unfortunate, was the declaration of Missouri friends in Minnesota that they could raise $100,000 to get us out of Stillwater.

But as the years went by, the popular feeling against us not only subsided, but our absolute submission to the minutest details of prison discipline won for us the consideration, I might even say the high esteem of the prison officials who came in contact with us, and as the Northfield tragedy became more and more remote, those who favored our pardon became more numerous, and yearly numbered in their ranks more and more of the influential people of the state, who believed that our crime had been avenged, and that Jim and I, the only survivors of the tragedy, would be worthy citizens if restored to freedom.

My Missouri friends are surprised to find that I prize friendships in Minnesota, a state where I found so much trouble, but in spite of Northfield, and all its tragic memories, I have in Minnesota some of the best friends a man ever had on earth.

Every governor of Minnesota from as early as 1889 down to 1899 was petitioned for our pardon, but not one of them was satisfied of the advisability of a full pardon, and the parole system provided by the enlightened humanitaria-nism of the state for other convicts did not apply to lifers.

Under this system a convict whose prison record is good may be paro-led on his good behavior after serving half of the term for which he was sentenced.

The reiterated requests for our pardon, coming from men the governors had confidence in, urging them to a pardon they were reluctant to grant, led to a feeling, which found expression finally in official circles, that the respon-sibility of the pardoning power should be divided by the creation of a board of pardons as existed in some other states.

It was at first proposed that the board should consist of the governor, attor-ney general and the warden of the prison, but before the bill passed, Senator Allen J. Greer secured the substitution for the chief justice for the warden, boasting, when the amendment was made:

"That ties the Youngers up for as long as Chief Justice Start lives."

A unanimous vote of the board was required to grant a pardon, and as Chief Justice Start had lived in the vicinity of Northfield at the time of the raid in 1876, many people believed that he would never consent to our pardon.

In the legislature of 1889, our friends endeavored to have the parole system extended to life prisoners, and secured the introduction in the legislature of a bill to provide that life prisoners might be paroled when they had served such a period as would have entitled them to their release had they been sentenced to imprisonment for 35 years. As the good time allowances on a 35-year sentence would cut it to between 23 and 24 years, we could have been paroled in a few months had this bill passed.

Although there was one other inmate of the prison who might have come under its provisions, it was generally known as the "Youngers' parole bill" and the feeling against it was largely identified with the feeling against us. I am told, however, since my release, that it would have passed at that session had it not been for the cry of "money" that was used. There never was a dollar used in Minnesota to secure our pardon, and before our release we had some of the best men and women in the state working in our behalf, without money and without price. But this outcry defeated the bill of 1899.

Still it did not discourage our friends on the outside.

At the next session of the legislature, 1901, there was finally passed the bill which permitted our conditional parole, the pardon board not being ready to grant us our full freedom. This bill provided for the parole of any life convict who had been confined for twenty years, on the unanimous consent of the board of pardons.

The board of prison managers promptly granted the parole.

And July 14, 1901, Jim and I went out into the world for the first time in within a few months of twenty-five years.

Rip Van Winkle himself was not so long away. St. Paul and Minneapolis which, when we were there in 1876, had less than seventy-five thousand people all told, had grown to cities within whose limits were over three hundred fifty thousand. A dozen railroads ended in one or the other of these centers of business that we had known as little better than frontier towns.

THE WEST'S MOST PROMINENT LAWMEN AND CRIMINALS TELL THEIR STORIES OF FIGHT, DEATH, AND SURVIVAL.

In the romantic narrative of the Old West, two larger-than-life characters emerged as the perfect foils for each other: the rampant outlaw and the heroic peace officer. Without the villain, sheriffs would not have needed to uphold the law; and without the sheriff, villains would have had no law to break. Together, both personalities fought, lost, and triumphed amid shootouts, train robberies, and bank holdups against the backdrop of the lawless American frontier.

This spectacular collection of true memoirs and autobiographies, told by the very people who lived these criminal and righteous lives during the Old West, reveal the outlaws and peace officers at their worst and best. Watch as Mark Twain introduces notorious gunslinger Jack Slade; hear about Theodore Roosevelt's encounters with men, women, and game from Roosevelt himself; read sheriff Pat Garrett's biography of Billy the Kid, the outlaw he killed; and listen as lawmen Bat Masterson and Wyatt Earp describe each other in their own accounts. Including other carefully curated stories by Tom Horn, Cole Younger, and more, *Outlaws and Peace Officers* invokes danger, honor, and the fight for survival during this perilous, but exciting, chapter in American history.

STEPHEN BRENNAN is an editor, teacher, and playwright. He is the editor of *The Best Cowboy Stories Ever Told*, *The Gigantic Book of Sailing Stories*, *The Gigantic Book of Pirate Stories*, and *Classic Adventure Stories*. He lives in New York City.

Skyhorse Publishing, Inc.
New York, New York
www.skyhorsepublishing.com

Cover design by Anthony Morais
Printed in the United States of America

ISBN-10: 1-63450-436-4
ISBN-13: 978-1-63450-436-2